Studies in Diplomacy and International Relations

General Editors: **Donna Lee**, Senior Lecturer in International Organisations and International Political Economy, University of Birmingham, UK and **Paul Sharp**, Professor of Political Science and Director of the Alworth Institute for International Studies at the University of Minnesota, Duluth, USA

The series was launched as *Studies in Diplomacy* in 1994 under the general editorship of G. R. Berridge. Its purpose is to encourage original scholarship on all aspects of the theory and practice of diplomacy. The new editors assumed their duties in 2003 with a mandate to maintain this focus while also publishing research which demonstrates the importance of diplomacy to contemporary international relations more broadly conceived.

Titles include

G. R. Berridge (*editor*)
DIPLOMATIC CLASSICS
Selected Texts from Commynes to Vattel

G. R. Berridge, Maurice Keens-Soper and T. G. Otte
DIPLOMATIC THEORY FROM MACHIAVELLI TO KISSINGER

Herman J. Cohen
INTERVENING IN AFRICA
Superpower Peacemaking in a Troubled Continent

Andrew F. Cooper (*editor*)
NICHE DIPLOMACY
Middle Powers after the Cold War

David H. Dunn (*editor*)
DIPLOMACY AT THE HIGHEST LEVEL
The Evolution of International Summitry

Brian Hocking (*editor*)
FOREIGN MINISTRIES
Change and Adaptation

Brian Hocking and David Spence (*editor*)
FOREIGN MINISTRIES IN THE EUROPEAN UNION
Integrating Diplomats

Michael Hughes
DIPLOMACY BEFORE THE RUSSIAN REVOLUTION
Britain, Russia and the Old Diplomacy, 1894–1917

Gaynor Johnson
THE BERLIN EMBASSY OF LORD D'ABERNON, 1920–1926

Christer Jönsson and Martin Hall
ESSENCE OF DIPLOMACY

Donna Lee
MIDDLE POWERS AND COMMERCIAL DIPLOMACY
British Influence at the Kennedy Trade Round

Donna Lee, Ian Taylor and Paul D. Williams (*editors*)
THE NEW MULTILATERALISM IN SOUTH AFRICAN DIPLOMACY

Mario Liverani
INTERNATIONAL RELATIONS IN THE ANCIENT NEAR EAST, 1600–1100 BC

Jan Melissen (*editor*)
INNOVATION IN DIPLOMATIC PRACTICE
Soft Power in International Relations

THE NEW PUBLIC DIPLOMACY
Soft Power in International Relations

Peter Neville
APPEASING HITLER
The Diplomacy of Sir Nevile Henderson, 1937–39

M. J. Peterson
RECOGNITION OF GOVERNMENTS
Legal Doctrine and State Practice, 1815–1995

Gary D. Rawnsley
RADIO DIPLOMACY AND PROPAGANDA
The BBC and VOA in International Politics, 1956–64

TAIWAN'S INFORMAL DIPLOMACY AND PROPAGANDA

Ronald A. Walker
MULTILATERAL CONFERENCES
Purposeful International Negotiation

A. Nuri Yurdusev (*editor*)
OTTOMAN DIPLOMACY
Conventional or Unconventional?

Studies in Diplomacy and International Relations
Series Standing Order ISBN 0–333–71495–4
(*outside North America only*)

You can receive future titles in this series as they are published by placing a standing order. Please contact your bookseller or, in case of difficulty, write to us at the address below with your name and address, the title of the series and the ISBN quoted above.

Customer Services Department, Macmillan Distribution Ltd, Houndmills, Basingstoke, Hampshire RG21 6XS, England

The New Multilateralism in South African Diplomacy

Edited by

Donna Lee
Department of Political Science and International Studies
University of Birmingham, UK

Ian Taylor
School of International Relations
University of St Andrews, UK

Paul D. Williams
Department of Political Science and International Studies
University of Birmingham, UK

First published in 2006 by
PALGRAVE MACMILLAN
Houndmills, Basingstoke, Hampshire RG21 6XS and
175 Fifth Avenue, New York, N.Y. 10010
Companies and representatives throughout the world.

PALGRAVE MACMILLAN is the global academic imprint of the Palgrave
Macmillan division of St. Martin's Press, LLC and of Palgrave Macmillan Ltd.
Macmillan® is a registered trademark in the United States, United Kingdom
and other countries. Palgrave is a registered trademark in the European
Union and other countries.

ISBN-13: 978–0–230–00461–0 hardcover
ISBN-10: 0–230–00461–X   hardcover

This book is printed on paper suitable for recycling and made from fully
managed and sustained forest sources.

A catalogue record for this book is available from the British Library.

Library of Congress Cataloging-in-Publication Data
    The new multilateralism in South African diplomacy / edited by
Donna Lee, Ian Taylor, Paul D. Williams.
        p. cm.
    Includes bibliographical references and index.
    ISBN 0–230–00461–X
    1. South Africa – Foreign relations – 1994– I. Lee, Donna, 1963–
II. Taylor, Ian, 1969– III. Williams, Paul, 1975–
DT1971.N48 2006
327.68—dc22   2006041680

10 9 8 7 6 5 4 3 2 1
15 14 13 12 11 10 09 08 07 06

Printed and bound in Great Britain by
Antony Rowe Ltd, Chippenham and Eastbourne

In memory of Lisa Jane Bloxham, 1965–2005

Contents

Preface

The idea for this book was developed at three one-day workshops exploring South African multilateral diplomacy during the academic year 2003–2004. We would like to thank the Diplomatic Studies Research Group and the Security Studies Research Group of the University of Birmingham for hosting two of the workshops. We would also like to thank the Department of International Relations at the London School of Economics for hosting the other workshop. The School of Social Sciences, University of Birmingham generously provided additional funding to cover the travel costs of visiting scholars from Africa. Without the financial support of these institutions this project would never have got off the ground.

The project benefited greatly from the active participation of staff and graduate students from both institutions as well as several visiting scholars from within the United Kingdom and Africa. In particular we would like to thank Chris Alden, George Lawson, Marie Muller, Tim Shaw, Keith Shear and Andy Williams for their helpful criticism on the papers presented at the workshop.

We would also like to thank the anonymous reviewers of an earlier draft of the manuscript for their supportive commentary and many useful suggestions for improvement.

This book is dedicated to the memory of Lisa Jane Bloxham – partner to James Hamill and mother to Sean and Finn – who died suddenly and tragically in April 2005. Lisa took a keen interest in South African politics, visiting the country many times in its post-apartheid era. She was greatly loved and will be deeply missed by family and friends.

Notes on Contributors

Scarlett Cornelissen is Senior Lecturer in Political Science at the University of Stellenbosch, South Africa.

James Hamill is Lecturer, Department of Politics, University of Leicester, UK.

Stephen R. Hurt is Senior Lecturer, Department of Politics and International Relations, Oxford Brookes University, UK.

Donna Lee is Senior Lecturer, Department of Political Science and International Studies, University of Birmingham, UK.

Sally Morphet is a Visiting Professor at the University of Kent at Canterbury, UK.

Mzukisi Qobo was awarded his PhD from the Department of Politics and International Studies, University of Warwick, UK.

Ian Taylor is Senior Lecturer, School of International Relations, University of St Andrews, UK.

Paul D. Williams is Senior Lecturer in Security Studies, Department of Political Science and International Studies, University of Birmingham, UK.

Introduction
Understanding South Africa's Multilateralism

Ian Taylor and Paul D. Williams

South Africa's multi-racial democratic elections in 1994 marked a major turning point in both the country's domestic politics and its role in international affairs. Internationally, the new South Africa emerged from its apartheid wilderness and was welcomed into a wide variety of multilateral forums. In turn, the new government committed itself to upholding the principles of multilateralism and to playing an active role within these institutions. Ten years on, the contributors to this volume participated in a series of workshops to reflect upon South Africa's involvement in, and contribution to, multilateral forums. This involved engaging with both the general literature on the concept of multilateralism within the discipline of International Relations and the more specific literature analysing South Africa's post-apartheid foreign policy. By providing a detailed analysis of how post-apartheid South Africa has participated in multilateral diplomacy in a variety of institutional settings we hope this volume can contribute to the broader debates about multilateralism in International Relations. Similarly, and in good dialectical fashion, we hope that readers primarily interested in understanding the new South Africa's foreign policy can benefit from an engagement with the general literature exploring the concept of multilateralism.

The chapters presented here do not conform to a single perspective but they all seek to explore and interrogate the political agendas that successive South African governments have pursued in a variety of multilateral forums. As a starting point, it is necessary to situate South Africa's multilateral diplomacy within the context of the country's political economy, for a state's foreign policy is intimately related to its domestic setting. In our opinion, this context is characterised in large part by the interrelationships between the concepts of race, class and democracy as South Africans have struggled to overcome apartheid's legacies, build a genuinely democratic society, and integrate that society within the global economy in ways that ostensibly allow all the country's citizens to flourish. But we must begin by explaining what we mean by multilateralism.

Approaches to multilateralism

As James Caporaso has pointed out, definitions of multilateralism are not neutral; they have consequences.[1] For Caporaso, multilateralism entails two defining characteristics. First, it suggests 'many' actors 'from a minimum of three to a maximum of all' and the various gradations in between. Second, multilateralism 'presumes cooperation' although not all cooperation is necessarily multilateral.[2] The coordination and cooperation referred to in this approach usually occurs through institutions and it is usually confined to the activities of states.[3] But restricting our understanding of multilateralism to cooperation and coordination between three or more states does not provide room for a sophisticated understanding of norm diffusion within world politics, nor does it explicitly address how power relations influence what at first sight may appear to be cooperative activities.

John Ruggie's notion of multilateralism as 'an institutional form that co-ordinates relations among three or more states *on the basis of generalised principles of conduct'* is thus a more helpful starting point as it encompasses the normative foundations of multilateral behaviour and hence opens up analytical space to discuss the ways in which power relations affect how certain principles of conduct rise to prominence and how others are marginalised.[4] Arguably the most fundamental but often unarticulated principle is the idea that multilateralism should entail non-discrimination between the members of a particular institution. As Philip Nel observed, the rationale is that in an interdependent world, stable orders are best promoted by applying

> generalised principles of conduct ... in a non-discriminatory way to all states that want to co-operate, without negating the individuality and autonomy of each actor; distributing the costs and benefits of interaction across the system (indivisibility); and developing incentives for actors to suspend the urge for instant gratification on every single issue, and to recognise and pursue joint satisfaction on many issues (diffuse reciprocity).[5]

The current efforts to create a rules-based system of international trade through the World Trade Organisation (WTO), for instance, are founded on the principle that once WTO members have signed up to free trade policies they should not discriminate against other members.[6] Even the fact that the WTO's more powerful members routinely ignore this ideal has not led states to discard the underlying principle of non-discrimination. Rather, weaker states have invoked it as a way of trying to exert influence over those members who violate the rules.

For Ruggie, the code of liberal values at the heart of multilateralism represents an off-shoot of American civic nationalism which promoted individualism rather than group rights, the capitalist rule of law and the ideal that humanity can be improved through deliberate actions and social learning. When incorporated into multilateralism these values reflected what Ruggie called 'embedded liberalism' or the internationalisation of American state–society relations.[7] In time, Ruggie's insights were to form a significant part of the Constructivist agenda in International Relations, which directed attention to how power and social purpose became fused as a set of norms to project political authority into the international system. During the Cold War period, multilateralism helped transform state–society relations within the Western bloc by influencing what was considered the legitimate social purposes of state power. In particular, 'the role of the state became to institute and safeguard the self-regulating market'.[8]

Writing from within the neo-Gramscian tradition, Craig Murphy also recognised multilateralism's role in constructing the liberal compromise of the post-war period. In addition, he demonstrated how the growth of international organisations stemmed in large part from particular types of political orders characterised by the expansion of capitalist markets through the spread of transportation and communication networks and the reduction of barriers to international trade. In short, Murphy highlighted how the origins of many of today's multilateral institutions lay within nineteenth century European imperialism and more recently during the Cold War, within the US-led capitalist bloc.[9] Consider the etymology of the concept of multilateralism in the United States (US). Before the Second World War the idea of multilateralism was rarely articulated. *Webster's New International Dictionary* (1934), for instance, did not include a reference to 'multilateralism' but defined multilateral as having many sides; many-sided, participated in by more than two states; as a multilateral treaty. The 1961 edition, however, included a reference to multilateralism as 'freedom of international trade and currency transfers so as to achieve for each country a trading balance with the total trading area but not necessarily with any one particular country'.[10] Hence over a couple of decades the concept of multilateralism entered into popular usage within the US and became associated with a specific normative agenda, namely, liberal free trade and the balancing of payments.

By far the most powerful supporter of this particular agenda was the US government, which recognised the need to secure its preferred political order by reassuring those states that signed up to it through the provision of constitutional guarantees about the principles that would govern state conduct within this particular multilateral system. As John Ikenberry has suggested, multilateralism was part of the constitutional order constructed by the US and its allies in the aftermath of the Second World War. This order aimed not just at reconstructing Europe after the devastation it had suffered during the war, but also in institutionalising US hegemony through a series of related multilateral institutions based upon the United Nations (UN) and its specialised agencies.[11] In this multilateral system the US could not simply control outcomes but it did form part of a hegemonic bloc whose values were institutionalised in a series of multilateral organisations. This required the US government to exercise what Ernst Haas called 'quiet' as opposed to 'conspicuous' leadership, or 'guidance' through 'continuous consultation'. It also meant that Washington had to accept compromises that fell short of its immediate goals and that there were real limits to what institutions could achieve.[12] In return, the US state remained the most important actor within a multilateral system based upon its preferred general principles of conduct.

It is this understanding of multilateralism as an inherently political enterprise that informed Robert Cox's critique of the ways in which international institutions – including those devised at Bretton Woods – help legitimise the existing world order and shape the parameters of acceptable or 'realistic' foreign policy. For Cox, international institutions (as sites of both ideas and material power) act at both the domestic and international levels to transmit hegemonic norms. This is because 'institutions reflect the power relations prevailing at the point of origin and tend, at least initially, to encourage collective images consistent with these power relations'.[13] In this schema, hegemony is understood in broadly Gramscian terms as

> a sociopolitical situation ... in which the philosophy and practice of
> a society fuse or are in equilibrium; *an order in which a certain way of*

life and thought is dominant, in which one concept of reality is diffused throughout society in all its institutional and private manifestations, informing with its spirit all taste, morality, customs, religious and political principles, and all social relations, particularly in their intellectual and moral connotation. An element of direction and control, not necessarily conscious, is implied.[14]

Hegemony thus represents a fluid form of social order characterised by a combination of coercion and popular consent 'in which a certain way of life and thought is dominant'. Within such an order international institutions contribute to the articulation of the hegemonic ideology wherein certain policies are considered more legitimate and realistic than others.[15] This can be done through a variety of mechanisms but international institutions have played particularly influential roles in constructing international regimes in a variety of issue areas.[16]

Approaches to South Africa's multilateralism

The neo-Gramscian approach to multilateralism exemplified by Robert Cox's work has important implications for understanding the roles multilateral institutions play within the current world order. For those of us interested in post-apartheid South Africa's foreign policy this approach raises several preliminary points. First, although, as Cox has suggested, multilateral institutions act as transmitters for hegemonic norms, they also act as forums for counter-hegemonic ideas and social forces. In short, multilateral institutions are a site of political struggle, the results of which are not preordained. As a consequence, many political elites within the South view multilateral institutions as one of the few places in which the North's power can be challenged.[17] Given first Mandela's and then Mbeki's desire to be seen as playing a leading role in constructing a more just and equitable world order, it is hardly surprising that Pretoria has invested considerable effort in multilateral diplomacy.

But while counter-hegemonic forces are always present within multilateral institutions, there is no guarantee that they will successfully displace the existing hegemonic principles. Indeed, since the early 1990s, the African National Congress (ANC) has become so enamoured with neoliberal political economy that its leaders appear to believe that there really is no alternative to the currently dominant strain of liberalism at the international level.[18] Consequently, they appear to have resigned themselves to the fact that the best they can expect from the current world order is to get the rich industrialised states to play by their own liberal rules instead of protecting their own economies through various mercantilist strategies. In this way, South Africa hopes to extract the maximum material benefits and modify the worst aspects of a far from perfect system, without necessarily challenging the rules upon which the system is based. Nel dubbed this approach instrumental or tactical multilateralism.[19]

Yet such a tactical approach is not without its problems. Just as the historic compromise surrounding South Africa's transition from apartheid has engendered contradictions within the domestic polity between competing class fractions and within the government's own ranks, acceding to neoliberal principles has also caused a fundamental tension in Pretoria's overall foreign policy.[20] On the one hand, South Africa consents to international liberalisation and tries to ensure that the powerful industrial states play by the liberal rules of the game they have created. On the other, however, South African representatives commonly question the most negative consequences of neoliberal globalisation, especially for states and societies within the South in general and Africa in particular. What this tension suggests is that ANC elites are continually playing to many different audiences both at home and abroad. At home, the ANC elite is conscious of the need to maintain an alliance with its Leftist-inclined constituency and elements linked to organised labour and/or the South African Communist Party (SACP) while at the same time courting domestic capital and foreign investors present within South Africa. As one commentator suggested of Mbeki, he 'wants to have it both ways: to be regarded by business leaders as a responsible economic manager, and by the political left as a champion of the downtrodden'.[21] Abroad, Pretoria has tried to appeal to both the powerful Western states by selling itself as a pro-Western bridge-builder capable of smoothing the differences between the North and the South, while simultaneously seeking to champion the values of the weaker Southern states in general and of an 'African Renaissance' in particular.

Within this historical context numerous analysts have presented their thoughts on Pretoria's interaction with the outside world.[22] The major fault-line in these accounts appears to be between those largely uncritical descriptions of Pretoria's multilateralism and those utilising more critical theoretical frameworks. More precisely, the vast majority of accounts have worked within the assumptions of neorealist and neoliberal theories, or what might be termed the 'neo-neo consensus'. These accounts have tended to lack both theoretical sophistication and critical reflexivity. As Vale and Taylor put it in 1999, neo-neo thinkers ... effectively control what (little) thinking there is regarding the nation's foreign policy. Indeed, securocrats and free-marketeers dominate South Africa's foreign policy debates – exactly why descriptions (and 'descriptions' not 'reflections' is the right adjective) are so pedestrian and non-informative. ... [M]uch is made, of embassies opening in Pretoria, of sojourns abroad by South African ministers, of receiving kings and queens on state visits, even of the bureaucratic politics inherent in the ongoing transformative process in the Department of Foreign Affairs. Yet little attention is directed to the overall thrust of South African foreign policy: the normative principles that underlie Pretoria's interaction with the international community. Even less attention or effort is aimed at explaining or analyzing why South Africa has 'bought into the programme'. It is as if South Africa's essential at oneness with the dominant discourse of neo-liberalism and neo-realism is teleological, with no material or ideological basis.[23]

As discussed below, critical analysts, on the other hand, have been more explicit about the normative foundations of their scholarship and have asked 'what (and who) South Africa's foreign policy is for?' and 'who has benefited and who has lost out from Pretoria's chosen policies?'

A few examples of some neo-neo thinking are perhaps in order. From a self-styled 'pragmatic' perspective, Gerrit Olivier and Deon Geldenhuys argued that after 1994 South Africa changed its foreign policy in a 'pragmatic and reasoned manner'.[24] In so doing, Pretoria apparently disappointed the (unidentified) 'ideologues' who had argued for a 'total' break from the past. In this approach, a pragmatic perspective became synonymous with objective analysis of the 'realities' imposed upon South Africa by contemporary international structures. This approach did not examine the ambiguities in South Africa's multilateralism although it did attempt to de-legitimise alternative views about the policies Pretoria should pursue. Other self-styled 'realists' repeatedly cautioned against South Africa taking too 'radical' a stance in solidarity with the concerns of the developing world. For these writers, South Africa's 'national interest' was self-evident and defined in very specific and objective terms. Greg Mills, for instance, cautioned against Pretoria forging links with 'pariahs' such as Cuba and Libya, and questioned whether South Africa's limited resources were best committed to greater interaction with Africa.[25] For some, the only explanation for engaging with such pariahs and risking the displeasure of the most powerful

Western states was the paying off of old, anti-apartheid struggle debts.[26] The fact that South Africa later gained considerable plaudits in the West for its mediatory role in bringing the Libyans suspected of the 1988 Lockerbie bombing to trial was apparently lost on such critics. In short, attempts to capture the 'realistic' ground were one of the hallmarks of this type of analysis as it sought to proffer 'scientific' and 'objective' advice to those making Pretoria's foreign policy.[27]

In contrast, a more critical and reflexive approach to South African foreign policy was pioneered by Peter Vale, who in the early 1990s fought a long campaign against the 'slash and burn realism' prevalent in much of the country's academy.[28] Vale rejected the objectivist epistemology and state-centric ontology that were central characteristics of most 'neo-neo' analyses of South African foreign policy and argued that the current world order was neither natural nor the best of all possible worlds.[29] For Vale, it was frustrating that most analyses of South African foreign policy made

> no effort to problematise the world, and certainly [had] no intention to challenge the cultism which holds that states are always the central player in international politics. Such perspectives turn on received notions of control: they re-circulate words, rather than seeking out new explanations or offering alternative understandings of the world. By using them pundits can certainly provide easy answers, but because punditry is rooted in problem-solving theory, its pronouncements are invariably mundane – concerned only with the maintenance of the status quo.[30]

In many ways, Vale's work was reminiscent of Cox's approach with its emphasis on challenging conventional wisdoms and asking how the present order had come about, what assumptions it left unspoken, and who benefited from it? It also stood as a pertinent local reminder that economics did not begin with Margaret Thatcher, nor did South Africa's history start with F. W. de Klerk's famous 2 February 1990 speech.[31] Although Vale's work focused on South African foreign policy, this did not include much analysis of South Africa's multilateralism. As a result, work undertaken at the University of Stellenbosch from the late 1990s sought to help fill this gap in the emerging critical literature.[32] From the outset, this work remained acutely aware of the implications of the ANC's shift towards neoliberalism.[33] Specifically, it sought to advance the idea (then relatively novel, in South African International Relations circles) that foreign policy is not only intimately related to domestic politics and domestic interests, but also that foreign policies advance certain domestic interests over others rather than advancing some objectified and mythical notion of South Africa's 'national interest'. As a result, Vale and Taylor argued that

> Any competent analysis of South Africa's foreign policy must begin with the fundamental question; how does it affect the country's citizens? Which segments benefit from the policies being pursued, and which do not? Whose interest is being served by, for example, South Africa playing an activist role in the WTO? Is such a role consummate with a government committed to 'A Better Life for All', or, after the rhetoric and the bluster have been stripped aside, is only a limited fraction of the country's peoples being served by such posturing.[34]

This approach to South African multilateralism also rejected the objectivist claims made by the neo-neo analysts and shared Cox's dictum that 'theory is always *for* someone and *for* some purpose'.[35] Surprisingly, even this limited degree of theoretical reflexivity was a scarce commodity among South Africa's International Relations scholars.[36]

As noted above, post-apartheid South Africa was keen, for several reasons, to make multilateralism a central plank of its foreign policy. Through its participation within, and contribution to the development of institutions such as the United Nations' Conference on Trade and Development (UNCTAD) and the Non-Aligned Movement (NAM), Pretoria could pursue the reformist – or to use Cox's term, problem-solving – strategy identified above whereby it would not challenge the fundamental principles of the liberal world order but would attempt to make them work to its advantage as best it could. Why South Africa's foreign policy-makers embarked upon this strategy is obviously open to debate but we believe a large part of the explanation lies in two interrelated factors. First is Pretoria's desire to appeal to a variety of audiences that often pursued fundamentally different agendas and held very different expectations about what politics and foreign policy should deliver. Second, despite considerable evidence of the very real opportunities for states to pursue distinct and varied responses to globalisation, successive ANC governments have failed to conceive of, let alone develop, a viable alternative to the prevailing neoliberal orthodoxy.[37] Although rarely stated explicitly, the rationale behind Pretoria's strategy seems to run along the lines that because there is no feasible alternative to neoliberal political economy the most realistic option is to act as a 'middle power' and promote technical reform within multilateral institutions such as the World Bank, the IMF (International Monetary Fund) and the WTO. The ANC government can thus feign at least a superficially plausible concern with global inequity to its domestic constituency, including the SACP and Congress of South African Trade Unions (COSATU).

At this point it is important to note that a reformist or problem-solving agenda successfully pursued could indeed result in significant changes within both international society and the global economy. Persuading the world's most powerful states to play by the rules they have devised for themselves would be a major achievement and would undoubtedly result in a more just, democratic and equitable world order. However, it would not eradicate some of the fundamental tensions and contradictions within neoliberal political economy most famously described by Karl Polanyi.[38] Whether such a strategy will continue to satisfy all the ANC's audiences remains an open-ended question. But the ongoing arguments within the tripartite alliance and the hostility from working class organisations to the macroeconomic policies pursued by Mbeki's administration suggest that what Gramsci referred to as 'a rift between popular masses and ruling ideologies' is opening up and, arguably, getting wider.[39]

As noted above, after a period of conversion away from the principles articulated in the Freedom Charter, the ANC's vision of a post-apartheid South Africa now conforms to neoliberal principles of political economy in several important respects. In particular, this ideological perspective has helped define what the ANC government sees as the 'limits of the possible' and 'credible' policy options both at home and abroad.

Simultaneously, to use Gramsci's terminology, a new historic bloc is forming in post-apartheid South Africa composed of elite fractions of the ANC; a developing and increasingly strident black bourgeoisie; and white business elites. The last group continue to control most of South Africa's financial markets, their accumulation patterns are primarily export-oriented, and they are acutely sensitive to trends and developments initiated outside South Africa within the capitalist core. The dominant interests within this historic bloc are among the local beneficiaries of neoliberal globalisation yet they represent only a small portion of the ANC's constituency, the rest of which is either indifferent or hostile to the way in which the new South Africa has been integrated into the global economy. Pretoria's reformist stance within a variety of multilateral forums allows it to claim – with at least a degree of credibility – that it is working in alliance with 'the South' to ameliorate the most blatant injustices and inequalities within the current world order. This was evident, for instance, during South Africa's period as chair of the NAM between 1998 and 2003. It also helps explain the Mbeki government's frequent and high profile engagements with the G-7/8 and the European Union (EU) to discuss how globalisation is affecting the South. South Africa's roles in devising the New Partnership for Africa's Development (NEPAD) or its support for the UK-funded Commission for Africa can be understood as the latest examples of this strategy.

In this sense, the rationale underlying Pretoria's multilateralism is twofold: to gain the best deal possible for South Africa within the current – apparently inflexible – structures of the global economy and international society, and to persuade its Leftist critics that it has not 'sold out' in the ongoing struggle to build a more just and democratic world order. Successive ANC governments have pursued the first goal by challenging the hypocrisy of Western governments who constantly lecture Southern states about the universal benefits of international free trade but consistently adopt mercantilist policies when it suits them. In other words, Pretoria has bought into – and consequently helps legitimise – the notion that international free trade would bring benefits (albeit uneven benefits) for Southern states and societies but that at present the world trading system contains too many protectionist barriers of one sort or another. However, and often simultaneously, South African governments have also deployed the rhetoric of fair trade in an attempt to help redress the legacy of the unequal structures of the global economy that continue to benefit the strongest players within global markets at the expense of the weaker ones. And here, Mbeki has expressed – forcefully at times – his concerns about the negative downsides of an increasingly globalised world. The problem is that Pretoria's multilateralism is attempting to placate numerous audiences who have very different political agendas and expectations. At best, this will require the ANC government to pull off a difficult balancing act. At worst, it represents an unstable and ultimately untenable strategy. As one analysis summed it up, 'there is quite obvious tension between on the one hand supporting global free trade, and on the other committing oneself to changing the rules of the system to ensure greater equity'.[40] Pretoria's 'solution' to this tension appears to be, 'talk left, walk right'.[41]

The reasons behind the ANC's shift towards neoliberalism are of course multiple, complex and contested. But the discussion so far suggests that analyses of South Africa's multilateralism need to recognise the implications that this shift in perspective has had (and is having) upon both Pretoria's domestic and foreign policy. It is not surprising perhaps that the ANC governments have not sought to fundamentally challenge neoliberal principles within explicitly neoliberal institutions such as the WTO. But given the enormous amounts of empirical evidence challenging the development claims and practical results of neoliberal macroeconomic policies, it is surprising that South Africa has promoted this agenda within more broadly focused institutions such as UNCTAD, the NAM or the Commonwealth. Within these forums Pretoria has played a bridge-building role between the North and South. However, it is noticeable that Pretoria has frequently played an active role directing traffic across this bridge and that the flow has been primarily in one direction as it has persuaded other Southern states to accept the 'global realities' and Northern agendas.[42] Such a role has allowed South African governments to enhance their international profile, depict themselves as credible economic managers (a necessary move in the international competition to attract foreign investment) and ingratiate themselves with the dominant states within world politics.

There is no clearer example of this strategy than the NEPAD, which itself grew out of a variety of earlier African initiatives, including Thabo Mbeki's version of an African Renaissance. Both Mbeki's renaissance vision and the NEPAD have been criticised for their faith in the ability of the market to deliver positive political results for ordinary Africans and for pandering to Western definitions of Africa's predicament, and, arguably, the West's preferred solutions.[43] As Peter Vale and Sipho Maseko argued,

> The African Renaissance suggests a continental effort led by South Africa to advance the familiar 'end-of-history' thesis ... South Africa's African Renaissance (this choice of words is important) is anchored in a chain of economies which, with time, might become the African equivalent of the Asian Tigers ... In this rendition, the African Renaissance posits Africa as an expanding and prosperous market alongside Asia, Europe and North America in which South African capital is destined to play a special role through the development of trade, strategic partnerships and the like. In exchange for acting as the agent of globalisation, the continent will offer South Africa a preferential option on its traditionally promised largesse of oil, minerals and mining.[44]

What these initiatives highlight is that within a broader concern for multilateralism, a more focused version of pan-Africanism has emerged as one strand of the new South Africa's foreign policy.

Once again, however, Pretoria's attempts to play to both Western and African governments proved difficult. The contradictions inherent in

South Africa's efforts to champion both liberal values of human rights, democracy and the rule of law, and the idea of African solidarity were made dramatically clear in the two separate crises in Nigeria in 1995 and in Zimbabwe since 2000. In both these cases, Pretoria found itself torn between two different types of multilateralism: one infused by liberal values about what constitutes appropriate conduct within a state's borders, and another informed by ideas of sovereign autonomy, pan-African solidarity, and the virtues of private rather than public criticism. The crisis in Nigeria developed during October and November 1995. It culminated in General Sani Abacha's decision to execute Ken Saro-Wiwa and eight other activists at the same time as Commonwealth leaders were meeting at their summit in Auckland, New Zealand. Abacha had taken power after annulling the 1993 presidential elections in Nigeria. According to Deputy Minister for Foreign Affairs, Aziz Pahad, Pretoria's objectives in the crisis were to prevent the execution of Saro-Wiwa and his colleagues, to secure the release from prison of Chief Moshood Abiola (the supposed winner of the 1993 elections) and to encourage the democratisation process in the country.[45] Unfortunately, South Africa's preferred strategy of quiet diplomacy failed to have the desired effect upon Abacha's junta. After the executions, Mandela publicly accused Abacha of 'judicial murder' and stated, 'If Africa refrains from taking firm action against Nigeria, then talk about the renaissance in Africa is hollow, is shallow.'[46]

In relation to our theme of multilateralism, South Africa's response to the crisis was notable in several respects. First, Pretoria's initial instincts were to engage in quiet, bilateral diplomacy with Abacha's regime rather than multilateral initiatives. Second, Pretoria refused to speak out against Abacha's actions at the UN, probably to avoid breaking ranks with other African states. Third, despite Mandela's personal efforts to ostracise Abacha's regime after the executions – such as recalling South Africa's High Commissioner to Nigeria, arguing for the US and UK (United Kingdom) to impose oil sanctions, and summoning the local Shell manager before him[47] – when he called a SADC summit in December to discuss the organisation's policy on Nigeria, SADC leaders refused to take a stance and handed the issue to the Commonwealth. Finally, after the Commonwealth created its Ministerial Action Group, in large part to address the Nigerian crisis, despite being a member, 'Pretoria did very little on CMAG and got off it as soon as it decently could.'[48] In sum, not only was Pretoria revealed to be a reluctant multilateralist, its desire to champion African solidarity was directly at odds with its stated foreign policy principles of speaking up for liberal values of human rights, democracy and the rule of law.

A similar story was evident in South Africa's relationship with Zimbabwe after 2000. Once again, Mbeki was seen to be a reluctant multilateralist, preferring instead to engage in quiet, bilateral diplomacy with Mugabe's regime. Once again, this strategy brought few, if any, tangible results, although it is fair to say that South Africa had less leverage over Mugabe's regime than many observers believed.[49] Nevertheless, this strategy had a significant impact on the multilateral responses to the crisis. In particular, it was notable that South Africa did not call for the UN to play a leading role in relation to Zimbabwe. Nor did Pretoria speak out against the SADC leaders who publicly supported Mugabe's actions. Similarly, South Africa's actions helped create division within the Commonwealth. This was in spite of the fact that the actions of Mugabe's government clearly breached the principles of state conduct set out in the Commonwealth's Harare Declaration.[50]

On the one hand, as Zimbabwe's crisis intensified, Mbeki repeatedly tried to reassure both white South African and international capital that his government would never pursue the sort of policies evident under Robert Mugabe. On the other, he vocally depicted himself as standing up to the so-called white countries that took a more forceful stance against Mugabe's authoritarianism. Writing in *ANC Today*, for instance, Mbeki accused the 'White world' of possessing a 'stubborn and arrogant mind-set [that] at all times must lead ... its demands must determine what everybody else does'. Commonwealth leaders who sought to punish Mugabe were quickly dismissed as racists 'inspired by notions of White supremacy' and who felt uneasy at their 'repugnant position imposed by inferior Blacks'.[51] It is the contradictions and tensions such as these within South Africa's multilateral diplomacy that the chapters in this volume explore in more detail.

Overview of the book

In Chapter 1, Scarlett Cornelissen examines Pretoria's role within the UN, seeing the General Assembly in particular as one of the key forums through which international society's relations with South Africa thawed dramatically after the end of white minority rule. On the South African side, full readmission to the UN system, exemplified by a reinvigorated and activist role in many of the UN's agencies, publicly demonstrated that Pretoria was no longer the 'world's polecat' but had resumed its place within international politics as a regular – if not 'just another' – member state. Certainly, the UN played a distinctive position in South Africa's early post-apartheid international relations and Pretoria's multilateralism was first practised and tested within UN forums.

Interestingly, as Cornelissen discusses, Pretoria used its multilateral engagement within the UN to project itself as an ostensible 'leader' of the developing world in general and of Africa in particular. This involved various attempts by South Africa to drive an Africa-centred policy at the UN. In practical terms this appeared in Pretoria's attempts to ground its UN policies under an overarching framework closely tied to its ambitions in Africa. This was graphically shown in South Africa's role as a key promoter of the NEPAD, but also by the way in which Pretoria repeatedly engaged with the UN over matters pertaining to the continent. On the other hand, as the crises in both Nigeria and Zimbabwe attest, South Africa was at times reluctant to involve the UN in ostensibly 'African' disputes. Pretoria's desire to engage with the UN also encountered problems when other African states resented what they saw as South Africa's hegemonic ambitions within the continent. And in projecting South Africa as the 'leader' of Africa, Mbeki opened himself up to criticism for his lethargic response to Zimbabwe's crisis while preaching about Africa's democratic 'renaissance'.[52] As Cornelissen suggests, contradictions and tensions such as these have been apparent within South Africa's multilateral strategies at the UN.

In Chapter 2, Donna Lee focuses on South Africa's influence and strategies within the WTO. Although a comparatively recent member, Pretoria quickly became an active participant in WTO deliberations, especially through its attempts to play a facilitating or bridge-building role between the developed and less developed states. As a facilitator in the WTO, Lee argues, South Africa pursued diplomatic strategies designed to project its own trade policy interests, especially the need to gain increased market access within the agricultural sector. These strategies were conducted within a neoliberal framework. This reflected Pretoria's commitment to its 1996 Growth, Employment and Redistribution programme (GEAR), which emphasised the need for an export-led growth strategy. Not surprisingly, therefore, South Africa has been a keen supporter of the WTO's trade liberalisation agenda. At the same time however, it has supported the negotiating process within the WTO by working to try to reduce conflict and differences between Northern and Southern states by facilitating dialogue between these two blocs on divisive issues. South Africa's extensive network of bilateral and regional relationships with Southern states, particularly African countries and the so-called majors, provided Pretoria with the potential diplomatic leverage to successfully pursue its economic and strategic interests in the WTO utilising a familiar middle power facilitating diplomacy.

Indeed, South Africa emphasised its Southern identity through projects such as the NEPAD, as well as its active membership of various regional organisations such as the African Union, the Non-Aligned Movement and the SADC. But unlike most developing states, South Africa also enjoyed extensive and growing diplomatic and economic ties with Northern states, especially the US, the G8 and the EU. These include the EU–SADC agreement (see Chapter 4) and Washington's African Growth and Opportunity Act (AGOA). South Africa is also a member of the group of key finance ministers known as the G20. Although dominated by Northern states, the G20 has provided South Africa with close strategic ties to both the G7 and other key middle powers. In turn, this unique set of relationships enhanced Pretoria's ability to act as a facilitator, not least because it was well respected and well connected in Africa and the key Northern states. The effectiveness of this strategy, as Lee notes, largely depends upon how one interprets Pretoria's ability to simultaneously represent and carry Africa in the 'off the record' and 'green room' meetings within the WTO. In Lee's opinion, it is doubtful that South Africa can sustain such a diplomatic position, which requires Pretoria to encourage Southern members to sign up to the neoliberal agenda of the rich industrialised states. Resistance to this has been perennial within the WTO and has consistently undermined the effectiveness of South Africa's multilateralism and highlighted the tensions within Pretoria's bridge-building strategy.

In Chapter 3, Sally Morphet examines South Africa's role within the oft-overlooked Non-Aligned Movement, which South Africa chaired between 1998 and 2003. During this period, Morphet suggests that Pretoria's diplomats gained valuable practical experience of multilateral diplomacy, something that had been denied to the country during the years of isolation. Furthermore, Mandela's patronage of the organisation enhanced its legitimacy at a time when it was still struggling to define a clear role for itself after the end of the Cold War. In the post-Cold War era, the NAM experienced difficulties related to self-definition. In particular, its members found themselves having to answer questions about the organisation's identity, its purpose and its practical achievements.[53] In part at least, South Africa joined the NAM and assumed the role of chair as a means of repaying debts accrued to the body during the apartheid era. The NAM had consistently condemned apartheid, although it did little in practical terms. This was not unique to South Africa's relationship with the NAM. In the immediate post-apartheid years South African foreign policy was often driven by a desire to repay the ANC's perceived debts and not offend previous supporters of the liberation struggle. However, South Africa's participation within the NAM was about more than paying off old debts; it also offered, as Morphet points out, an important symbolic resource. In particular, it sent a powerful signal that post-apartheid South Africa identified with the South. It is this symbolic element of diplomacy that, arguably, was the central rationale behind South Africa's decision to chair the NAM from 1998 until 2003.

Stephen Hurt's analysis of South Africa's relations with the EU in Chapter 4 starts by situating the relationship within an understanding of Pretoria's domestic political economy. Hurt argues that the South Africa–EU relationship illustrates many of the central features of post-apartheid South Africa's integration into the global economy. As Hurt makes clear, Pretoria prioritised neoliberalism as the principal framework for understanding how the country could and should incorporate itself into the global economy. Unfortunately, this has been detrimental to the developmental needs of South Africa's poor black majority.

While Hurt notes that South Africa could not and should not avoid engagement with the global economy, it is the *nature* of this integration and the *importance* attached to it, which he argues should be opened up to more critical debate. The problem for South Africa's poorest citizens is that supporters of the idea that the needs of the black majority should be put before the perceived need to liberalise the country's economy have been marginalised by (and within) successive ANC governments. As a result, most official debate has taken it for granted that South Africa's 'national interest' requires the strengthening of ties with the EU. The 'debate' then simply revolved around deciding how best to do that, even though the subsequent deal left the region and many of its people worse off. This view is shared not only by the five conglomerates which dominate the South African economy, but also by local finance capital, their external allies in the form of the international financial institutions (IFIs) and, implicitly, by Thabo Mbeki. Problematically, as Hurt notes, unlike in other multilateral bodies, if South Africa chooses to act alone it cannot expect to form alliances with other Southern elites, which, in turn, raises questions about its avowedly reformist approach to the global economic order.

Issues of reform versus solidarity with Southern elites have also been evident in Pretoria's Africa policies. As James Hamill concludes in Chapter 5, under Mbeki's leadership, 'South Africa appears to be retreating from a vigorous defence of democratic principles, ... prioritising the interests of the continent's elites at the expense of its peoples and ... reducing the founding principles of these various regional and sub-regional organisations to so much political ephemera.' During Mbeki's government there emerged a distinctly Africanist and racialised strand to South Africa's multilateralism, articulated most clearly through Mbeki's notion of an African Renaissance. Hamill suggests that there were three main reasons for this. First, Pretoria was stung to refute charges from other Africans, notably a Nigerian Foreign Minister, that post-apartheid South Africa was a white state run by a black president. Second, successive ANC governments were keen to repay African states for their support during the national liberation struggle. Third, prudential considerations were also high on Pretoria's agenda. Specifically, the ANC quickly recognised that South Africa could not long 'flourish as an island of prosperity in a wider African sea of poverty, stagnation and conflict'.

The commitment to promote the African Renaissance threw up several important challenges for South Africa. First, as Hamill suggests, the renaissance rhetoric raised expectations across the continent and the wider world but failed to deliver many concrete changes for ordinary Africans. Without results, grandiose statements of intent will soon ring hollow. In order to deliver results, however, Pretoria may have to commit itself to expending large amounts of resources on renaissance projects. The difficulty comes from the fact that Pretoria lacks both the human and financial resources to play a leading role in managing all of Africa's crises. As a result it has faced a constant challenge of how to play a leading role in Africa without overburdening itself in the process. For Hamill, Mbeki's solution lay in trying to shape the continent's multilateral institutions to suit his government's agenda. A third challenge stemmed from the domestic sources of Pretoria's foreign policy. In particular, given the extent of poverty and underdevelopment at home, Pretoria had to be careful that its attempts to achieve an *African* renaissance did not jeopardise its ability to generate a *South African* renaissance. Finally, Hamill notes that if South Africa is widely perceived to be meddling in issues it does not fully understand, and the risk is especially high outside its own neighbourhood, it could generate resentment within the continent and damage Pretoria's newly acquired Africanist credentials.

A similar set of challenges and dilemmas was evident in South Africa's regional policies. In Chapter 6 Mzukisi Qobo argues that South Africa remains caught between various impulses that push its policy-makers in different directions in relation to other SADC states. While Pretoria sought to project an image of itself as an equal partner with the region's states, it consistently struggled to shake off the label of regional hegemon. This was made more difficult by the fact that Western pressure on South Africa to assume the role of a 'pivotal state' was a constant theme of the post-apartheid era. Indeed, several Western states argued Pretoria should not shy away from playing a visible leadership or hegemonic role in the region.[54] In Qobo's opinion, Mbeki's government resolved this balancing act by preserving solidarity among the region's state elites rather than making principled interventions to promote liberal democracy in the region. This was graphically illustrated in the case of Zimbabwe, which Qobo analyses in depth. Yet, clearly, Mbeki could not have it both ways. As a result, he found it increasingly difficult to balance the demands of 'African solidarity' put forward by many African statesmen with support for human rights. In this sense, two of the central stated objectives of South Africa's post-apartheid foreign policy often pushed in opposite directions. As Qobo highlights, performing a principled balancing act within the region assumes that Pretoria is clear about the principles it wishes to promote. When the principles that guide South Africa's foreign policy collide or the region does not share Pretoria's values, the balancing act will become untenable.

Ian Taylor's study of the Treaty on the Non-Proliferation of Nuclear Weapons (NPT) and South Africa's role within it is equally critical of Pretoria's official stance. In Chapter 7, Taylor argues that South Africa's involvement in the NPT reveals that its multilateralism has been conducted within the middle power role identified at the beginning of this Introduction. Close inspection of Pretoria's diplomacy shows that it has not criticised the fundamental characteristics of the current global nuclear order. Rather, South Africa exploited what space was available to play a largely technical role, namely, to smooth out sources of friction within that order.

Regarding the NPT specifically, the Treaty has helped to delegitimise the acquisition of nuclear weapons although at the cost of legitimising the status of the five nuclear weapons states (NWS). Where South Africa can be criticised, according to Taylor, is in that by abandoning a principled position in favour of bridge-building and the search for consensus, Pretoria advanced the no time-bound agreement which means that the NWS can effectively decide for themselves if and when their disarmament should take place. However, as Taylor further notes, the desire to take practical steps towards achieving a nuclear free world appeared to play only a relatively minor role in the policies of most non-nuclear weapons states. Instead, such decisive action appeared secondary to ensuring good relations with the NWS states. In this respect, South Africa was not unusual.

In the final chapter, Paul Williams analyses some of the challenges thrown up by South Africa's participation in peace operations. After an apartheid history of conducting 'war operations' on the African continent, South Africa is now seen by many Western states as being among the most effective contributors to keeping the peace in Africa. Williams starts by discussing two ongoing debates about contemporary peace operations, namely, what are they for, and which entities can legitimately authorise and conduct them? South Africa has tended to adopt a post-Westphalian approach to peacekeeping that considers it necessary to promote liberal structures of governance within states rather than just keep the peace between them. On the second question, Pretoria has adopted a pragmatic approach to multilateralism and conducted peace operations without securing the official authorisation of either the UN Security Council or the SADC. Williams then provides an overview of the conceptual thinking behind Pretoria's peacekeeping philosophy and its practical participation in peace operations by focusing on its missions in Lesotho, the Democratic Republic of Congo (DRC), and Burundi. In the final section of the chapter he reflects upon the main challenges that have emerged from Pretoria's current agenda.

In addition to the debates over the legality and effectiveness of Pretoria's track record and liberal approach to peacebuilding, Williams highlights three key challenges related to South Africa's domestic politics: consultation, cost and capability. Peace operations represent another area where the executive has acted with little or no consultation with parliament let alone wider South African society. In addition, the cost of mounting effective operations generated heated domestic debate, especially after the notorious arms deal in which South Africa purchased military equipment that was both hugely expensive and of little help in conducting peace operations. In relation to capabilities, the parlous state of the SANDF, not least because of the devastating impact of HIV/AIDS, suggests that South Africa is unlikely to be able to carry the burden of expectations which Mbeki's statements of intent and Western aspirations of finding 'African solutions to African problems' have placed upon it. As a result, Pretoria is likely to continue exploring pragmatic solutions to the multilateral dilemmas thrown up by the big issues of war and peace in Africa.

In many respects, the dilemmas, challenges and tensions evident across many areas of the new South Africa's multilateralism emerge from the government's inability to clearly answer the question: what and who are its foreign policies for? Although underpinned by liberal assumptions about diplomatic conduct, multilateralism is first and foremost a means of conducting foreign policies; it does not dictate the objectives foreign policies should strive to achieve.

Until Pretoria is clear about the values it wishes to promote, and the relative diplomatic weight it should give to protecting sovereignty, human rights, the rule of law or pan-Africanism, its new multilateralism will remain beset by some much older contradictions.

Notes

1. Caporaso, J., 'International Relations Theory and Multilateralism: The Search for Foundations', *International Organization*, 46:3 (1992) p. 601.
2. Both these elements are present in Robert Keohane's definition of multilateralism as the 'practice of co-ordinating national policies in groups of three or more states': Keohane, R., 'Multilateralism: An Agenda for Research', *International Journal*, 45:4 (1990) p. 731.
3. See, for example, Yarbrough, B. and Yarbrough, R., *The World Economy, Trade and Finance* (New York: Dryden Press, 1992).
4. Ruggie, J., 'Multilateralism: The Anatomy of an Institution' in John Ruggie (ed.), *Multilateralism Matters: The Theory and Practice of an Institutional Form* (New York: Columbia University Press, 1993) p. 11. Emphasis added.
5. Nel, P., 'In Defence of Multilateralism: The Movement of the Non-Aligned Countries in the Current Global Order'. Paper presented at a DFA/FGD workshop on 'South Africa and the NAM in an Era of Globalisation', Pretoria, 25–30 April 1998, p. 3.
6. Winters, A., *Trade Policy as Development Policy: Building on Fifty Years' Experience* (Geneva: UNCTAD, 1999).
7. Ruggie, J., 'International Regimes, Transactions and Change: Embedded Liberalism in the Postwar Economic Order', *International Organization*, 36:2 (1982) pp. 379–405.
8. Ruggie, 'International Regimes', p. 402.
9. Murphy, C. N., *International Organisation and Industrial Change: Global Governance since 1850* (Cambridge: Polity, 1994).
10. Miller, J., *Origins of the GATT: British Resistance to American Multilateralism* (Cambridge: Cambridge University and Levy Economic Institute Working Paper No. 318, 2000) fn. 49.
11. Ikenberry, G. J., *After Victory: Institutions, Strategic Restraint, and the Rebuilding of Order after Major Wars* (Princeton: Princeton University Press, 2001).
12. Haas, E. B., 'Collective Conflict Management: Evidence for a New World Order' in Thomas G. Weiss (ed.), *Collective Security in a Changing World* (Boulder: Lynne Rienner, 1993) p. 98.
13. Cox, R. W., 'Social Forces, States, and World Orders: Beyond International Relations Theory' in Robert Keohane (ed.), *Neo-Realism and Its Critics* (New York: Columbia University Press, 1986) p. 219.
14. Williams, G., cited in Anne Showstack Sassoon, 'Hegemony, War of Position and Political Intervention' in Anne Showstack Sassoon (ed.), *Approaches to Gramsci* (London: Writers & Readers, 1982) p. 94. Emphasis added.

15. Cox, R. W., 'Middlepowermanship, Japan and Future World Order', *International Journal*, 44:4 (1989) p. 172.
16. Gale, F., '*Cave "Cave! Hic Dragones"*: A Neo-Gramscian Deconstruction and Reconstruction of International Regime Theory', *Review of International Political Economy*, 5:2 (1998) p. 274.
17. Taylor, I., 'The "Mbeki Initiative": Towards a Post-Orthodox New International Order?' in Philip Nel *et al.* (eds), *South Africa's Multilateral Diplomacy and Global Change* (Aldershot: Ashgate, 2001).
18. Williams, P. and Taylor, I., 'Neoliberalism and the Political Economy of the "New" South Africa', *New Political Economy*, 5:1 (2000) pp. 21–40.
19. Nel, P., 'Approaches to Multilateralism'. Paper presented at biennial conference of the South African Political Science Association, Saldanha, 29 June to 2 July 1999, p. 6.
20. See Taylor, I., *Stuck in Middle GEAR: South Africa's Post-Apartheid Foreign Relations* (Westport, Connecticut: Praeger, 2001).
21. *Mail and Guardian* (Johannesburg), 7 August 2003.
22. See among others, Aly, A., 'Post-Apartheid South Africa: The Implications for Regional Cooperation in Africa', *Africa Insight*, 27:1 (1997) pp. 24–31; Bischoff, P.-H. and Southall, R., 'The Early Foreign Policy of the Democratic South Africa' in S. Wright (ed.), *African Foreign Policies* (Boulder: Westview Press, 1999); Carim, X., 'International Relations Theory, Global Change and a Post-Apartheid Foreign Policy', *Acta Academica*, 26:2–3 (1994); Carim, X., *South Africa and UNCTAD IX: New Beginnings?* (Pretoria: Institute of Strategic Studies, Occasional paper no. 7, 1996); Carim, X., 'Multilateral Trading, Regional Integration and the Southern African Development Community', *South African Journal of Economics*, 65:3 (1997) pp. 334–53; Hamill, J. and Spence, J., 'South Africa and International Organisations', in W. Carlsnaes and M. Muller (eds), *Change and South African External Relations* Halfway House, South Africa: International Thompson Publishing, 1997) pp. 211–30; Kromberg, M., 'SA's Niche in the Global Village', *SA Now*, 1:6, (1996); Legum, C., 'South Africa's Potential -Role in the Organisation of African Unity', *South African Journal of International Affairs*, 1:1 (1993) pp. 17–22; Makin, M., 'The Prodigal Returns: South Africa's Re-Admission to the Commonwealth of Nations, June 1994' *South African Journal of International Affairs*, 4:1, (1996); Muller, M., 'South Africa's Changing External Relations' in M. Faure and J.-E. Lane (eds) *South Africa: Designing New Political Institutions* (London: Sage, 1996) pp. 121–50; Nel P., *et al.*, 'Multilateralism in South Africa's Foreign Policy: The Search for a Critical Rationale', *Global Governance*, 14:3 (2000) pp. 43–60; Nel P., *et al.* (eds), *South Africa's Multilateral Diplomacy and Global Change* (Aldershot: Ashgate, 2001); Schoeman, M., 'South Africa as an Emerging Middle Power', *African Security Review* (online), 9:3 (2000); Solomon, H. (ed.), *Fairy Godmother, Hegemon or Partner? In Search of a South African Foreign Policy* (Halfway House: Institute of Strategic Studies Monograph Series No. 13, 1997); Solomon, H., 'Middle Power Leadership vs. Cooperative Leadership: Some Reflections on South Africa's Foreign Policy', *African Journal of International Affairs and Development*, 3:1 (1998) pp. 69–80; Spence, J. E., 'A Post-Apartheid South Africa and the International Community', *Journal of Commonwealth and Comparative Politics*, 31:1 (1993) pp. 84–95; Spence, J. E., 'The Debate over South Africa's Foreign Policy',

South African Journal of International Affairs, 4:1 (1996) pp. 118–25; Spence, J. E., 'The New South African Foreign Policy: Moral Incentives and Political Constraints' in Toase, F.and Yorke, E. (eds), *The New South Africa: Prospects for Domestic and International Security* (Basingstoke: Macmillan, 1998); Taylor, I., 'Rethinking the Study of International Relations in South Africa', *Politikon*, 27:2 (2000) pp. 207–20; Taylor, I., 'The Cairns Group and the Commonwealth: Bridge-Building for International Trade', *Round Table*, No. 355 (2000) pp. 375–86; Taylor, *Stuck in Middle GEAR*; Taylor, I. and Williams, P., 'South African Foreign Policy and the Great Lakes Crisis: African Renaissance Meets Vagabondage Politique?', *African Affairs*, 100: 399 (2001) pp. 265–86; Taylor, I. and Nel, P., ' "Getting the Rhetoric Right", Getting the Strategy Wrong: "New Africa", Globalisation and the Confines of Elite Reformism', *Third World Quarterly*, 23:1 (2002) pp. 163–80; Vale, P. and Black, D., *The Prodigal Returns: The Commonwealth and South Africa, Past and Future* (Working Paper No. 35, Bellville: Centre for Southern African Studies, 1997); Vale, P. and Taylor, I., 'South Africa's Post-Apartheid Foreign Policy Five Years On – From Pariah State to "Just Another Country"?, *The Round Table*, No. 352 (1999) pp. 629–34; Van der Westhuizen, J., 'South Africa's Emergence as a Middle Power' *Third World Quarterly*, 19:3 (1998) pp. 435–55; Williams, P., 'South African Foreign Policy: Getting Critical?' *Politikon*, 27:1 (2000) pp. 73–91.
23. Vale and Taylor, 'South Africa's Post-Apartheid Foreign Policy', p. 632.
24. Olivier G., and Geldenhuys, D., 'South Africa's Foreign Policy: From Idealism to Pragmatism', *Business and the Contemporary World*, 9:2 (1997) pp. 365–6.
25. Mills, G., 'Pretoria Discovers that with Greater Diplomatic Authority Comes the Duty of Engaging the Continent's Problems', *Sunday Independent* (Johannesburg), 11 May 1997.
26. Geldenhuys, D., 'Towards a New South Africa: The Foreign Policy Dimension', *International Affairs Bulletin*, 15:3 (1991) p. 19.
27. See, for example, Du Plessis, A., 'Revisiting South Africa's National Interest in an Era of Change and Transition: Theoretical Considerations and Practical Manifestations', *Strategic Review for Southern Africa*, 19:2 (1997).
28. Vale, P., 'Random Speaking Notes on South Africa's Foreign Policy', paper prepared for submission to ANC Study-Group on Foreign Policy, Cape Town, 14 March 1997, p. 22.
29. See, for example, Booth K. and Vale, P., 'Security in Southern Africa: After Apartheid, Beyond Realism', *International Affairs*, 71:2 (1995) pp. 285–304; Booth K. and Vale, P., 'Critical Security Studies and Regional Insecurity: The case of southern Africa', in Keith Krause and Michael C. Williams (eds), *Critical Security Studies: Concepts and Cases* (London: UCL Press, 1997); and Vale, P., 'Regional Security in Southern Africa', *Alternatives*, 21:3 (1996) pp. 363–91.
30. Vale, 'Random Speaking Notes', p. 23.
31. Vale, 'Random Speaking Notes', p. 25.
32. See, for example, Taylor *Stuck in Middle GEAR*; Nel, P., *et al.* (eds) *South Africa's Multilateral Diplomacy and Global Change: The Limits of Reform* (Aldershot: Ashgate, 2001); Taylor, 'Rethinking the Study of International Relations in South Africa'; Taylor, I. and Vale, P., 'South Africa's Transition Revisited: Globalisation as Vision and Virtue', *Global Society*, 14:3 (2000)

pp. 399–414; Nel, P., Taylor, I. and van der Westhuizen, J., 'Multilateralism in South Africa's Foreign Policy: The Search for a Critical Rationale', *Global Governance*, 6 (2000) pp. 43–60; and Taylor, I., 'Legitimisation and De-legitimisation Within a Multilateral Organisation: South Africa and the Commonwealth', *Politikon: South African Journal of Political Science*, 27:1 (2000) pp. 51–72.
33. On the ANC's shift see Adelzadeh, A., 'From the RDP to GEAR: The Gradual Embracing of Neoliberalism in Economic Policy', *Transformation*, 31 (1996) pp. 66–95; and Williams and Taylor, 'Neoliberalism'.
34. Vale and Taylor, 'South Africa's Post-Apartheid Foreign Policy', pp. 632–3.
35. Cox, 'Social Forces', p. 207.
36. The dominance of realist and liberal theories of international relations within South Africa is discussed in Vale, P., 'Whose World is it Anyway?' International Relations in South Africa', in Hugh C. Dyer and Leon Mangasarian (eds), *The Study of International Relations* (London: Macmillan, 1989) pp. 201–20; and Taylor, 'Rethinking the Study of International Relations in South Africa'.
37. For evidence that there are indeed alternatives see Hay, C., 'Contemporary Capitalism, Globalization, Regionalization and the Persistence of National Variation', *Review of International Studies*, 26:4 (2000) pp. 509–31.
38. See Polanyi, K., *The Great Transformation* (London: Beacon Press, 1957).
39. Gramsci, A., *Selections From the Prison Notebooks* (London: Lawrence and Wishart, 1971) p. 276.
40. Thompson, L. and Leysens, A., 'Comments: South African Foreign Policy Discussion Document' (unpublished paper, August 1996) p. 8.
41. Bond, P., *Talk Left. Walk Right: South Africa's Frustrated Global Reforms* (Scottsville: University of Kwa-Zulu-Natal Press, 2004).
42. See Taylor, *Stuck in Middle GEAR*.
43. For such a critique of the NePAD see Taylor and Nel, 'Getting the Rhetoric Right'.
44. Vale, P. and Maseko, S., 'South Africa and the African Renaissance', *International Affairs*, 74:2 (1998) p. 279.
45. See van Ardt, M., 'A Foreign Policy to Die For: South Africa's response to the Nigerian crisis', *Africa Insight*, 26:2 (1996) pp. 107–19.
46. Cited in Sampson, A., *Mandela: The Authorised Biography* (London: HarperCollins, 1999) p. 557.
47. Barber, J. *Mandela's World* (Oxford: James Currey, 2004) p. 109.
48. Mills, G., *The Wired Model: South Africa, Foreign Policy and Globalisation* (Capetown: Tafelberg, 2000) p. 268.
49. Schoeman, M. and Alden, C., 'The Hegemon That Wasn't': South Africa's Foreign Policy toward Zimbabwe', *Strategic Review for Southern Africa*, 23:1 (2003) pp. 1–28.
50. See Taylor, I., ' "The Devilish Thing": The Commonwealth and Zimbabwe's Denouement', *The Round Table*, 94:380 (2005) pp. 367–80.
51. Mbeki, T., 'Letter From the President, "Zimbabwe: Two Blacks and One White" ', *ANC Today*, 2:10 (8–14 March 2002), www.anc.org.za/ancdocs/anc-today/200218.
52. See Taylor, I., 'The New Partnership for Africa's Development and the Zimbabwe Elections: Implications and Prospects for the Future', *African Affairs*, 101:404 (2002) pp. 403–12.

53. For how it has answered some of these questions see Morphet, S., 'Multilateralism and the Non-Aligned Movement: What is the global South doing and where is it going?', *Global Governance*, 10:4 (2004) pp. 517–37.
54. See Chase, R., *et al.*, 'US Strategy and Pivotal States', *Foreign Affairs*, 75:1 (1996) pp. 33–51; and Schoeman, M., 'South Africa as an Emerging Middle Power', *African Security Review* (online), 9:3 (2000).

1
Displaced Multilateralism? South Africa's Participation at the United Nations
Disjunctures, Continuities and Contrasts

Scarlett Cornelissen

As a forum the United Nations (UN) has historically posed a challenge to South Africa's international relations. South Africa featured prominently on General Assembly (GA) agendas for a great portion of the latter's existence, and Assembly resolutions were an important instrument through which international admonishment of apartheid South Africa was expressed. However, by the 1990s the GA was one of the most important forums through which the international community's rapprochement towards South Africa manifested itself as the country embarked on its path of democratisation. For South Africa, reacceptance into the community of sovereign states was contingent upon resuming its place in the UN. In this light, the UN can be said to have occupied a distinctive position in South Africa's early post-apartheid international relations.

At the same time the UN was itself emerging from the bipolar rivalry of the Cold War. By the beginning of the 1990s, the UN, like South Africa, faced the challenge of grafting a new role for itself. In the twelve years since the end of institutionalised apartheid, South Africa has sought to do this by defining itself as a leader of the developing world. A strong focus on multilateralism in its foreign policy propels this.[1] The UN constitutes an important element of this multilateral thrust, although South Africa's political engagement in the world institution has been distinctly mottled and paradoxical, as will be detailed below. Indeed, this chapter analyses the nature, direction and implications of post-apartheid South Africa's involvement in the UN. In particular it examines two dimensions: South Africa's overall orientation to, and participation in, the various UN organs since 1994, and the connections and contrasts with its wider multilateral foreign policy. The first section sketches the context by outlining the various ways in which South Africa has been involved in the UN since 1994. The country's increased participation contrasts starkly with its position in the organisation during the apartheid era. Several factors tied to its wider foreign policy goals underlie this. The second section more fully explores the main themes that characterise the country's connections to the world body. These include the strong attempts by South Africa to use the UN as a forum to project or showcase itself as a representative of the developing world, and of Africa more specifically; and how it seeks to model itself as a middle power through its involvement in important international initiatives such as the Ottawa and Kimberley Processes, where in typical middle power fashion it has sought to play a proactive role in directing the development of new regimes within the framework of the UN.

Overall, South Africa's UN involvement is strongly shaped by its desire to increase its global stature as a progressive and African power. This has resulted in an opportunistic orientation to the world body and as a consequence, several misapplied strategies. While there has been increased activism by South Africa in an assortment of fora and for diverse causes, its overall foreign policy is characterised by contradictions, inconsistencies and incongruities.[2] Indeed, the general trend has been an oscillation between an idealist orientation where emphasis is placed on supposedly universal normative goals, and in actual implementation, a realist gestalt to foreign policy. These tensions detract from Pretoria's ability to successfully use the available opportunities within the UN to advance itself as a multilateral leader. Such opportunities include rallying, through various processes of alliance formation and advocacy, for stronger action on key international development initiatives (such as the Millennium Development Goals (MDGs)) and, where it is involved in movements to shift norms regarding security (such as in the Ottawa and Kimberley Processes) doing so with the aim of producing more robust and binding accords.

Contextualising South Africa at the UN: From outcast to participant

In historical perspective, South Africa's part in the UN's output has been transient. In contrast to the high profile the country enjoyed in the UN's early days, especially with General Smuts's involvement in the drafting of the founding Charter, for the next five decades South Africa's participation in UN affairs was curtailed by a series of hostile General Assembly and Security Council initiatives and resolutions. South Africa's policy of apartheid repeatedly appeared on the GA's agenda. In 1961, for instance, the GA adopted its first resolution condemning apartheid as constituting a threat to international peace and security, and requested member states to implement a variety of embargoes against South Africa. In 1962 the GA established the Special Committee Against Apartheid, which was to become the principal channel through which the UN engaged with the issue of apartheid. In 1974 a resolution was adopted that denied South African government participation in the Assembly, although anti-apartheid movements gained observer status. The year before, the GA in its adoption of the International Convention on the Suppression and Punishment of the Crime of Apartheid famously declared apartheid a 'crime against humanity'. Declarations adopted by the GA in the 1970s and 1980s against racial segregation in sport (e.g., the International Declaration Against Apartheid in Sports of 1977 and the 1985 International Convention Against Apartheid in Sports) played an important part in South Africa being banned, or withdrawing, from many international sporting tournaments. In 1986 the GA's entreaty to countries to enlarge the existing oil embargo against South Africa proved an effective additional strain to bilateral and UN Security Council sanctions imposed in that period.

However, by the early 1990s, resolutions were being passed to encourage democratisation within South Africa. Thus by 1993, when sustained domestic and international pressures triggered policy reform and led to multiparty negotiations in South Africa, the GA invoked a resolution to lift the oil embargo. This followed two resolutions by the Security Council in 1992 (numbers 765 and 772) for greater international assistance to South Africa's democratisation efforts, and the establishment of a UN Observer Mission to South Africa (UNOMSA) in preparation for the country's first broad-based elections.

Thus to South Africa's new political leaders, the UN played an instrumental part in cohering and transmitting international censure of apartheid South Africa, and in supporting domestic efforts at reform. It was thus logical and understandable that the post-apartheid government adopted a positive stance towards the world body, proclaiming that 'South Africa's people look forward to our country's return as a full and active member of the United Nations family.'[3]

More significantly, however on a rhetorical level, the UN and the values that underlie it (such as cooperation and non-discrimination) have proved strategically useful for the international orientation and goals of the current African National Congress (ANC) government. Shortly before the country's first democratic elections, Nelson Mandela's outline of key external objectives and strategies for post-apartheid South Africa heralded a new era in the country's foreign policy.[4] The strong focus on certain fundamental principles (i.e., democratisation, human rights, respect for the rule of law) and the formulation of foreign policy on core pillars (interdependence, maintaining international stability and a commitment to Africa) were to be continuous features of Pretoria's foreign policy. Despite marked differences in output between the Mandela and Mbeki presidencies, the central aims and content have broadly remained the same.[5]

These principles and pillars (albeit quite contradictory) have formed the basis of much international activism and have manifested themselves in intense multilateral and bilateral engagement and involvement in a series of conventions, treaties, declarations and other forms of lobbying. The UN is an important arena for South Africa's rapid reintegration into the world and in the twelve years since its full re-entry into the General Assembly, South Africa has sought to increase its profile in the body, with varying success. Early on, Pretoria demonstrated an enthusiasm for taking a leadership role within the organisation. Thus in 1996 the country assumed leadership of the United Nations' Conference on Trade and Development (UNCTAD) IX for a four-year period and in 1997 it was elected a vice-president of the Assembly. In the same year it became chair of the UN Commission on Human Rights for a three-year term, and Pretoria was elected to the council of the UN's Educational, Scientific and Cultural Organisation (UNESCO), whilst also chairing the Session of the Preparatory Commission for the Implementation of the Comprehensive Nuclear Test-Ban Treaty. In addition to this it had also been elected member of the executive board of the UN Development Programme (UNDP), the UN Population Fund (1998–2000) and several other UN bodies.[6] Most recently, the country was elected as vice-chairperson of the GA's Economic and Financial Committee in 2003. Since this committee is generally viewed as one of the most influential, it was regarded as a particularly significant achievement by the South African government.[7]

South Africa's chairmanship of UNCTAD IX can be seen as the first expression of the country's active reintegration into the world organisation and of its intentions at the UN.[8] As a body that enjoys some degree of status within the UN as a mouthpiece of the developing world, chairing UNCTAD IX provided the opportunity for South Africa to raise its international profile and to attempt to define itself as a leading voice in the developing world. The time frame and context within which South Africa assumed chairmanship were very significant. As with other political alliances of developing countries (the Non-Aligned Movement being key among them – see Chapter 3), UNCTAD faced a growing level of questioning of its relevance after the end of the Cold War. It had the additional challenge of maintaining a role as broker of favourable international trade conditions for the developing world, even though the newly established World Trade Organisation made this increasingly difficult.

In this context, South Africa defined its role as taking a leading position in resuscitating UNCTAD. This was reflected in the Midrand Declaration, adopted at the end of the ninth Conference, and drafted by South Africa's Minister of Trade and Industry. The Declaration emphasised that UNCTAD still had a role to play in addressing the specific developmental challenges faced by the Least Developed Countries (LDCs) and specifically the African continent.[9] As chair, South Africa undertook to proactively foster cooperation and coordination among members. In retrospect it is clear that some of the early optimism that surrounded South Africa's chairmanship was misapplied, as UNCTAD's ability to influence international trade negotiations continues to wane and the body seems to be eclipsed by other, emerging alliances among developing countries.[10] This is reflective of the shifting dynamics of international trade bargaining as new groupings (such as the G20+ and the India–Brazil–South Africa Dialogue Forum – see Chapter 7) form and fragment.[11] From South Africa's vantage point, UNCTAD certainly provides less opportunity to affect international decision-making and the country has accordingly attached less and less importance to it after it gave up its chairmanship of the body. UNCTAD IX nonetheless gave the country a means to raise its own political visibility in the first years of its global reintegration.

Indeed, chairing UNCTAD IX allowed South Africa to fulfil a major platform of its multilateral diplomacy: using key UN events or conferences to raise its stature and to mark foreign policy priorities. This may be seen as part of a broader external orientation whereby, over the past decade, South Africa has used international events of various sorts – cultural, sports and international political meetings – as a means of international engagement and to attain foreign policy goals, such as boosting its visibility or attracting foreign investment. This includes the country's increased participation in international competitions to host major sports events such as the Olympic Games or the FIFA World Cup. A general feature of today's sports events bidding competitions is a particular means of political framing and imaging. South Africa's sports bids have characteristically cast it as a major African power that seeks to assist in the continent's renaissance.[12] Such eventing strategies may be seen as a subset of a wider foreign policy that claims to accord Africa a central place.[13]

Thus in 2001 and 2002 South Africa hosted two major UN conferences, respectively, the World Conference Against Racism, Racial Intolerance, Xenophobia and Related Intolerance (WCAR) and the World Summit on Sustainable Development (WSSD). Given the size and high profile of the conferences, hosting them proved a major diplomatic feat for South Africa. More significantly however, the conferences provided Pretoria with the opportunity to cast itself as a leader of the developing world and a campaigner for a transformed world order. This is in tandem with the country's general multilateral foreign policy that advocates a more equitable international economic system and the promotion of a particular global development agenda that counteracts imbalances and carries various benefits for the developing world.[14] In recent times South Africa has become deeply engaged in multilateral lobbying over specific issues such as the abolishing or reduction of agricultural trade subsidies (e.g., its participation in the Cairns Group and the G20+) or the reform of the Bretton Woods institutions, but the WCAR and the WSSD provided the first high-profile opportunities for the country to attempt to overtly advance its global development agenda.

However, the WCAR and WSSD were also significant for their discordant nature and the controversies surrounding the conduct and outcomes of the conferences that exposed many of the limitations of South Africa's efforts to place itself at the diplomatic forefront of the developing world. The weeks leading to the WSSD were characterised by disputes between developed and developing countries on the central purpose of the summit and how 'sustainability' should be conceived. From the vantage point of developed countries, the WSSD was devised as a successor to the UN Earth Summit in Rio and was hence aimed at assessing progress since the adoption of the Rio Declaration. The position adopted by South Africa and others was that while sustainable development consisted of an environmental facet, it primarily also had to refer to the balanced use of environmental and economic resources, and that poverty alleviation and development needed to receive priority attention on the summit agenda.[15] This divergence in objective played a significant role in diluting the WSSD outcome, which rather than producing a strong programme of action, tended to be an uneasy political compromise.[16] Procedures at the WCAR were equally jarred, but given the strong normative dimension of South Africa's foreign policy, and its stance regarding racism, this conference had perhaps a more lasting, negative impact on the country's international relations. The WCAR was marked by acute disagreement over definitions of racism and hampered by opposing positions over compensation for the trans-Atlantic slave trade. It eventually deteriorated into a diplomatic stand-off between Middle East and other Arab participants and Israel, the latter challenging references equating Zionism with racism and the Israel/Palestine conflict as emulating apartheid. Preparations prior to the conference also raised tensions among other participants, for example, India and the People's Republic of China (respectively over the race elements of India's caste system and Chinese treatment of Tibetans and other minorities).[17] It was however the withdrawal of the US (United States) and Israeli delegations that plunged the conference into a diplomatic debacle. For South Africa this proved a particular misfortune as it undermined the country's normative authority on racial matters, and, importantly, subverted its self-proclaimed position as representative of the 'dispossessed' (i.e., the developing world) juxtaposed against the ravages of the developed world (the 'oppressors').

But the fracas concerning the content of the conferences aside, it is significant that the two events did *not* succeed in their wider goals of promoting South Africa as a – if not *the* – representative of the developing world. Instead, on key issues there was marked division between South Africa and some other developing countries. For instance, the country was not able to unite all developing countries on aspects regarding environmental trade and there was a significant divergence of opinion among African states over whether reparations should be sought for the slave trade. In part this reflected the variable and complex nature of diplomatic events such as these, but it also demonstrates that states, despite often proclaiming collective normative goals framed by a supposedly communal identity, invariably act according to parochial preferences and interests. A body such as the UN is not immune from these pressures, and even though there may be a greater degree of predictability of outcomes based on established patterns of alliance formation – cohering and bloc formation within organs such as the GA– there is still significant potential for fragmentation and disunity.

Having said that, South Africa's framing of itself as a leader of the developing world through such events as the conferences is part of an emerging tendency in its involvement in UN bodies and initiatives. Importantly, Pretoria appears to have miscalculated about how best to gain the support of developing countries and there are tensions and contradictions in a whole range of South Africa's activities within the UN. The following section investigates some of these through an analysis of two key aspects of South Africa's UN involvement. The first explores political showmanship by South Africa on issues in which a large part of its politicking in the UN is built around particular notions and projections of itself as representative of the developing world. Much of this revolves around its membership of an amorphous developing world or even 'Afro' bloc within the GA. Its position and activities regarding three dimensions are focused on: the reform of the UN, human rights, and its promotion of a specific global development agenda that includes certain positions regarding Africa.

The second theme relates to activities geared towards the development and adoption of new regimes and that may be viewed as instances of South Africa's middle power behaviour in the UN. Its participation in wider international initiatives such as the Ottawa and Kimberley Processes and the role it sought to play in incorporating these processes into wider UN structures is investigated. In this analysis, a middle power refers to a state that is not a superpower or great power but still possesses international capabilities and influence. Its foreign policy is characteristically shaped by the desire to fulfil a mediating role in the international system, to bridge-build as it were. Customarily middle powers seek to influence international policy in a delimited range of issue areas, to shape or transform norms in such issue areas and to precipitate change more generally. Activism in the creation or mediation of international regimes is a general feature of middle powers.[18] By examining South Africa's participation in major, middle power projects such as the Global Campaign to Ban Landmines (or the Ottawa Process, as it has become known) and the Kimberley Process, the nature, motives, dynamics, effectiveness and implications of its UN involvement can be surveyed.

Showcasing Pretoria as leader of the developing world

Voting bloc formation, particularly as it manifests itself in GA deliberations, is widely acknowledged as an important indicator of political preferences within the UN.[19] Bloc voting generally takes place within the five officially recognised regions of the UN, that is, Africa, Western Europe, GRULAC (Latin-America and the Caribbean Islands), Asia and

Eastern Europe. A very significant component of South Africa's UN participation is shaped by the country's identity as a member of the developing bloc, and more narrowly the African bloc, within the GA. As a general rule, South Africa orients itself in GA and other UN body procedures to preferences and directions given by other African or developing states. There are often important differences, however, in viewpoints or voting behaviour. It is these differences that highlight the important political processes influencing South Africa's UN multilateralism: first, Pretoria often seeks to distinguish itself or raise its visibility by championing certain positions on key issues; second, it frequently presents itself as a leader or a/the representative of the developing world bloc. Tensions that arise from the latter are both a result of other countries competing for this leadership status (and thus rejecting South Africa's claim), and Pretoria's insensitivity towards the intricacies of political bargaining. In this regard, it is often overlooked that with its re-entry into the UN, South Africa had in many respects to create new diplomatic ties with a grouping of countries that functioned according to their own dynamics and from which South Africa was for a very long time excluded. This lack of institutional memory and the presence of countries who had long been influential in many agencies of the UN (such as India) may go some way to explaining Pretoria's evident lack of success in its attempt to be the vanguard of the developing world. Three dimensions of South Africa's UN participation are examined below, each providing indications about the country's priorities and shortfalls.

South Africa's global development agenda and Africa

It is fair to characterise South Africa's engagement with the UN as consisting of two overarching elements. The first is a desire to raise the profile of poverty and development on the UN agenda, based around set notions of human security and constructed within a particular neoliberal prioritising of objectives. This is linked to a deep-seated (if misconstrued) claim to an identity as a custodian of the developing world and particularly, the African continent. The country *does* make extensive attempts to have more focus placed on Africa within the UN, most recently manifested mainly in its promotion of the New Partnership for Africa's Development (NEPAD).

A second element is through its emphasis on promoting stability and security on the African continent, and its attempt to steer policies and goals surrounding African peace and security initiatives in the UN. Of this, its involvement in the peace negotiations and subsequent operations in the Democratic Republic of Congo (DRC) and Burundi is significant for indicating a different dimension in the relationship between itself and the UN as far as the African continent is concerned (see Chapter 5).

Indeed, whilst South Africa has gained increased commitment from the international body to Africa, it has come at a price: Pretoria has had to entrust a considerable degree of its own resources to lend credence to its professed Africa focus.

But South Africa's increased contribution, in various forms in the resolution of the conflicts and, in the case of the DRC, its political reconstruction, is significant for signalling a gradual but clear development of Mbeki's claims regarding the 'African Renaissance'.

However, it is arguable that the decision taken by the South African government in July 2004 not to extend its forces in the DRC upon the UN's request points to an ambivalence between the UN and South Africa as far as African peacekeeping is concerned. Certainly, while South Africa's activism within the UN clearly requires a greater commitment from Pretoria, there is a considerable degree of unwillingness and inability (due in part to an ageing armed forces with a high incidence of HIV/AIDS infection) by South Africa to yield to such demands. This begs the question of whether there is any actual substance to South Africa's proclaimed allegiance to helping solve Africa's conflicts.

The country has nonetheless found many creative ways of infusing 'Africa' and its global development agenda more broadly into its policies at the UN. One example is the way the government has linked international sentiment against the US-led war on terrorism with its campaign (championed by Mbeki) for an international economic system that is based on a more equitable distribution of resources. This is encapsulated in Mbeki's statement to the fifty-sixth session of the UN General Assembly:

It would seem obvious that the fundamental source of conflict in the world today is the socio-economic deprivation of billions of people across the globe, co-existing side-by-side with islands of enormous wealth and prosperity within and among countries. This necessarily breeds a deep sense of injustice, social alienation, despair and a willingness to sacrifice their lives among those who feel they have nothing to lose and everything to gain, regardless of the form of action to which they resort.[20]

In this, the South African government also strongly advocates reforming and fortifying the UN as a multilateral forum. As a result, the government postures its position (in a rather maudlin fashion, it might be said) as being an advocate of

> a strong, effective and popularly accepted UN ... because we are poor. We do so because of the place our country and people occupy in the contemporary world. That place is defined by the fact that we are a developing country, whose central challenge is the eradication of poverty and underdevelopment, a challenge we share with the rest of the African continent.[21]

This theme has persisted up to the Millennium Review Summit that was held in September 2005. The summit was aimed at assessing progress that had been made with the implementation of the eight Millennium Development Goals agreed to by the GA five years earlier.[22] Many governments in the developing world had hoped to use the summit to secure financial commitments by industrialised states to help them reach development targets. The reform of the UN was a further major topic of deliberation and the summit was meant to reach some concrete conclusion in this respect. Instead, diplomatic wrangling specifically over the Security Council restructuring both prior to and during the summit caused discussion on the MDGs to be subsumed under the politically more challenging issue of UN reform. In response, Mbeki lamented the summit process and the diluted nature of the summit outcome document as 'half-hearted, timid and tepid', indicative of the lack of a 'security consensus ... because of the widely disparate conditions of existence and interests among the Member States of the UN as well as the gross imbalance of power that define the relationship among these Member States'.[23] Given that sub-Saharan Africa is evaluated the region least likely to meet the MDGs, this statement is consonant with Pretoria's foreign policy emphasis on African development. Yet, it jars with another recent incident, where the South African government vehemently criticised the 2004 UNDP report that indicated that inequality in the country had sharply risen during the ten-year post-apartheid period. The government was particularly scathing in its criticism, admonishing the UNDP for misrepresenting and misapplying facts and data.[24] It would seem therefore that Pretoria aims to administer specific rhetoric on global and African development in a range of UN fora but that it has little tolerance for the reciprocate from the world body.

In short, it is clear that championing the plight of the poor, at least rhetorically, is a prime element of South Africa's UN focus. The strategy of coupling this with other issues such as approaches to global terrorism or the reform of the UN however can have drawbacks, as it can fragment rather than encourage alliance formation. Each issue area also characteristically has its own coagulation of interests tied to it that determine processes of bargaining and outcomes. This is particularly evident in the debate on the reform of the UN, which has followed a fractious pattern even in established voting blocs.

Reform of the UN

The reform of the UN has been one of the issues that developing countries have collectively pursued in recent years. This has also been an issue on which South Africa has attempted to take a leading position, seeking not only to direct the debate and prioritise certain goals, but also aiming to gain a permanent seat on the Security Council. Pretoria first entered the debate on UN reform in 1997 when at the opening of the fifty-second session of the GA the then Foreign Affairs Minister argued the necessity to 'redress existing imbalances and transform [the UN] into a transparent organisation accountable to its broader membership'.[25] South Africa adopted the position held by the Non-Aligned Movement (NAM – see Chapter 3) that proposed an expanded Security Council (SC) with Africa gaining at least two permanent and five non-permanent SC seats and the elimination or extension of the veto. In recent years more attention has been given to reforming and democratising other elements of the UN, on improving the role of the Economic and Social Committee (ECOSOC) and redefining the relationship between the Bretton Woods institutions and the UN system.[26] More emphasis has also been placed on the 'revitalisation' of the GA. South Africa's efforts to advance the Assembly's role and authority are aimed at offsetting what it perceives as a shift towards unilateralism, triggered by the US-led war on Iraq and the increasingly peripheral position of the UN in the wake of this war.

By siding with the NAM and mainly using the channels of this body to signal its position regarding UN reform, that is, effectively structuring its multilateral lobbying on an issue within one organisation through another, South Africa has remained part of the lobbying cluster within the UN from which the NAM largely draws its membership. Rather than strengthening its position, however, South Africa's bid for one of the projected permanent African seats on the SC has drawn extensive criticism from other major African states such as Nigeria and Egypt, who are lobbying their own permanent seats. Within the NAM, jostling among other developing countries for Council membership has served to weaken the overall bargaining position of the organisation. Rivalry within the African Union (AU) over UN reform is similarly intense, as seven states have responded to the continental body's request and put themselves forward for permanent membership on the Council. The divisive impact of the competition for SC membership was demonstrated in an AU summit held shortly before the Millennium Review Summit, where several influential African states (such as Kenya, Egypt and Algeria) declared as 'non-negotiable' an expanded Council with the extension of veto rights to all new permanent, including African, members. This is in opposition to what is proposed by Germany, Japan, India and Brazil, the so-called G4 – the grouping that had thus far gained the greatest level of support in the GA for its reform vision. The bellicose attitude of African members poses a particular problem to South Africa, for whom assuming a more powerful position in the UN is commensurate with its attempts to establish itself as a continental leader. This is part of a wider emerging antipathy by many African countries towards South Africa and the rising reaction against many of Pretoria's initiatives on the continent. For instance, recently some African countries have started to criticise South Africa's participation in the India, Brazil and South Africa (IBSA) Dialogue Forum, a tripartite body set up to lobby for the eradication of global economic and social injustices and a more humane face to globalisation. IBSA was created on the premise that the three states are major players in the developing world and in their respective regional spheres, and that combined, they will have a greater ability in shifting international policy. Many other developing countries have questioned the presumed dominance of these three, and particularly their implied claim to permanent Council membership. In Africa, leaders have taken Thabo Mbeki's attendance at the inauguration of the Brazilian president, rather than that of the newly elected Kenyan presidential candidate (which took place at the same time), as a negation of his professed allegiance to the continent's renaissance.

In this context it is significant that South Africa has to date not actively sought to gain a non-permanent seat on the Council. This could be read as one means by which the country attempts to placate African fears while at the same time increasing support for its claim to a permanent seat. Overall, Pretoria's contribution to the deliberations on UN reform has been significantly shaped and constrained by the broader processes of intense political bargaining and jostling for positions of influence.

Human rights

Human rights is a further issue on which South Africa has sought to increase its prominence in the UN. A strong commitment to human rights is one of the professed cornerstones of the country's foreign policy. Yet, as with many other elements of its foreign policy, its attempt to advance human rights internationally has been fraught with contradictions.[27] The theme of divisions between South Africa and other African and developing countries that counteract the country's claims to being a representative of the developing world is also one that pervades South Africa's activities concerning human rights at the UN. An early example of such discord was Pretoria's decision in 1997 to vote against a key measure by the People's Republic of China (PRC) that aimed to prevent its censure by the Human Rights Commission of its human rights record. The PRC had for the previous seven years been successful in mustering sufficient votes to defeat or block Commission resolutions that demanded it release political prisoners and ease controls on political and religious expressions. South Africa's vote against the PRC's blocking measure was significant in that Pretoria broke from the NAM, which voted in support of China. In the same year, South Africa broke ranks with other African countries by voting in support of a motion to have a UN investigation of human rights abuses in Nigeria. This action followed a similarly highly public (if diplomatically naïve) censure by the government in 1995, after the execution of human rights activist, Ken Saro-Wiwa. Pretoria in fact advocated the expulsion of Nigeria from the Commonwealth. Such stances were part of a more principled human rights-driven foreign policy, characteristic of Mandela's presidency. This approach did have important drawbacks, however, as the diplomatic fracas that surrounded it soon led South Africa to reframe its position.

Under Mbeki, South Africa's human rights policies at the UN have been much more in line with wider African and NAM standpoints, to the extent that it actively promoted the election of Libya as chair of the Human Rights Commission in 2003 and rarely speaks out against human rights abuses in the developing world. South Africa, itself a member of the Commission until 2006, took the lead in nominating and garnering the votes in support of the North African country. In defence of widespread international criticism, the South Africa government justified its actions in terms of the goals of the African Renaissance, of which having Libya chair the Commission was an important symbol of Africa's ability to transcend past failures. In truth, its actions were part of broader politicking related to the African Union and its attempt to inveigle African support for its bid for many key positions within the continental body. This event is a good example of the paradoxical nature of South Africa's UN involvement, as it both seeks to project an image as a moral leader *and* increase its political influence. Clearly, its actions are often not in accordance with its rhetoric.

An example where there has been greater congruence between its ostensible 'ethical foreign policy' and its actual behaviour is its activism regarding the International Criminal Court (ICC) and, particularly, its belligerent attitude towards the US on this issue. South Africa has been a vocal supporter of the ICC since its conception and was one of the signatories of the Rome Statute, the agreement that constituted the ICC in 1998. The country has promoted a strong enforcement and punitive capability for the institution and criticised the concessions reached in later deliberations on the ICC. Key amongst these was the draft Security Council resolution 1422, adopted in 2002, which agreed to exempt from prosecution personnel of states not signatory to the Rome Statute but who are involved in UN missions. This resolution came largely due to pressures from the US, who had lobbied against the ICC since its inception. South Africa adopted a strong position against the renewal of resolution 1422 during the fifty-eighth session of the GA when it contended that such an action 'would be unacceptable'.[28] It took more concrete steps when it refused to sign an 'impunity agreement' with the US in July 2003, a scheme set up by the American government whereby it bilaterally accords with countries not to have US troops prosecuted by the ICC. As a consequence of this, the US suspended military aid to South Africa.[29] In contrast, Nigeria, another vocal sponsor of the ICC and who also argued against the renewal of the exemption clause in resolution 1422 in the GA, signed the bilateral impunity agreement with the US, along with other countries such as Botswana, Senegal and Uganda.

Its activism on the ICC notwithstanding, on the whole South Africa's participation on human rights at the UN has been informed and constricted by its larger political ambitions in other multilateral fora such as the AU, and as a consequence it has been ambiguous and has not enhanced its claim as an ethical leader. Indeed, a criticism of Mbeki's diplomacy is that he has allowed South Africa's commitment to human rights and democracy to be undermined by often cynical realpolitik.

Middle powering for new security regimes: The Ottawa and Kimberley Processes

A further theme that can be discerned in South Africa's UN behaviour is its involvement in activities geared towards the establishment of new regimes within the framework of the world body. This can be seen as part of a wider, conscious attempt to advance itself as a global middle power, one that seeks to create for itself a niche of influence within a limited range of issue areas.[30]

Pretoria's participation in the Ottawa and Kimberley Processes is a good example of such middle power activism. These processes were international state and non-state based campaign networks, seeking to effect changes on key security issues and to create global regulatory instruments that would be applied in conflict areas. They are distinguished by their strong normative underpinnings and attempt to assist in the emergence of new security regimes, based on particular understandings of human security. The Ottawa Process – the collective name given to the series of deliberations on banning the use of anti-personnel landmines in wars – sought to devise an international agreement whereby signatories refrain from using landmines. The Kimberley Process sought to curtail the international trade in conflict (or 'blood') diamonds, that is, those gems mined from conflict areas and whose sale in international markets often provide the financial resources to rival belligerent groupings.[31]

Arising from initial campaigns by international non-governmental organisations (INGOs), they eventually developed into multilateral state-driven initiatives. In the case of the Ottawa Process, it eventually became subsumed under the regulatory agenda of the UN. South Africa participated in the early stages of state negotiations in both processes and sought to influence the outcomes of the various stages of deliberation. Given that both campaign networks were comprised of disparate groupings of NGOs and states, with varying objectives, South Africa sought to encase the issues of anti-personnel landmines and blood diamonds within a particular framing of security and development in Africa, emphasising its security agenda for the continent.

The Ottawa and Kimberley Processes are important for being the normative projects of a collection of middle powers. The Canadian government was a driving force in both processes, while states such as Sweden and other Scandinavian countries were influential in propelling the later bargaining phases, particularly in the Global Campaign to Ban Landmines. Through its involvement in the two processes South Africa attempted to impress upon the processes an outcome that would be of greatest benefit to the African continent.

With regard to the Ottawa Process, Pretoria played a leading role in many of the state negotiations that followed the initial campaigning by NGOs.[32] It is important, however, to regard South Africa's role within the context of its broader foreign policy goals and the fact that its involvement stemmed from the larger recognition it could gain from participating. Indeed, it was a reluctant entrant to the process, and then only upon sustained pressure by local NGOs. Disarmament has emerged as one of the issues that South Africa has strongly pursued in various international forums in recent years. However, the South African government's participation in the Global Campaign to Ban Landmines, and the various declarations and conventions that emanated from this, has been well documented as a process that essentially emerged from civil society lobbying in the country during the mid-1990s.[33] It is therefore significant that from its initial unwillingness to support a complete international ban on landmines, the South African government later became a strong advocate for this objective, particularly in the GA. What underlay this shift was the government's realisation that assuming a leading position in an international moral campaign would carry great political benefits.

Under the broad provisions of the 1980 Convention on Prohibition or Restrictions on the Use of Certain Conventional Weapons Which May be Deemed to be Excessively Injurious or to have Indiscriminate Effects (CCW), to which South Africa acceded in 1995, the use of landmines, booby traps and other devices in conflicts, covered by Protocol II of the Convention, is restricted. Generally regarded as the most significant and most open to various interpretations of the four Protocols of the CCW, states convened in 1995 to revise the provisions of Protocol II. The outcome of this saw the scope of Protocol II being enlarged, to cover non-international or internal conflicts also. In an attempt to strengthen the humanitarian restrictions of the Protocol, the amendments also aimed to make provision for more rigid discrimination between civilian and military targets, requiring advance warning of the use of mines, booby traps and other devices.

While party to the amended Protocol II, the South African government did not support a complete ban on landmines at that stage, focusing its attentions rather on supporting demining activities in Southern Africa.[34] By 1996, however, yielding to increased pressure from domestic and international NGOs and other civil society organisations, South Africa became actively involved in the Ottawa Process, which aimed at fast-tracking the complete global ban on the use of landmines. This developed out of dissatisfaction with the UN initiatives on the issue. The principal UN bodies charged with disarmament are the UN Conference on Disarmament (CD), a body established in 1979 to provide a forum for international negotiations, and the UN Disarmament Commission, whose main task is to implement disarmament decisions taken at the tenth Special Session of the GA in 1978 and to monitor broad progress on international disarmament. The CD follows an incremental approach to global disarmament, based on deliberations between member states. This stems from the political complexity that surrounds the issue of landmines, with states such as India, Pakistan, Cuba, Syria, Sri Lanka, South Korea, China and Libya consistently opposing various attempts to place this on the CD agenda. The Ottawa Process emerged out of impatience with the slow progress made on the banning of landmines in the CD.

The resulting Ottawa Declaration of 1996 saw 50 states, including South Africa, undertake to ensure the prompt conclusion of a legally binding international agreement to ban anti-personnel landmines. This move by the South African government also stemmed from an important shift in its foreign policy objectives at the time, and it rationalised its involvement that it would help reframe demining as a humanitarian and development issue, rather than simply being a security matter. The South Africa government views this as a vital prerequisite for post-war reconstruction and rebuilding on the African continent, and particularly in the context of the Southern African region.[35]

South Africa's participation signalled its wish to adopt a much more proactive international stance on the issue of landmines, and it implicitly censured the UN as a forum through which to attain this. Nonetheless, South Africa subsequently played an important role in coupling the Ottawa Process with UN procedures. In 1994 and 1995, South Africa co-sponsored two GA resolutions on a 'Moratorium on the export of anti-personnel landmines'. Indicative of the lack of consensus on restrictions applied to the use of landmines, Resolutions A/RES/49/75D and A/RES/50/70O merely concluded that further attempts would be made to 'seek solutions to the problems caused by anti-personnel landmines with a view to the eventual elimination of anti-personnel landmines'.[36]

In 1996 more concrete progress was made when, through Resolution A/RES/51/45S, 'An international agreement to ban anti-personnel landmines', co-sponsored by South Africa, was adopted. This resolution encouraged the conclusion of an 'effective, legally binding international agreement' banning the use, stockpiling, production and transfer of anti-personnel landmines. The acknowledgement of the Ottawa Declaration in the Resolution signified the first accreditation of the Ottawa Process in a UN forum.

By 1997 South Africa had more completely enmeshed itself in the international movement towards the banning of the use of landmines, through its involvement in the Oslo Diplomatic Conference on an International Total Ban on Anti-Personnel Landmines and its adoption of the Convention on the Prohibition of the Use, Stockpiling, Production and Transfer of Anti-Personnel Mines and on their Destruction. Significantly, South Africa chaired the Conference, a far cry from its refusal to support the banning of landmines in 1996.

Since then a series of GA resolutions has followed, incrementally shifting the focus from restricting the export of landmines to the wholesome proscription of their use. Resolution A/RES/52/38 of 1997, for instance, calls upon all states to sign and promptly ratify the convention prohibiting the use and stockpiling of anti-personnel mines.[37] This Convention entered into force on 1 March 1999. More recent GA resolutions have sought to fortify the move towards the ban on landmines.[38]

In short, the international discourse on disarmament and landmines, as reflected in GA resolutions, has clearly swung from a limited restriction on the use and exports of landmines to an outright ban. South Africa's early involvement in various international conferences and its role as co-sponsor of various GA resolutions suggest that it has played a part in this shift. The motives that underlie this, however, may have less to do with a virtuous turnaround on the part of the government after being put under a significant degree of domestic pressure, than with a particular understanding that it would allow the government to posture itself in an important diplomatic forum. In this regard, South Africa's behaviour may be defined as stemming from the interplay between its foreign policy objectives, and the opportunistic use of the GA as an international stage.

South Africa's involvement in a related aspect of international disarmament – attempts to stem the illicit trade in small arms and light weapons – may also be seen in this light. By 2001 the South Africa government set out to steer international negotiations in the UN on disarmament away from a focus on weapons of mass destruction to incorporate the adequate control and non-proliferation of small arms and light weapons. The government sees this as an important aspect of its attempts to establish a link between disarmament and human rights in international discourse. In recent years, however, this has become a central part of its efforts to counter the predominant focus on weapons of mass destruction driven by US attempts to garner support for its military campaign against Iraq, and what it perceives to be a weakening of the GA as a consequence of the Bush administration's foreign policy. This is also in tandem with its persistent efforts to raise the profile of

African problems of which, in terms of armaments, the illicit trade in small arms and light weapons is far more imposing than weapons of mass destruction.

In contrast to its initial unenthusiastic involvement in the Ottawa Process, South Africa played a more active role in the Kimberley Process from an early stage. Set in motion by Northern-based NGOs who lobbied for the development of instruments to control the international diamond market, by 2000 a number of states had started the embryonic process of dialogue. The Kimberley Process, named after the diamond-mining city of Kimberley, South Africa, where the first meeting was held in May 2000, evolved into a larger network of state negotiations. By 2003 the Kimberley Process Certification Scheme, the main mechanism of diamond sale oversight, went into effect. Signatories to the Certification Scheme undertake to issue certificates with all diamonds bought and sold stating that they do not originate from illicit sources. Both the UN Security Council and GA have adopted resolutions that censure the illicit trade of rough diamonds that fund armed conflicts. GA resolution (A/RES/57/302) was introduced by South Africa. Beyond this, however, criticism by some states, most notable among them the US, about the deficiencies of the Certification Scheme[39] and calls to have a more binding framework developed within the UN, such as a treaty that sets up international law to regulate the international diamond trade, have not had much effect on changing the Scheme. The Certification Scheme has also been criticised for lacking the ability to enforce compliance or to properly oversee the issuing of certificates, and not being an adequate instrument.[40] Aside from a normative argument, South Africa's involvement in the Kimberley Process, along with that of other African states such as Sierra Leone and Botswana, can be seen as an attempt to avert the potentially devastating consequences that rising negative public sentiment could have on an important cash-generating industry.[41] As with its involvement in the Ottawa Process, therefore, in the main, self-interest, based on assessments of the economic significance of the diamond industry, and evaluations of what benefits may be yielded from participation (for example, restoring the legitimacy of South African diamonds on overseas markets), rather than wholesale altruism, were important reasons for South Africa becoming part of the Kimberley Process. Pretoria's desire to ward off a full-scale international diamond consumer boycott by initiating a multilateral process was evident from an early stage, when Nelson Mandela stated that 'the diamond industry is vital to the Southern African economy. Rather than boycotts being instituted it is preferable that through our own initiative the industry takes a progressive stance on human rights issues'.[42]

It is significant that in both cases South Africa's involvement came after prolonged lobbying and criticism by local NGOs. To a great extent the country's participation in the two processes was a means to offset the pressure from a vocal, if small, domestic constituency[43] who, given their linkages to international NGOs, could do much to harm the international image of the government. Within the broader forum of the UN, South Africa however also realised the political value of advocating the cause of improved human security and using these to showcase itself as a global moral champion. Its involvement in the two processes hence had great rhetorical utility. This may be a disabling strategy, however, as South Africa is seldom able to perform beyond its rhetorical flourishes and be instrumental in the creation and enforcement of effective legal and regulatory instruments within the framework of the UN. A good example is the flawed nature of the Certification Scheme set up to control diamond transactions. More active leadership by South Africa on the design of a more powerful instrument would be of greater long-term political benefit for the country. Similarly, the 2005 Millennium Review Summit presented an occasion for the South African government to advance more concrete action on the MDGs, stronger commitments for support from industrialised states and to adopt a more cogent position on the issue of UN reform (which up to now has been subsumed and constrained by the county's desire to achieve certain diplomatic goals on the continent). In the end, the lacklustre process and outcome of the Summit can be seen as a missed opportunity and as a further instance where Pretoria has not been capable of translating its middle power claims into practice. While pragmatic impulses and considerations around trade, economic ties and political objectives account for much of the country's behaviour at the UN (as it does for the general tone of its foreign policy), it can still be argued that a more thoughtful crafting of foreign policy that privileges and indeed gives force to the ethical dimensions of the policy may in the long term be a more sagacious approach to the world body.

Conclusion

An uneasy history between South Africa and the UN initially set the context for diplomatic ties between the two entities during the mid-1990s. But since the end of institutional apartheid, South Africa has coupled an aggressive multilateral foreign policy with a progressively more proactive role in the UN and made a vigorous attempt to raise its visibility and stature within the organisation. A keen desire to use the

UN to project itself as a leader of the developing world mainly underlies this. In recent years, as the UN became a spectator in the build-up to the current US-led war against Iraq in 2003, South Africa has sought to craft a new role for itself aiming to resuscitate the UN as a multilateral agency. The country has also driven a self-conscious Africa-centred UN policy, at least rhetorically, where it has attempted to ground all of its engagements with the world body under the framework of its ambitions regarding Africa. While this is concomitant with its use of the UN to position itself as a leader of the developing world, there have been contradictions and tensions with other major African players. These have often neutralised and stymied many of South Africa's attempts.

Overall, South Africa's conduct in and relations with the UN reflect many of the difficulties experienced by its wider multilateral foreign policy: in sum, an over-ambitious policy offset by a less than adequate level of political support and often diplomatic miscalculation.

Notes

1. See for example Bischoff, P.-H., 'External and Domestic Sources of Foreign Policy Ambiguity: South African Foreign Policy and the Projection of Pluralist Middle Power,' *Politikon*, 30:2 (2003) pp. 183–202; Nel, P., Taylor I. and van der Westhuizen, J. (eds), *South Africa's Multilateral Diplomacy and Global Change: The Limits of Reformism.* (Aldershot: Ashgate, 2001); and Taylor, I., 'Legitimisation and De-legitimisation within a Multilateral Organisation: South Africa and the Commonwealth', *Politikon*, 27:1 (2000) pp. 51–72.
2. See for instance Nathan, L., 'Consistency and Inconsistencies in South African Foreign Policy,' *International Affairs*, 81:2 (2005) pp. 361–72.
3. Mandela, N., 'South Africa's Future Foreign Policy', *Foreign Affairs*, 72:5 (1993) p. 89.
4. Ibid.
5. Landsberg, C., 'Promoting Democracy: The Mandela-Mbeki Doctrine,' *Journal of Democracy*, 11:3 (2000) pp. 107–22.
6. South Africa served as a member of the World Meteorological Association (1998–2000), the executive board of the UN Children's Fund (1998–2000), and the councils of the Food and Agricultural Organisation (1997–1999), the International Telecommunications Union (1994–1998) and of the UN Commission for Social Development (1997–2000).
7. Personal communication, Department of Foreign Affairs official, 28 April 2004. GA matters are dealt with by six committees. Agenda items relating to disarmament and international security are allocated to the First Committee. The Second Committee is responsible for economic and financial matters, while the third deals with social, humanitarian and cultural matters. Decolonisation and other related aspects, and administrative and budgetary matters fall under the remit of, respectively, the Fourth and Fifth Committees. Agenda items relating to legal matters are allocated to the Sixth Committee.

8. See ITaylor, I., *Stuck in Middle GEAR: South Africa's Post-Apartheid Foreign Relations* (Westport, Connecticut: Praeger, 2001).
9. UNCTAD (1996). The Midrand Declaration. Text submitted by the President of the Ninth Session of the United Nations Conference on Trade and Development, Midrand, 10 May 1996.
10. See for instance Carim, X., 'South Africa and UNCTAD IX: New beginnings?' (Cape Town, South Africa, Institute for Security Studies, Occasional Paper No. 7, 1996).
11. See Taylor, I., 'South Africa, the G-20, the G-20+ and the IBSA Dialogue Forum: Implications for Future Global Governance', Paper presented at the UN University, Buenos Aires, Argentina, 19–21 May 2004.
12. See for instance Cornelissen, S., ' "It's Africa's Turn!" The Narratives and Legitimations Surrounding Morocco and South Africa's Bids for the 2006 and 2010 Fifa Finals,' *Third World Quarterly*, 25:6 (2004) pp. 1293–309.
13. This strategy has borne mixed results. South Africa's hosting of the Aids conference in 2000 was a tumultuous affair and counter-productive as it underscored the divisions between the ANC government on the one hand and domestic and international pressure groups on the other on how to most effectively deal with the country's AIDS pandemic. Instead of neutralising many of the negative sentiment that controversial viewpoints by key state leaders such as the Minister of Health and Thabo Mbeki elicited (one of the key aims of the conference), the government appeared increasingly isolated.
14. Nel *et al.* argue that a significant element of South Africa's current multilateral relations is based on the rhetoric of transforming the international system. They contend however that in practice, South Africa's multilateralism can at best enable limited reformism. See Nel *et al.*, *South Africa's Multilateral Diplomacy*.
15. Swatuk, L., 'From Rio to Johannesburg and beyond,' *Round Table*, 92:371 (2003) pp. 465–76.
16. Steiner, M., 'NGO reflections on the World Summit – Rio + 10 or Rio −10?', *Review of European Community and International Environmental Law*, 12:1 (2003) pp. 33–9.
17. Harris, S., 'Tampering with the World Conference Against Racism,' *Social Alternatives*, 21:3 (2000) pp. 20–7.
18. See for example Cooper, A., Higgott, R. and Nossal, K., *Relocating Middle Powers: Australia and Canada in a Changing World Order*, (Vancouver: University of British Columbia Press, 1993) and Hamill, J. and Lee, D., 'A Middle Power Paradox? South African Diplomacy in the Post-Apartheid Era,' *International Relations*, 15:4 (2001) pp. 33–59.
19. Extensive analyses are provided by Ball, M., 'Bloc Voting in the General Assembly,' *International Organization*, 5 (1951) pp. 3–31 and Holloway, S. and Tomlinson, R., 'The New World Order and the General Assembly: Bloc Realignment at the UN in the Post-Cold War World,' *Canadian Journal of Political Science*, 28:2 (1995) pp. 227–54.
20. Mbeki, T., Address at the 56th session of the UN GA, 10 November 2001.
21. Mbeki, T., Address at the 58th session of the UN GA, 23 September 2003.
22. The Millennium Development Goals that were adopted during the 55th session of the GA in 2000, are: to halve poverty by 2015; to achieve universal primary education; to further gender equality and the empowerment

of women; to reduce child mortality; to increase maternal health; to fight HIV/AIDS and malaria; to work towards environmental sustainability; and to develop a global partnership for development. Together the goals are meant to provide common direction for international development.

23. Mbeki, T., Address at the 59th session of the UN GA, 15 September 2005.
24. The Minister of Finance, Trevor Manuel, scornfully referred to the report as 'flawed' and the product of 'a UN that doesn't have a refined methodology', *This Day*, 11 May 2004. Ironically, South Africa had fared even worse in the 2005 UNDP report, having fallen 35 places on the body's Human Development Index.
25. 'Restructuring Security Council "Central to Revitalising Body" ', *Business Day*, 23 September 1997.
26. Dumisani Kumalo, South Africa ambassador to the UN, statement to General Assembly on Agenda Item 55: Revitalisation of the work of the General Assembly, 27 October 2003.
27. As noted by David Black, for instance, its major weapons procurement transaction, the Strategic Defence Procurement Package, implemented since the late 1990s, strongly belies the country's foreign policy proclamations. See Black, D., 'Democracy, Development, Security and South Africa's "Arms Deal" ', in Philip Nel and Janis Van der Westhuizen (eds), *Democratizing Foreign Policy: Lessons from South Africa* (Maryland: Lexington Books, 2003) pp. 137–55.
28. Dumisani Kumalo, Statement to the Security Council on extending the draft resolution exempting States not party to the Rome Statute, 12 June 2003.
29. 'South Africa must Remain Uncowed before Goliath,' *Sunday Times*, 6 July 2003.
30. See Hamill and Lee, 'A Middle Power Paradox?'.
31. See Andrew Grant, J. and Taylor, I., 'Global Governance and Conflict Diamonds: The Kimberley Process and the Quest for Clean Gems', *Round Table*, 93:375 (2004) pp. 385–401.
32. Van der Westhuizen, J., 'Working with the Good, the Bad and the Ugly: South Africa's Role in the Global Campaign to Ban Landmines,' in Nel *et al*, *South Africa's Multilateral Diplomacy*, pp. 31–44.
33. Wixley, S., *A Case Study of Advocacy Initiatives: The South African Campaign to Ban Land Mines*, 1997 (mimeo).
34. For example, in 1995 at a UN International Meeting on Mine Clearance, South Africa undertook to assist the UN Stand-by Capacity for training programmes for mine clearance. It also signed a Declaration of Intent with the Mozambican government in 1995 to cooperate in demining in the neighbouring country.
35. Department of Foreign Affairs, 'Convention on the prohibition or restrictions on the use of certain conventional weapons', www.dfa.gov.za/foreign/Multilateral/inter/treaties/ccw.htm, Accessed 30 January 2005.
36. A/RES/50/70O, 'Moratorium on the export of anti-personnel landmines,' 12 December 1995.
37. A/RES/52/38, 'Convention on the Prohibition of the Use, Stockpiling, Production and Transfer of Anti-personnel Mines and on their Destruction,' 9 December 1997.
38. For instance, A/RES/57/74 and A/RES/58/53, respectively on the 'Implementation of the Convention on the Prohibition of the Use,

Stockpiling, Production and Transfer of Anti-personnel Mines and on their Destruction,' 22 November 2002 and the 'Implementation of the Convention on the Prohibition of the Use, Stockpiling, Production and Transfer of Anti-personnel Mines and on their Destruction,' 8 December 2003.

39. In 2002 the United States General Accounting Office released a report criticising aspects of the Kimberley Process such as the shortage of formal risk analysis procedures and that many of its controls are not compulsory, but recommended.

40. See for instance Burkhalter, H., 'A Diamond Agreement in the Rough,' *Foreign Policy*, 73:2 (2003) pp 72–3 and Grant and Taylor, 'Global governance and conflict diamonds'.

41. The threat of a consumer boycott played a major role in the South African mining giant, De Beers, partaking in the Kimberley Process. In its 2000 annual report, the company for instance stated, 'the possible effect of conflict diamonds on consumer confidence is a threat to the entire legitimate diamond industry'. Cited in Burkhalter, 'A Diamond Agreement'. See also Taylor, I. and Mokhawa, G., 'Not Forever: Botswana, Conflict Diamonds and the Bushmen', *African Affairs*, 102:407 (2003) pp. 261–83.

42. Mandela, N., media statement, 17 November 1999.

43. In the case of the Ottawa Process, lobbying in South Africa was driven by the South African Campaign to Ban Landmines, a loose amalgamation of NGOs, religious- and community-based organisations, anti-apartheid activists and at times veteran associations tied to the Azanian People's Liberation Army and Umkhonto we Sizwe. In 1996 veteran associations often made appeals to the South African government to support the then nascent international move to ban landmines. The campaign against conflict diamonds was initiated by two Northern NGOs, Global Witness, a British-based organisation and Partnership Africa-Canada. Together, these two organisations set off a consumer awareness campaign around conflict diamonds that soon drew in and was supported by smaller South African NGOs and activists.

2
South Africa in the World Trade Organisation

Donna Lee

The World Trade Organisation (WTO) is an enormously powerful and, therefore, significant international institution for South Africa. Its 148 members account for 90 per cent of world trade in which exports account for around a quarter of world GDP. The mandatory nature of WTO agreements, the single undertaking,[1] the strengthened dispute settlement system, the robust trade review process, as well as its widening trade agenda means that it has a major impact on the economic well-being of all its members, including South Africa. Indeed no country, but especially developing countries, can afford to remain outside the WTO regime. Moreover, few developing countries can afford to remain politically isolated within the institution and given the structural and diplomatic capability asymmetries within the WTO, most countries seek alliances with others in order to counter these inequalities and thus strengthen their hand in negotiations.

The WTO has strategic as well as economic importance for Pretoria. The WTO remains a vital international forum for both the projection of South African foreign policy as well as its international status in the post-apartheid era. It provides a world platform on which Pretoria can project and perhaps increase its power at international levels as well as increase its international status by constructing a positive image of good citizenship and responsible leadership to contrast with its pariah-state image of the apartheid era. Such a positive leadership image increases the potential for Pretoria to play a middle power role at international, regional and sub-regional levels.[2]

In this chapter I explore South Africa's middle power role in multilateral negotiations through an analysis of its influence in the WTO. Although a relatively recent member, as with most international and regional organisations, South Africa became a member of the WTO in 1994.[3]

Pretoria has quickly become a more active participant in WTO deliberations attempting to play, as I will argue here, a facilitating role between
the developed countries and the developing and less developed countries. As a facilitator in the WTO, South Africa pursues diplomatic strategies that seek to project its own trade policy interests – with a key
priority being increased market access, particularly in agriculture –
within the neoliberal agenda. Since it introduced the Growth,
Employment and Redistribution programme (GEAR) in 1996 the ANC
(African National Congress) government has stressed the need for an
export-led growth strategy and so it has a keen interest in supporting
the WTO's trade liberalisation agenda.[4] At the same time it supports the
negotiating process within the WTO by working to try to reduce
the conflict and differences between the North and South[5] and facilitate
dialogue between these two blocs on divisive WTO issues.[6] Its deep and
extensive network of bilateral and regional relationships with developing countries, particularly African countries, as well as with the majors
provides at least diplomatic potential for Pretoria to be able to successfully pursue its economic and strategic interests in the WTO utilising a
middle power facilitating diplomacy. Its Southern identity is well
established, and its Southern commitments are far-reaching and
illustrated by policy programmes such as the New Partnership for
Africa's Development (NEPAD), as well as its active membership of various regional organisations such as the African Union, the Non-Aligned
Movement and the Southern African Development Community
(SADC). In addition Johannesburg has hosted development summits
such as the 2003 Growth and Development Summit and the 2003 Africa
Investment Forum. But like most developing countries, South Africa has
extensive, and growing, diplomatic and economic ties with the major
powers, and especially the United States (US) and the European Union
(EU). These include the EU–SADC agreement (discussed in detail in
Chapter 6), the 1999 Trade and Investment Framework Agreement
signed with the US, as well as Washington's African Growth and
Opportunity Act (AGOA) and Generalised System of Preferences (GSP)
for South African exports.[7] South Africa is also a member of the group of
key finance ministers dominated by the North known as the G20. This
group provides Africa with close strategic ties to other key middle powers as well as the G7.[8] Essentially, Pretoria's potential to act as facilitator
rests with its unique position as an important regional middle power in
the African context.[9] It's influence vis-à-vis the US and the EU largely
depends upon how the two interpret Pretoria's ability to both represent

as well as carry Africa in the off the record 'green room' and 'mini-ministerial' meetings of the WTO.[10]
Whether South Africa is able to carry off and successfully propitiate agreement around the neoliberal agenda between the developed and developing countries in the Doha Development Round from its launch at the Doha Ministerial in November 2001 to the completion of the Round is, however, questionable.[11] Principally, facilitation requires South Africa to be able to encourage Southern members to also sign up to the neoliberal agenda of the majors. Whether it can do this depends, to a large extent, on its influence within the various developing country groupings in the WTO such as the G20+,[12] the Africa Group[13] and the G90.[14]

One of the more interesting, and welcome, developments in the WTO during the Doha Round has been the increased activism of developing countries *per se*. As Kapoor notes, Southern members authored 'almost half of the submissions' for the Ministerial Declarations at both Seattle and Doha.[15] This increased participation reflects a greater willingness on the part of the majors to draw key developing countries like Brazil, India and South Africa into the negotiations process, but it also reflects developments within the South that have increased their strength. Two developments in particular are worth noting. First, developing countries have increased their deliberative capacity by enhancing the skills of their delegations through increased manpower, training and better preparation.[16] More noticeable, however, has been the establishment of the G20+ of Southern members that has actively opposed the majors on agriculture and the so-called Singapore Issues – investment, competition, government procurement, and trade facilitation.

Recent studies have provided much needed details of the involvement of the South in WTO deliberations.[17] As these studies show, however, Southern activism is largely restricted to the upper-income level developing countries and the middle powers. Most developing countries, and especially the less developed countries, are seldom involved in key decisions and seldom consulted during the deliberative process despite their involvement in alliances such as the Least Developed Countries (LDC) Group,[18] G20+, G90, Africa Group and the Like-Minded Group.[19] Moreover, even most of the countries that do participate – including South Africa – seem to have little impact on the drafts and final texts of Ministerial Declarations and other agreements though, of course, as Cancún illustrated, they can have a decisive impact on whether final agreement is reached in the Ministerial Conferences.

On substantive issues, however, increased participation by developing countries has not resulted in their increased influence during the Doha Round. As Lal Das notes, the Work Programme for the Doha Round that emerged from the 2001 Doha Ministerial Conference was authored by the dominant powers who did not engage in 'give-and-take negotiations' on any of the issues but rather 'put up their proposals and asked the developing countries to accept them'.[20] How might this limited impact, despite greater levels of participation, be explained?

Most studies explain developing-country participation – and in particular alliance formation – in the context of material asymmetries. Southern members are generally unable to influence WTO negotiations because of the structural and deliberative asymmetries within the WTO. Unequal material power relationships within the WTO 'predispose developing countries towards certain negotiating strategies'[21] with the optimal choice of strategies being coalition formation. According to such approaches, the asymmetrical power politics of the WTO creates the conditions in which coalitions become a 'crucial instrument' for developing countries to bolster their bargaining power and 'offer a way out of their weak position'.[22] That is, to solve the problems of power asymmetries states pursue collective action strategies. In this respect, rationalist approaches are highly prescriptive and seem intent on solving the problem for developing countries by identifying various typologies of coalitions and explaining which kind works for which group of developing country under which conditions.

The key assumption in this approach seems to be that if developing countries can increase their deliberative capacity by forming alliances to challenge the major powers, then they can look forward to significant influence in the negotiations. Unfortunately this has not been the case in the Doha Round. The G20+ countries have not been able to enjoy significant influence on issues of key interest to them despite the fact that several of these countries were part of the 'green room' and 'mini-ministerial' meetings. Perhaps developing country impotence in the WTO has as much to do with ideational factors as with material factors. That is, the key problem for Southern members is the dominance of neoliberal principles within the WTO; there simply is no way of challenging the political economy model of the major powers at present. Quite apart from the hegemony of neoliberalism, Southern members have not been able to articulate an alternative hegemonic model.

Developing countries like South Africa might be more active in the WTO, but the extent to which they can influence the rules and substantive issues of the Doha Round – rather than simply forcing a collapse of talks – has as much to do with the hegemony of neoliberalism as it does with their ability to form and sustain alliances, that is, their strategic positioning. It is necessary, therefore, to go beyond rationalist approaches to Southern participation in the WTO which tend to neglect ideational factors in order to more fully understand the limitations of developing country activism.

It is worth making a further theoretical point. Rationalist approaches view the WTO and the multilateral processes within it as neutral rule-making and procedural instruments. We usually have to turn to critical approaches to find discussion of the normative dynamics within liberal governance structures such as the WTO.[23] Rationalist scholars tend to assume that multilateralism is merely an instrument and framework in which to negotiate rules and procedures. As rules become more binding and procedures more judicial – as they have in the WTO – power politics is replaced by the rule of law.[24]

Rationalist approaches tend to explain negotiation outcomes in multilateral institutions using formal modelling which is then used to evaluate the pros and cons of the strategic choices of states within known incentive structures.[25] A similarly formal approach sees coalition formation within the context of developing country mediation roles.[26] Both approaches, in common with rational choice theory, share assumptions about states' interests in international organisations such as the WTO. In sum, they assume that state interests are known, that they are self-evident and singular, and that states can calculate which strategies will best serve their interests.

Because they do not unpack the state, such approaches ignore the socio-economically constructed nature not only of states but also of the WTO regime and of multilateral diplomatic processes. Differing trade interests within states are constantly played out prior to, during and after (when implementation issues come to the fore) WTO negotiations and as such state interests cannot be fixed, singular or even known during the negotiations.[27] For example, we cannot even begin to understand the EU's stand-off position on agricultural subsidies in the Doha Round without analysis of the political economy of agriculture within EU states. Furthermore, the notion that the WTO and multilateral diplomacy simply provides a rule-based negotiation framework ignores their socially constructed nature too. Like the states acting within it, the WTO is a product of hegemonic social forces within developed states that maintain power and domination through the prevalence of their neoliberal knowledge-claims.

Thus to fully understand the diplomatic strategy of some developing countries, and in this case South Africa (which I acknowledge may well be an exception), and the limitations of the particular middle power model Pretoria pursues, we need to go beyond a focus on the material constraints and incentives placed on states to reach agreement and conform (as rationalist approaches do) to a focus on the ideational constraints and incentives developing country states face in WTO negotiations; constraints that manifest themselves at structural, regional, as well as state levels.[28]

Clearly we need to make room for analysis of the ideational dimension to South African activism in the WTO in order to secure a better understanding of its middle power diplomatic strategy which, I will argue, is driven by material *and* ideational factors. Both explain increased South African activism as well as the limited impact this is having in WTO multilateralism.

South Africa – middle power facilitator

South Africa's goals in the WTO are to advance its own trade interests while firmly positioning itself within the neoliberal orthodoxy. Thus it has argued for improvement rather than transformation of the WTO trade system; for fairer trade policy and practice rather than new trade policies and practices. In this context, middle power facilitation is limited to a strategy of seeking an expansion of the common ground that the developed and developing countries occupy on the various trade issues.

The key features of this limited facilitation strategy are threefold: (1) increasing activism in WTO processes; (2) uncritical support for the WTO system and its neoliberal agenda; and (3) alliance formation and maintenance. This chapter now turns to an analysis of each.

Increasing activism in the WTO system

South Africa has quickly become an active and high profile actor since it joined the WTO in 1994, and especially during the current Doha Development Agenda. It was a frequent participant in the informal and much criticised 'green room' meetings at the Seattle Ministerial Conference in 1999.[29] It was also an ever-present member of the several mini-ministerial meetings that took place between the Singapore, Doha and Cancún Ministerial Conferences throughout 2001, 2002 and 2003.[30] South Africa even ascended to the role of 'green man', that is, 'Friend of the Chair', at the Doha Ministerial Conference in November

2002 when Alec Erwin, South African Minister of Trade and Industry, chaired meetings on rule-making in the WTO.[31]

At the same time that South Africa has ascended to key developing country participant, the WTO has become a far more influential body in the international political economy. Its binding rules already cover trade in goods, services and intellectual property, and, if the developed countries get their way, will in the future cover the Singapore Issues. In addition, dispute settlement has been toughened up and a robust trade policy review mechanism is now in place. With so much at stake in WTO negotiations it is no wonder South Africa seeks to position itself as an influential and active member. While this might be expected of most countries, and certainly of middle powers, we can note that not all countries have the capacity to be active members. Less developed countries in particular have such limited resources that the size of their delegations are too small and lack the necessary technical specialisation to be influential. Indeed, around half of the less developed countries have no delegations at all in Geneva and do not attend the meetings. South Africa's delegation is well above average with a permanent staff of five but below that of Brazil which has eight. This compares with Botswana with a staff of two.[32] For South Africa, as with most other small and medium sized countries, influence at the WTO rests to a large extent on its ability to join or build and sustain alliances with other countries, both developing and developed. In this respect South Africa has been a key member of important developing country coalitions such as the G20+, the Africa Group and the Trilateral Group (Brazil, India and South Africa). Indeed, South Africa was instrumental in the creation of the G20+ that, for some, is perhaps the most active of the various alliances within the WTO during the Doha Round.[33] Pretoria has also found a place in the Cairns Group – a mixed coalition of developed and developing countries united by common interests in agriculture.[34]

Despite activism in each of these groups, South Africa's chief position, and one that is controversial given the ANC's historically leftist ideology, is best described as one of bridge-building between the North and the South. This involves pushing the Northern members, and particularly the US and the EU, to follow through on their liberal commitments, particularly in agriculture where they have yet to implement Uruguay agreements on subsidy reduction and market access (which most of the developing countries, including South Africa, have already implemented). And on the other side of the bridge, South Africa works with the South to try to get them to go along with demands from the major powers to launch the Doha Round and include the new Singapore Issues in the negotiations. This facilitator positioning enhances Pretoria's relations with the US and the EU and is a likely explanation for the willingness of Washington and Brussels to accept South Africa's self-proclaimed role as key developing country and main bridge-builder between North and South (this willingness being best illustrated by South Africa's selection as a green room and mini-ministerial meetings' participant and 'green man').[35] Given the structure of South Africa's trade relations (see Table 2.1 below), however, this positioning vis-à-vis the US and the EU is hardly surprising and seems to be a sober and pragmatic response to South Africa's economic dependence upon the two. At the time the Doha Round began for example, the EU accounted for around 40 per cent of South Africa's total foreign trade while the US was the largest single trade partner, described by the ANC as its 'number one trading partner in terms of total trade'.[36]

At the same time, however, this pro-US/EU positioning leads to mistrust of Pretoria by some of its African and developing country coalition partners such as Nigeria, Uganda, India, Zimbabwe, Pakistan and Bangladesh who are far more critical of, and less willing to compromise on, US and EU positions on the new Singapore Issues and implementation of the agricultural agreements. These acute differences undermine South Africa's leadership credibility and influence within the G20+ and the Africa Group. It is notable that South Africa is not a member of the Like-Minded Group. This Group adopted the most critical stance against the US and the EU. Such problems highlight the inherent difficulties and contradictions of South Africa's middle power

Table 2.1 South Africa's key trade patterns, 2003[1]

Exports	% of total	Imports	% of total
Product		*Product*	
Agriculture	8.6	Agriculture	6.4
Mining products	23.6	Mining products	14.6
Manufactured products	67.4	Manufactured products	69.6
Country		*Country*	
European Union (15)	35.6	European Union (15)	42.2
United States	12.2	United States	9.9
Japan	9.9	Japan	7.0
China	2.8	China	6.4
Zimbabwe	2.7	Saudi Arabia	5.7

Note: 1. These figures are for merchandise trade only. South Africa's services trade is small.
Source: World Trade Organisation.

diplomatic strategy in the WTO. Because of their influence over the WTO Director General and Secretariat, the US and EU effectively selects South Africa to take part in the deliberations in the hope that it can carry the G20+ and the Africa Group, but Pretoria's close relationship with the two severely diminishes its ability to do this.

Yet this middle power strategy is vital not only in terms of the strategic and economic interests of Pretoria in the international political economy, it is also important for the effectiveness of the WTO regime. As a social construct, the WTO needs legitimacy and support from within as well as outside. South Africa can help provide this legitimacy, if only symbolically, by playing – or at least attempting to play – the role of facilitator between the North and South on some of the key trade conflicts that have dominated the organisation during the Doha Round. According to this view, South African participation can increase the common ground between the majors and the Southern members, thus opening the way for agreement and the smoother working of the institution. Furthermore, Pretoria's activism, and Southern members activism more generally, lends much needed legitimacy to the WTO as a governance institution in an age when it is roundly criticised as undemocratic.[37] That South Africa has become an active developing country member – involved in the many informal as well formal meetings – is seen by some, including the ANC government itself, to signal an increasingly democratic WTO. But clearly this is a very naïve position and one that goes against all the evidence. The WTO decision-making process continues to be undemocratic and 'tilted towards richer countries'.[38] A very small number of countries are involved in the early consultation process in the 'green room' meetings and the mini-ministerials organised and chaired by the WTO Director General.[39] 'Green room' meetings and negotiating committee meetings lack transparency; no minutes are produced, instead the chair submits a briefing to the WTO of his 'sense' and 'understanding' of the meeting. These briefings are then reflected in WTO Drafts such as ministerial texts. Ministerial texts act as agendas for Ministerial Conferences, forming the basis for the negotiations. Developing countries feel marginalised in this process and are, not surprisingly, often very critical of this procedure – which Kwa refers to as the 'manufacture of consent'[40] – since their positions get lost in the system and are often absent from the ministerial texts. This was certainly the case with the notorious 'Harbinson Text' which went through various drafts before it was submitted as the final draft for the November 2001 Doha Ministerial Conference. Throughout its various drafting stages during 2001, developing countries submitted their positions on matters such as the Trade Related Aspects of Intellectual Property Rights (TRIPS) and Singapore Issues, but these, according to many members, were not reflected in the final draft.[41] The Nigerian delegation, for example, complained that the Harbinson Text 'gives the impression that the whole membership is agreed to it … you know we have not agreed on this Draft. Our views and positions are not reflected'.[42] And because there is no record of the meetings – since minutes are not taken and no records produced – the developing countries cannot substantiate their complaints. Developing countries may well be more active in the WTO, but most remain powerless in the decision-making process. Their influence is severely restricted because the WTO remains undemocratic and opaque. Developing country proposals to reform the institution – such as the African Trade Minister's 'Abuja Declaration' – have been ignored by the WTO Secretariat and the majors.

While it is easy to identify South Africa's symbolic impact, it is much more difficult, however, to identify substantive or procedural impact on WTO policy in key areas such as agriculture, cotton and the Singapore Issues. And procedurally, Pretoria's attempts at North–South facilitation failed to prevent the collapse of the Seattle or Cancún conferences – though this is a harsh judgement since it is difficult to imagine how South Africa could have prevented either conference from collapsing given the deep fault lines between members on issues and procedures.

In light of these failures it seems more appropriate to refer to South Africa's middle power positioning as one of co-option vis-à-vis the major powers rather than simply facilitation between North and South since Pretoria was largely isolated in its key Southern alliances as I will show below. Moreover, the notable absence of South Africa during informal WTO meetings in July 2004 where a modified post-Cancún agreement was reached suggests, perhaps, that the US and the EU recognise the limitations of South Africa's middle power strategy. In the post-Cancún months of 2004 both appear to have concluded that South Africa cannot successfully deliver Africa and the other developing countries.[43] They are certainly turning their attention to other potential facilitators. During the Cancún and post-Cancún stage of the Doha negotiations for example, Botswana, as leader of the G90, emerged as a strategically important potential ally for the US and the EU and was invited to a number of informal multilateral meetings.

Advancing the neoliberal agenda in the WTO

The middle power strategy of South Africa has been more successful in advancing the neoliberal agenda in trade in the WTO.[44] Kapoor offers insights into how we might understand South Africa's conformity with neoliberal orthodoxy by pointing out that

> power fixes or privileges certain types of knowledge, and ignores and suppresses others, so that it is the knowledge claims of the dominant participants that tend to get naturalised.[45]

South Africa's middle power strategy is founded on a commitment to the neoliberal policy priorities of trade liberalisation as well as on a belief in the ability of the WTO to deliver development.[46] Indeed, Pretoria sees no alternative for achieving development other than working within a robust rules-based liberal WTO. How has this ideological commitment come about?

Studies of the political economy of South Africa point to the prominence of liberal social forces – international capital and business groups – within the state that have forced an alignment to neoliberalism within the ANC government.[47] As we might expect, the business community in South Africa has long been an advocate of neoliberal policy at state, regional and global levels. As it has come to dominate the ANC government (rather than the ANC movement which remains a leftist organisation) so also it has come to dominate public policy. A key feature of the ANC government is the rich array of public–private partnerships that serve to embed the business community within the formal governance structures. This is particularly the case in trade and investment policy. In 2003, for example, the ANC government hosted an Africa Investment Forum in collaboration with the Commonwealth Business Council to formulate strategies on investment.

As a result of this business influence, South Africa's trade negotiators at the Doha Round define the state's interests in terms of trade liberalisation. The key policy goal during the Doha Development Agenda has been to secure market access to the developed country economies as well as an end to agricultural subsidies that lead to the dumping of products in South Africa's markets. At regional levels, too, and in the ongoing SADC–EU and US–SACU trade negotiations, South Africa is pursuing these same liberal policy priorities.

This is equally true with regard to South Africa's proposals on development. South Africa maintains that if the WTO can address trade liberalisation decisively in the Doha Round then development can be delivered. South Africa's view of development is that developing countries can industrialise if they can access markets currently protected or dominated by the protectionist measures and subsidisation policies of the developed countries. Trade liberalisation would foster development by relocating production and investment to developing countries in sectors such as agriculture where developing countries enjoy comparative advantages.[48] In this way, South Africa's own classical liberal view of the development process is not so different from the view of Mike Moore, the former Director General of the WTO, who, on a 2002 visit to South Africa, stated that 'development is trade and trade is development'.[49] South Africa also appears confident that the other development provisions with the current Doha Round – the special and differential treatment with respect to market access, flexibility and reciprocity, as well as the commitment to increase technical and capacity skills – can also help deliver development to all members of the WTO.

It would be overly optimistic to expect developing countries to be able and willing to advance an alternative vision of development to challenge the hegemonic neoliberal paradigm. It would also be harsh to criticise developing countries for not doing so since development theory itself seems to have run out of steam in the 1980s and the primacy of neoliberal theory has been further entrenched by the discrediting of the Asian state-led model of development following the Asian crisis of the 1990s.[50] The neoliberal paradigm might have refiners (for example, Sen's neoliberal capabilities thesis) but it has few effective challengers within the WTO since the civil society groups have few opportunities to exercise real influence within the WTO.[51] Those less committed to neoliberalism have many doubts that special and differential treatment will do anything beyond fill the gaps in the international trade system by giving these states more time to adjust their economies to market forces,[52] and other developing countries such as India have seriously questioned the extent to which the Doha Round can and will deliver on development.[53]

Going into the Cancún negotiations, Xavier Carim, South Africa's Chief Director of Multilateral Trade Negotiations, summarised South Africa's key objective in the WTO stating that success at the Conference 'rests on developed countries to advance agricultural issues in order to advance the interests of developing countries'.[54] Similarly, Alec Erwin stated that at Cancún, Pretoria sought to

> Promote structural adjustment in the North, notably through reform of agricultural trade regimes and eliminating the protection of sunset industries. However, the only way to secure the necessary concessions is to participate in a broad round of negotiations in which the interests of the North (such as services, investment and competition policy) are on the table.[55]

Carim and Erwin are voicing exactly the middle power strategy of facilitating agreement between North and South in the context of the neoliberal agenda and showing what others feel is a naïve confidence in the WTO multilateral process. Indeed the facilitating strategy was devised at the start of the Doha Round. A Department of Trade and Industry 2000 document sets out the diplomatic agenda of Pretoria stating that

> Part of our preparations externally has been to draw together key developing countries (i.e. Nigeria, India, Egypt and Brazil) around a common agenda and shared objectives in the WTO. This would also include developing common positions with our SADC partners ... we have also shared the substance of our position at the OECD level.[56]

On all the key issues within the Doha negotiations, South Africa has advocated and supported neoliberal principles. No other Southern country has so comprehensively conformed to the orthodoxy. In the area of services, for example, South Africa supports developed country proposals to increase market access despite the almost complete lack of comparative advantages for developing countries in areas such as financial services, telecommunications, energy and transport. This position might be explained by the fact that South Africa enjoys some comparative advantage in services within African economies because it has an advanced financial sector. In agriculture, South Africa positions itself with other developing countries advocating fairer trade practices, supporting proposals that would increase market access and reduce Quad (Canada, US, EU and Japan) country subsidies. In the area of industrial tariffs South Africa again wants to see trade liberalisation. Pretoria also supports proposals to eliminate tariff peaks and tariff escalation in the clothing and textile sectors of the economy where developing countries again have comparative advantages over the developed countries. On the Singapore Issues, South Africa's approach is that new disciplines in these areas can 'contribute positively to development' and 'not merely provide advantage to advanced economies'.[57]

In sum, South Africa's commitment to neoliberal principles is sweeping and consistent. While most developing countries rejected US and EU calls for the launch of a new round at the 1999 Seattle Ministerial Conference on the grounds that they wanted the WTO to concentrate on implementing the Uruguay agreements before negotiating new issues,[58] South Africa greeted the proposal with enthusiasm, and throughout the Doha Development Agenda, the South African delegation has worked tirelessly to try to keep the negotiations on track. While most members of the G20+ and the Africa Group adopted a 'won't do' diplomatic strategy in the negotiations – to use US Trade Representative Robert Zoellick's characterisation – South Africa was quite clearly a 'can do' member. Indeed, as already stated, South Africa was a keen member of a whole range of informal and formal meetings, eventually rising to the insider status of 'green man' at the Doha Ministerial Conference.

As a 'can do' country, South Africa has adopted a 'trade-off ' strategy in the Doha negotiations. This strategy sets it apart from most of its alliance partners in the G20+ and the Africa Group, who tended to adopt a 'stand-off' strategy vis-à-vis the US and the EU over agriculture, cotton and the Singapore Issues. At each point when the stand-off between the North and South threatened to de-rail the negotiations, South Africa lobbied within the G20+ and the Africa Group for trade-offs with the US and EU. Most notable was that rather than see negotiations collapse, South Africa consistently supported the US and EU proposal to include negotiation of the Singapore Issues in the Doha Round. A few other developing states were also prepared to include the Singapore Issues, but these countries attached detailed conditions in agriculture.[59] When the EU Trade Commissioner, Pascal Lamy, dropped his insistence on inclusion of all four of the Singapore Issues and reduced his stand-off position to one issue – trade facilitation – it seemed that the South African strategy might indeed be working. But the developing countries wanted movement on agriculture prior to negotiations on any of the Singapore Issues. The EU, however, was not prepared to acquiesce, and so the talks collapsed.[60] Most developing countries were happy with the outcome, taking the position that 'No deal is better than a bad deal.'[61] The South African press and business community tended to interpret Pretoria's diplomatic strategy favourably.[62] To these sections of the community, South Africa's position was a pragmatic one, involving a sober assessment of what could and could not be achieved. This is compared to the G20+ position that was seen in some South African quarters such as the conservative press, as well as in Brussels and Washington, as unrealistic and, ultimately, unachievable.[63]

Despite the collapse of the Cancún talks South Africa maintains support for the WTO process. In particular, Pretoria points to the break-through in the TRIPS negotiations to illustrate the usefulness of WTO multilateralism to developing countries.[64] But for others the manner in which agreement on this issue was sealed in the weeks leading up to the Cancún Conference illustrates the fundamental problems within the

WTO. First, the final deal was very limited and represented a 'deeply flawed compromise'[65] because of the numerous terms and conditions that were attached to the compulsory licensing process. Critics also pointed to the undemocratic methods used to secure deals; only five countries – the US, Brazil, South Africa, India and Kenya – were actively involved in the decision to accept the US offer on TRIPS in September 2003.[66] As a result, many developing countries opposed the deal because they had not been consulted during the deliberations.

While South Africa seldom criticises the processes or policies of the WTO, most other developing countries are deeply critical of both. They point to the lack of transparency and the existence of a 'democratic deficit' in the WTO as well as the growing trade imbalances and inequalities between North and South,[67] but since South Africa has enjoyed a privileged position as a member of the decisive 'green room' and mini-ministerial meetings as well a 'green man' status, we might reasonably expect an uncritical stance from Pretoria on procedural matters.

On substantive issues, the WTO fares no better in the eyes of many developing countries as well as scholarly critics of the WTO who argue that the WTO system fails the South on development policy issues. A clear case in point being the passing of the interim deadlines on agriculture and special and differential treatment without new agreement as to progress on development in the Doha *Development* Agenda:

> No progress was made before Cancún on the development issues (Special and Differential Treatment for developing countries and implementation issues arising from the 1994 Uruguay Round Agreements). In the Geneva draft, to the anger of the Africa Group and other developing countries, the priority of the implementation issues was downgraded, and the twenty-four Special and Differential Treatment (SDT) provisions were of little or no economic value.[68]

And all this despite record levels of developing country participation in the WTO on which Alec Erwin concluded:

> This is the first time we have experienced a situation where, by combining our technical expertise, we can sit as equals at the table ... This is the change in the quality of negotiations between developing and developed countries.[69]

While South Africa points to its frequent visits to the 'green room' and its chairing of the Rules Negotiating Group as evidence of a shift towards

including developing countries in the negotiating process, critics again see
this as evidence of the co-opting of hand-picked developing countries into
the process.[70] Many developing countries are suspicious of South Africa's
'green man' status. Moreover, developing countries have chaired what are
rather insignificant negotiating groups such as rules (South Africa), as well
as the so-called miscellaneous group (Ghana) and the development group
(Kenya). The relatively low importance of these groups compared to the
Singapore Issues and agriculture groups, chaired by the majors, has added
to the mistrust of the system. As a Japanese commentator recently pointed
out, developing countries' appointment as 'Friends of the Chair' was
'meant to give the impression that the third world is participating in trade
discussions as an equal partner, but that is not the case'.[71] Developing
countries are only participating at the behest of the Secretariat and they
cannot hope to negotiate on an equal footing with the North in the WTO.
Southern members are constrained by their dependence upon the North
and the inequalities within the international political economy.[72] The EU
and the US in particular are able to dominate trade negotiations because
they enjoy material and ideational command in the WTO.[73]

Critics also point to the inequities in the 'reciprocity dynamics' of the
WTO negotiating process in which 'developing countries offer enough
to OECD countries to induce them to take on the interests that benefit
from protection'.[74] Bowing to the reciprocity dynamic – South Africa's
willingness to trade-off agriculture for the Singapore Issues – in order to
save the negotiations – can be interpreted as an act of appeasement to
EU and US interests.

Supporting the WTO system is a key arm of South Africa's middle
power strategy and one that largely advances the neoliberal agenda.
Trying to pursue this strategy within the context of active participation
in developing country coalitions within the WTO illustrates well the
contradictions inherent in South Africa's multilateralism. Such tensions
are probably inherent in any bridge-building strategy.[75]

Alliance membership and formation

South Africa's pursuit of alliance partners is typical of most middle and
small powers in the WTO who have always tended to forge geographi-
cally based as well as issue-orientated blocs, and just as the other two elements of the middle power strategy – activism and advancing the
neoliberal agenda – exposed contradictions in this strategy, so too does
this third element.

Participation in a number of Southern member alliances in the WTO
requires South Africa to publicly identify with the trade problems of the

developing countries while at the same time positioning its trade interests and policies very much within the neoliberal paradigm of the developed countries. On the one hand it prioritises the concerns of the South, while on the other it pushes for trade liberalisation. Since South Africa is an exporting economy as well as the key developing country investor in Africa this is not surprising. But its dual nature as a symbolic leader of Africa and major exporting country means that Pretoria has to develop what can be described as a promiscuous diplomatic strategy vis-à-vis various WTO members – that is, it has to seek out numerous and varied negotiating partners and groups. It is, therefore, actively involved in a range of groups within the WTO, while simultaneously conducting bilateral and regional free trade negotiations with many WTO members outside the framework of the Doha Agenda. Other WTO members adopt similar strategies. Mexico, for example, is a member of a number of coalitions within the WTO as well as regional agreements such as the North American Free Trade Association. But it is South Africa's unique position as symbolic leader of Africa, as well as a large exporting middle-income country with a broad range of trade partners in the North and the South, that makes such promiscuity a strategic necessity. This promiscuity presents a number of strategic dilemmas, not least that its negotiating partners are very diverse, politically and economically. They include the G20+ bloc of developing countries, the Cairns Group (which includes developed countries such as Australia and New Zealand), the Africa Group, the G90 and the Trilateral Group (India, Brazil and South Africa). Not only is this perverse on the grounds that it stretches the limited resources of the negotiating team, it can also leave South Africa fairly isolated within these alliances when differences over policy or diplomatic strategy arise, or when differences between the alliances and the US and EU arise.[76]

In the Africa Group, for example, South Africa has spent much of its time in an isolated position on the key issue for this group, cotton. And from the onset South Africa also breached the consensus position of the Africa Group to oppose the launch of the new Doha Round.[77] Although the Africa Group is one of the largest blocs in the WTO, dwarfed only by the G90, it is probably the weakest vis-à-vis the dominant powers. It suffers from internal divisions and high levels of vulnerability because the members are particularly exposed to bilateral pressure from the majors due to existing preferential trade agreements and aid and finance programmes such as the AGOA and the Cotonou Agreement. But, apart from the cotton issue where the Group found a consensus position, there are also fundamental policy splits within the Group on agriculture.

Uganda, Kenya, Senegal and Nigeria, for example, argue against substantive negotiations because they want to retain subsidies since they rely on imports of subsidised food and already enjoy access to EU markets through existing preferential trade agreements. South Africa and Tanzania, however, seek greater access to agricultural markets and therefore support negotiations on the removal of subsidies, anti-dumping and increased market access. The differences on agricultural subsidies left the 'continent polarised into two camps'.[78] Indeed, some less developed countries within the Africa Group remain deeply suspicious of South Africa's position in agricultural negotiations because they experience the dumping of South African products onto their markets. Most of the products in Kampala markets, for example, come from South Africa. In sum, there seems little opportunity for South Africa to enlarge the common ground within the Africa Group let alone between the Africa Group and the majors.

During the Doha Round South Africa also became increasingly isolated within the G20+ group (a group it claimed to 'lead') and was at loggerheads with its key strategic partners in that Group, India and Brazil. The differences between India and South Africa were particularly pronounced since India was adamantly opposed to any inclusion of the Singapore Issues and took a hard line stance vis-à-vis the EU and the US. This contrasts with the more flexible negotiating stance of South Africa.

Alec Erwin recognises the uncertainty in South African multilateralism in the WTO and has been critical of the poor negotiating strategies of the Africa Group.[79] Faizel Ismail has also argued that many developing countries lacked diplomatic skills in the negotiations which meant they could not be responsive to new turns in the deliberations.[80]

Pretoria's differences with its alliance partners were most pronounced during the final hours of the Cancún Conference where its delegation found itself isolated over the Singapore Issues. While South Africa offered trade-offs on the Singapore Issues – agreeing to demands from the US and the EU to include them in the negotiations for movement on agriculture – the G20+ refused to consider their inclusion. An impasse developed with both the majors and the developing countries holding fast to their respective positions. Alec Erwin made a last ditch attempt to break the deadlock, pleading with the Africa Group to support the final EU offer of including just one of the Singapore Issues – trade facilitation.[81] But his move failed and since the deadlock could not be broken, the Chair of the Conference, Luis Ernesto Derbez was forced to close the Cancún Conference without agreement.[82] At this brinkmanship stage (which Jawara and Kwa argue may well have been deliberately contrived by the US to prevent agreement on cotton[83]), countries like Kenya in the Africa Group, and Mauritius in the G20+, fashioned a stand-off strategy that contrasted sharply with the trade-off strategy of South Africa. Clearly, South Africa's willingness to submit to some US and EU demands were at odds with the more strident position adopted by the Africa Group and G20+.

Not surprisingly, South Africa viewed the collapse of the Cancún Ministerial Conference as a major blow for development. Others, however, saw it as a slap in the face for the EU and US who might now have to take more notice of the demands of the developing countries in the Doha Round. However, the July 2004 agreement – which gives a green light to negotiations on trade facilitation without any significant movement by the EU and the US on agriculture or cotton – indicates the false optimism in this latter view.

Conclusions

This chapter has shown that South Africa has become an increasingly active member of the WTO, especially during the Doha Round. It has also shown the limitations of this activism such that, despite participation in influential meetings and membership of apparently influential alliances within the WTO such as the G20+, Pretoria can claim very little influence over substantive and procedural matters. Since its key goals were to secure greater market access, the continued failure of the WTO to make progress on agricultural issues means that the Doha Round is yet to yield anything meaningful in trade for South Africa.

Occupying the position of facilitator proved to be a problematic diplomatic strategy for South Africa. Not for the first time, middle power diplomacy has failed to generate meaningful outcomes for the ANC government in the international system and the contradictions of its middle power strategy were all too apparent at Cancún.[84] The attempt to expand the common ground between the developed and the developing world by advancing neoliberal policies and ideas left South Africa isolated within the G20+ and the Africa Group and thus unable to deliver the South to the US and the EU on the key Singapore Issues. Pretoria's decidedly Northern approach to trade policy brought it into conflict with other leading developing countries. India, Brazil and Kenya led the G20+ and the Africa Group in challenging the EU and the US on key issues, pursuing a stand-off strategy at Seattle and Cancún. South Africa, by contrast, insisted on offering a trade-off on the Singapore Issues for movement on agriculture. Probably because they have greater experience of WTO negotiations than South Africa, other Southern members such as India and Brazil were better able to see the dangers in acquiescing to the major powers and therefore tended to adopt more strident negotiating positions on the key issues.

Rather than accede to US and EU demands, most members of the G20+ and Africa Group grasped a rare opportunity to delay the inclusion of the Singapore Issues onto the WTO agenda until the promise of satisfactory progress had been made on implementing the Uruguay agreements on agriculture. When this promise did not materialise, the talks collapsed.

South Africa's trade-off strategy left many developing countries, and African states in particular, feeling that the South African delegation had been too close to US and EU positions throughout the Doha negotiations. In supporting the launch of the Doha Round against the opposition of the Africa Group, and in supporting the inclusion of the Singapore Issues when the G20+ and the Africa Group rejected their inclusion, South Africa did appear to rally round EU and US positions.

South Africa was strategically and tactically naïve in the Doha Round negotiations. In accepting the launch of the Doha Round without conditions, and in agreeing to include the Singapore Issues ahead of any new US and EU commitment on agricultural issues, the South African delegation showed its hand too quickly without having a fall-back position.[85]

As we survey the wreckage of the collapsed Cancún Conference there are many disappointments, not least the continued lack of progress on development matters and the continued marginalisation of the less developed countries in the process. While some middle power developing countries can rightly claim some influence in the negotiations – even if this is only a negative influence in preventing agreement – the smallest and poorest nations remain spectators rather than players. The ANC government, too, must feel disappointed by the failure of its middle power strategy in the Doha talks. As a result of this failure it will struggle to carve out for itself an influential role in future Doha deliberations because it has damaged its credibility vis-à-vis the US and the EU as well as damaged the trust of the G20+ and the Africa Group. That South Africa was not invited to participate in the post-Cancún mini-ministerial meetings that led to the modified agreement of July 2004 is evidence of this diminished credibility.

The contradictions in the middle power strategy at the WTO cannot be easily overcome. This chapter has argued that South Africa's middle power strategy has a neoliberal dimension at its core. Given the deeply embedded nature of the neoliberal political economy at the state and international level, it is unlikely that South Africa will weaken its commitments to neoliberal multilateralism. Neither can it easily ignore its commitments, however rhetorical, to working with other developing countries to address developing-country development – as embodied in the NEPAD. The attempt to satisfy its neoliberal patrons in the North (as well as those within the South African state) and its development partners in the South was ineffectual. South African middle power diplomacy in the WTO appears to have reached its limits in view of the growing North–South divide within the organisation.

Notes

1. In contrast to the GATT where members could decide which obligations they would adopt and which they would not, members must adopt all of the WTO agreements as a 'single undertaking'.
2. For a detailed analysis of the international, regional and sub-regional middle power strategy of South Africa in see Hamill, J. and Lee, D., 'South African Diplomacy in the Post-Apartheid Era: An Emergent Middle Power?', *International Relations*, 15:4 (2001) pp. 33–59.
3. Although a founding member of the GATT in 1948, the Apartheid Government played no role in the various negotiating Rounds. South Africa entered the very last stages of the Uruguay Round as the 'The National Economic Forum' (the Apartheid regime, the ANC and COSATU). The ANC government ratified the Marrakesh Agreement of December 2004 and thus the new South Africa became a founding member of the WTO as it was established – South Africa Department of Foreign Affairs, http://www.dfa.gov.za/foreign/multilateral/inter/wto/htm, Accessed 11 June 2004). See also Erwin, A., 'Statement on the 5th Ministerial Meeting of the WTO held in Cancún, Mexico in September 2003' available at http://www.sarpn.org.za/documents/d0000545/index.php. Accessed 8 June 2004.
4. For discussion of the GEAR see Williams, P. and Taylor, I., 'Neoliberalism and the Political Economy of the New South Africa', *New Political Economy*, 5:1 (2000) pp. 21–40; Taylor, I., *Stuck in Middle GEAR: South Africa's Foreign Relations* (Westport, CT: Greenwood Press, 2001).
5. I use the terms 'North' and 'Northern' to refer to the industrialised countries and the terms 'South' and 'Southern' to refer to developing and less developed countries.
6. I am conceptualising South Africa's middle power diplomacy within the WTO in a similar way to Robert Cox who sees middle powermanship as a 'problem-solving' strategy. See Cox, R. W., 'Middlepowermanship, Japan and the Future World Order', in Robert W. Cox with Timothy J. Sinclair, *Approaches to World Order* (Cambridge: Cambridge University Press, 1996). This, according to Cox, entails seeking distributive economic benefits in the liberal trade regime without challenging the neoliberal rules and principles governing that regime. Others have also used a Coxian approach to South African middle power diplomacy. See Taylor, I., 'South Africa, the G20, the G20+ and the IBSA Dialogue Forum: Implications for Future Global Governance.' Paper presented

at the UN University conference, Buenos Aires, Argentina, May 19–21 2004; Van Der Westhuizen, J., 'South Africa's Emergence as a Middle Power', *Third World Quarterly*, 19:3 (1998) pp. 435–56.

7. The GSP provides duty-free access to some 4500 South Africa products.
8. The G20 members are Argentina, Australia, Brazil, Canada, China, France, Germany, India, Indonesia, Italy, Japan, Mexico, Russia, Saudi Arabia, South Africa, South Korea, Turkey, Great Britain, the US, as well as IMF, World Bank and EU representatives. For details of South Africa's relations with the G20 see Taylor, 'South Africa, the G20, the G20+ and the IBSA Dialogue Forum'.
9. Peter Draper, 'To Liberalise or Not to Liberalise? A Review of the South African Government's Trade Policy', Working Paper, South African Institute for International Affairs, May 2003.
10. By 'off the record' I refer to the fact that no minutes of these meetings are taken or produced by the Secretariat.
11. The original date set for completion of the Round was January 2005. A more likely date for completion is the forthcoming Hong Kong Ministerial in December 2005 although this might be an optimistic deadline.
12. The G20+ group includes Argentina, Bolivia, Brazil, Chile, China, Colombia, Costa Rica, Cuba, Ecuador, Egypt, Guatemala, India, Indonesia, Mexico, Pakistan, Paraguay, Peru, the Philippines, Nicaragua, South Africa, Thailand and Venezuela. El Salvador was originally a member but it withdrew at the Cancún Conference.
13. The Africa Group consists of 44 members from the African Union.
14. The G90 comprises all the developing and less developed country members of the WTO.
15. Kapoor, I., 'Deliberative Democracy and the WTO', *Review of International Political Economy*, 11:3 (2004) p. 530.
16. The WTO has provided funds and technical assistance to help developing countries improve their negotiating skills.
17. Akyüz, Y., *Developing Countries and World Trade: Performance and Prospects* (London: Zed Books/UNCTAD/Third World Network, 2003); Jawara, F. and Kwa, A., *Behind the Scenes at the WTO: The Real World of International Trade Negotiations*, Updated edition. (London: Zed Books, 2004); Kapoor, 'Deliberative Democracy'; Martin, W. and Winters, A. (eds), *The Uruguay Round and the Developing Countries*, (Cambridge: Cambridge University Press, 1996); Kufour, K. O., *World Trade Governance and Developing Countries: The GATT/WTO Committee System* (London and Oxford: The Royal Institute of International Affairs/ Blackwell,(2004); Narlikar, A., *International Trade and Developing Countries: Bargaining Coalitions in the GATT & WTO* (London: Routledge, 2003); Narlikar, A. 'Developing Countries in the WTO' in Brian Hocking and Steven McGuire (eds) *Trade Politics*, Second edition. (London: Routledge, 2004); Narlikar, A. and Odell, J. S., 'Explaining Negotiation Strategies and Bargaining Outcomes: The Like-Minded Group and the 2001 Doha Agreements'. Paper presented at the annual general meeting of the International Studies Association, Montreal, 2004; Smith, J., 'Inequality in International Trade? Developing Countries and Institutional Change in WTO Dispute Settlement', *Review of International Studies*, 11:3 (2004) pp. 542–73.
18. The LDC Group was created in 1999 and has 31 less developed country members most of which are African. For a breakdown of membership see Narlikar, *International Trade and Developing Countries*, Table 2.2.

19. The Like-Minded Group was formed in 1996 and consists of Cuba, Egypt, India, Indonesia, Malaysia, Pakinstan, Sri Lanka, Tanzania, and Uganda.
20. Das, B. L., *WTO: The Doha Agenda. The New Negotiations on World Trade* (London: Zed Books/Third World Network, 2003) p. 5.
21. Narlikar, 'Developing Countries in the WTO', p. 143. See also Hoekman, B. M. and Kostecki, M. M., *The Political Economy of the World Trading System*, chapter 4; Narlikar and Odell, 'Explaining Negotiation Strategies'. For studies of developing coalition building during the GATT see Kahler, M. and JOdell, J., 'Developing Country Coalition-Building and International Trade negotiations' in John Walley (ed.), *Trade Policy and the Developing World*. (Ann Arbour: University of Michigan Press, 1989); Tussie, D.and Glover, D. (eds), *The Developing Countries in World Trade: Policies and Bargaining Strategies* (Boulder: Lynne Rienner, 1995).
22. Narlikar, *International Trade and Developing Countries*, p. 13. See also Wolf, R., 'Crossing the River by Feeling the Stones: Where the WTO is Going after Seattle, Doha and Cancún', *Review of International Studies*, 11:4 (2004) pp. 574–96.
23. See for example Jawara and Kwa, *Behind the Scenes*; Peet, R., *Unholy Trinity: The IMF, World Bank and WTO*. (London: Zed Books, 2003).
24. For a discussion of this apparent shift see Donna Lee, 'Understanding the WTO dispute settlement system', in Hocking, B. and McGuire, S. (eds), *Trade Politics*, Second edition (London: Routledge, 2004). See also Steinberg, R. H., 'In the Shadow of Law or Power? Consensus-Based Bargaining and Outcomes in the GATT/WTO', *International Organization*, 56:2 (2002) pp. 339–74.
25. For a detailed exposition of rational actor negotiating theory see Odell, J. S., *Negotiating the World Economy* (Ithaca: Cornell University Press, 2000).
26. Hampson, F. O., 'Lilliputians to the Rescue: Small and Middle Power Mediation in International Multilateral Negotiations'. Paper presented at the annual general meeting of the International Studies Association, Montreal, 2004. For a seminal study of mediation in negotiation see Zartman, W. I. and Berman, M. R., *The Practical Negotiator* (New Haven: Yale University Press, 1982).
27. Note that Robert Putnum uses formal models to develop a two-level approach to trade diplomacy that includes the domestic level as well as the international level – and the links between the two. Robert Putnum, 'Diplomacy and Domestic Politics: The Logic of Two-Level Games', *International Organization*, 42:3 (1988) pp. 427–60. Since Stephen Woolcock correctly argues that state-level forces play an increasingly significant role in shaping state incentives and strategies in the WTO, the rationalist approach to WTO negotiations seems increasingly problematic. See Woolcock, S., 'The ITO, the GATT and the WTO' in Nicholas Bayne and Stephen Woolcock (eds), *The New Economic Diplomacy* (Hampshire: Ashgate, 2003).
28. For an analysis of the WTO using a critical approach in the tradition of Habermas see Kapoor, 'Deliberative Democracy'.
29. The 'green room' process has been roundly criticised by Non Governmental Organisations (NGOs), as well as some WTO members, and academics. For example, in August 2003 several NGOs including Christian Aid, the World Development Movement and Actionaid wrote an open letter to Patricia Hewitt, UK Secretary of State for Trade and Industry, expressing deep concerns about the 'lack of democracy and accountability' in the WTO

negotiating and decision-making procedures. In particular they point to the lack of transparency and exclusive nature of the 'green room' process. See the full text of the letter at http://www.rspb.org.uk/Images/ Joint%20NGO%20Cancun%20Challenge%20to%20Patricia%20Hewitt% 20August%202003_tcm5-45149.pdf#search='wto%20democratic%20deficit' (accessed 17 January 2005). See also Third World Network, *The Multilateral Trading System: A Development Perspective* (New York: United Nations Development Programme, 2001). Kwa's explanation for the collapse of the Seattle Ministerial meeting in September 1999 was that many developing countries refused to accept a 'green room' decision to launch a new round. See Kwa, A., *Power Politics in the WTO* (Bangkok: Focus on the Global South, 2002). The Like-Minded Group was highly critical of the 'green room' and submitted a set of proposals for procedural reforms. See Narlikar, *International Trade and Developing Countries*, table 2.2 and pp 179–82.. For academic analysis and criticism of the 'green room' process and WTO decision-making more broadly see Keet, D., ' The WTO-led System of Global Governance: Tactical options and strategic debates amongst civil society organisations worldwide' (Institute For Global Dialogue Occasional Paper No. 32, Braamfontein, South Africa: Institute for Global Diaolgue, 2002); Peet, *Unholy Trinity*; Kwa, *Power Politics*; Narlikar, A., *WTO Decision-making and Developing Countries* (Oxford: South Centre, 2001). Schott, J. J. and Watal, J., 'Decision-making in the WTO' in Jeffrey. J Schotte (ed.), *The WTO After Seattle* (Washington, DC: Institute for International Economics (2000).

30. 'Green room' meetings, which began during the Uruguay Round, are informal meetings of between 20 to 25 invited members. The WTO's director general organises and manages these meetings which are closed with no minute taking. Mini-ministerials are a more recent feature in the WTO process. Very similar in make-up and process to the green room meetings and equally lacking in transparency, they have become, essentially, an executive council of the WTO. Jawara and Kwa, *Behind the Scenes*, pp. 230–1.

31. Erwin was one of six 'Friends of the Chair'. The other five chaired groups meetings on agriculture, the Singapore Issues, implementation issues, environment, TRIPS and Health. Clearly in this context, rule-making was the least contentious and least significant, but it is nevertheless an indication of South Africa's increased status within the WTO. Chairs played a facilitating role, consulting with members and ensuring that member's views were included in the draft text of the Ministerial. But as Jawara and Kwa point out this public role was undermined by the more important private role played by the Secretariat who dominated the administration of this process in close cooperation with the Quad countries (Canada, the United States, the European Union, and Japan). Kwa, *Behind the Scenes*, p. 91.

32. The average size of developed country delegations in Geneva is 7.38 while for developing countries it is 3.51. See SSharma, S., 'A Mockery of a Multilateral Trading System: Who is accountable?' at http://www.model-wto.org/ Documents/A%20Mockery%20of%20a%20Multilateral%20Trading% 20System%20%28Sharma%29.doc, Accessed 17 January 2005. For a detailed breakdown of delegation size see Jawara and Kwa, *Behind the Scenes*, pp. 20–1.

33. Jawara and Kwa, *Behind the Scenes*, p. xxxvi.

34. The Cairns Group was formed in 1986 and now consists of Argentina, Australia, Brazil, Canada, Chile, Columbia, Hungary, Indonesia, Malaysia, New Zealand, the Philippines, Thailand and Uruguay. Fiji was briefly a member.
35. Membership of the 'green room ' meetings is by invitation from the WTO Director General or the Chair of the negotiating group, supposedly on the basis of representation of the various alliances within the WTO. The 'Friends of the Chair' were also chosen by the WTO Director General. See Jawara and Kwa, *Behind the Scenes*, p. 18. It is worth noting that all the chairs were taken from the delegations of the countries that supported the launch of the Doha Round.
36. By contrast, the rest of Africa accounts for around 16% of total South African exports and 4% of imports, South African Government *Yearbook 2002–03*.
37. See Jawara and Kwa, *Behind the Scenes*; Kwa, *Power Politics*; Peet, *Unholy Trinity*.
38. Jawara and Kwa, *Behind the Scenes*, p. 65.
39. Green room meetings and mini-ministerials typically have around 15 members present. The Quad always participate but other members come and go.
40. Kwa, *Power Politics*, pp. 41–67.
41. Jawara and Kwa, *Behind the Scenes*, pp. 50–79.
42. Ibid., p. 70.
43. The key delegations involved in the negotiations on a post-Cancún agreement were Australia, Brazil, the EU, India and the US. For details of the WTO 'July Package' see http://www.wto.org/english/tratop_e/dda_e/dda_package_july04_e.htm, Accessed 1 September 2004.
44. For detailed analysis of how South Africa has advanced the neoliberal agenda in other international and regional organisations see Bond, P., *Talk Left, Walk Right: South Africa's Frustrated Global Reforms* (Stocksville: University of Kwazulu-Natal Press, 2004).
45. Kapoor, 'Deliberative Democracy', p. 534. The increasing (liberal) legalism of WTO decision-making and rule-making only serves to increase the power of the knowledge claims of the developed countries especially since trade issues are becoming increasingly technical.
46. For a detailed critical view of South Africa's role in promoting the WTO see Keet, D., 'South Africa's Position and Role in Promoting the World Trade Organisation and a New Round of Multilateral Trade Negotiations', Paper presented to the Conference on The Multilateral Trading System and the Road to Doha: Challenges for South Africa, 7–8 August 2001.
47. See Bond, *Talk Left, Walk Right*; Williams, M., 'The World Trade Organisation and the Developing World: Convergent and Divergent Interests'. Paper presented at the annual general meeting of the International Studies Association, Montreal, 2004; Williams and Taylor, 'Neoliberalism and the Political Economy of the 'new' South Africa'.
48. For a critical perspective on South Africa's development policy position see Keet, D., 'Proposals on the New Role of Trade within the New Partnership for African Development (NEPAD)', Paper presented at workshop for African trade unions organised by the National Labour and Economic Development, Johannesburg, South Africa, 22–23 May (2003). Available at http://www.tni.org/fellows/keet.htm. Accessed 24 July 2004.
49. *Public Agenda*, 22 December 2003. Outside of the WTO, Pretoria has also put forward regional proposals for development based on neoliberal policies and

prescriptions, for example, the New Partnership for African Development (NEPAD) which Bond pithily describes as a home-grown version of the Washington Consensus. Bond, *Talk Left, Walk Right*. See also Taylor, I., *NEPAD: Toward Africa's Development or Another False Start?* (Boulder, CO: Lynne Rienner, 2005).

50. For an excellent discussion of the current state of development theory see Payne, A. (ed.), *The New Regional Politics of Development* (Basingstoke: Palgrave, 2004).
51. See Scholte, J. A., 'The WTO and Civil Society' in B. Hocking and S. McGuire (eds), *Trade Politics*.
52. Kapoor, 'Deliberative Democracy', p. 535.
53. Jawara and Kwa, *Behind the Scenes*.
54. *BuaNews*, 4 September 2003.
55. *Business Day*, 10 May 2004.
56. South African Department of Trade and Industry, International Trade and Economic Development Division, 'Note on South Africa's Approach to the WTO and Key Elements of a Negotiating Position', December 2000, Available at http://www.dti.gov.za/07_itedd/downloads/sa_wto_approach_and elements. pdf. Accessed 18 January 2005.
57. Ibid., For a more detailed analysis of South African trade policy, see Draper, 'To Liberalise or not to Liberalise?'
58. Jawara and Kwa, *Behind the Scenes*.
59. These include Columbia, Morocco, Uruguay and Peru.
60. There are a number of theories as to who was actually to blame for the collapse of the Cancún talks. See Jawara and Kwa, *Behind the Scenes*, for details.
61. Ibid., p. xxiii.
62. The conservative and pro-business newspaper Business Day consistently backed South Africa's trade-off positioning in the Doha Round.
63. Pascal Lamy says that the USA referred to the G20+ as a 'coalition of para-lyzers' (Jawara and Kwa, Behind the Scenes, p. xxxvii) who did not negotiate but 'made demands' and 'believed in fairy tales' (Jawara and Kwa, ibid., p. lii) and EU Agriculture Commissioner Franz Fischler commented that the G20+ were in 'different orbits entirely' and wanted 'the moon and stars' (Jawara and Kwa, *Behind the Scenes*, p. xxxvi).
64. The August 2004 agreement stated that poor countries can import generic versions of patented medicines from countries such as India and Brazil; but it was a limited agreement as some feel that it will not drive prices down because global patents rules are still in force.
65. Jawara and Kwa, *Behind the Scenes*, p. xxxii.
66. *The East African*, 8 September 2003.
67. For details of the trade imbalances see Akyüz, *Developing Countries and World Trade*.
68. WTO, 2003, Cited in Jawara and Kwa, *Behind the Scenes*, p. xxxv.
69. Ibid., p. xxiii.
70. Ibid; Kwa, *Power Politics*; Peet, *Unholy Trinity*.
71. *The Monitor*, 15 September 2003.
72. For details of the inequalities between North and South in the international political economy see Hoogvelt, A., *Globalisation and the Postcolonial World: The New Political Economy of Development* (Basingstoke: Macmillan, 1997); Seligson, M. A. and Passé-Smith J. T. (eds), *Development and*

Underdevelopment: The Political Economy of Global Inequality, Third edition (London: Lynne Rienner, 2003).
73. For a detailed discussion of the dominance of the EU and US in the WTO and other international organisations see Shaffer, G., 'Power, Governance, and the WTO: A Comparative Institutional Approach' in Michael Barnett and Raymond Duvall (eds), *Power in Global Governance* (Cambridge: Cambridge University Press, 2005).
74. Bernard Hockman in the *Public Agenda*, 24 November 2003.
75. Note, for example, the tensions in the UK's bridge-building strategy on the issue of the 2003 war with Iraq. The UK strategy was to try to find common ground between the US and the UN (and to a lesser extent Germany and France) and to try to get consensus on a second UN resolution on Iraq.
76. There are concerns that South Africa's participation in the G20+ bloc has undermined the negotiations to create a free trade agreement between the US and the Southern African Customs Union since the US has publicly criticised the positioning of the G20+ during the Cancún negotiations.
77. The negotiations on cotton were dominated by an impasse between the Africa Group and the US. The Africa Group proposed a stand-alone agreement on cotton that would eventually eliminate all cotton subsidies. They also sought the creation of a US$250 million compensation package. The G20+ supported this proposal. The US rejected the proposal and argues for the cotton issue to be negotiated as part of the agricultural deliberations. Jawara and Kwa, *Behind the Scenes*, pp. xxvii–xxxi.
78. *The East African*, 23 June 2003.
79. On this point Erwin is not alone. Botswana's Ambassador to Geneva, Charles Ntwaagae, also noted the lack of coherent discussion among Southern African countries in the Doha negotiations. *Financial Gazette* (Harare), 29 May 2003.
80. Ismail, F., ' "An Insider's Insight" in Development through Trade Project, "Africa after Cancún: Trade Negotiations in Uncertain Times" ', South African Institute of International Affairs, 2003. Avaiable at www.wits.ac.za/saiia/TradePolicyBrief/TR2Cancun.pdf. Accessed June 2004.
81. Jawara and Kwa, *Behind the Scenes*, pp. 106–7.
82. Although the G20+ almost collapsed over the 'Museveni letter' issue. This letter – which was unsigned but was supposedly penned by the President of Uganda – called upon the Ugandan negotiating team to withdraw support for the G20+ bloc position on the Singapore Issues. Serious questions remain as to the actual authorship of this letter with some suspecting that the US team wrote it.
83. Jawara and Kwa, *Behind the Scenes*, p. xiiv.
84. For further analysis of the failings of South Africa's middle power strategy in a broader context see Hamill and Lee, 'Middle Power Paradox?'; Taylor, 'South Africa, the G20, the G20+ and the IBSA Dialogue Forum'; Van Der Westhuizen, South Africa's emergence as a middle power'.
85. See Keet, D., 'South Africa's Official Position'. Others have also criticised the South African delegation. The EU, for example, criticised the South African delegation in 1997 for 'having no detailed' proposals and 'being unprepared' for meetings. *Bridges Weekly Trade News Digest*, 1:1 (3 February 2003).

3
South Africa as Chair of the Non-Aligned, September 1998–February 2003

Sally Morphet

The non-aligned had adjusted to the end of the Cold War[1] by the time it became clear that South Africa was likely to be chosen to be the next chair of the movement at the Cartagena Summit in 1995 once the Africa Group had agreed. South Africa in its new guise had joined the non-aligned movement (NAM) with great acclaim at the Cairo Foreign Ministers Meeting in June 1994 and had quickly become part of its moderate mainstream by eschewing radicalism though continuing to work against unipolarity. South Africa in accepting the chair was both paying off an historic debt to the non-aligned for their struggle against apartheid and taking on a symbolic role which, as Ian Taylor notes, enabled it to gain 'international respectability'.[2]

The following looks at the origins and development of the non-aligned including their fight against apartheid and dealings with African issues; the non-aligned system; the 1998 Durban Summit; and how South Africa handled its chairing role at the United Nations (UN) and beyond. It then assesses its achievement within a group which 'contains rising great powers and major centers of economic growth' and which has to try and deal with many urgent security issues, population problems and development approaches that will profoundly affect the global environment.[3] The involvement of China as an Observer in the non-aligned since 1992 is one example of the continuing relevance of the movement. This chapter is more empirical than theoretical. It is informed by work at and on the UN and attendance at all summits and most foreign ministers meetings beginning with the 1979 Havana Summit.

Putting the Non-Aligned into Context

The South Africans were probably not entirely aware of the complex background of the non-aligned movement which had been a focal point for Third World (later Global South) thinking about how to tackle major global, political and economic issues since its first Summit at Belgrade (1961). It was established primarily through the efforts of Tito, Nasser and Nehru who were trying to find ways for their own and other weaker countries to influence the major powers, break down the bloc system, and to further their foreign policy interests on such issues as disarmament, decolonisation, apartheid, Palestine, Great Power military bases, natural resources and economic development. They were much influenced by UN Charter principles and adopted many as their own. Other major non-aligned principles include the struggle against imperialism, hegemony and racism; peaceful coexistence; freedom of all states to determine their political system and pursue their economic, social and cultural development; the right of self-determination; peaceful settlement of disputes; and the non-use of force or threat of the use of force.

Like-minded countries saw the importance of working and voting together at the UN once it came into operation in 1946. The voting on General Assembly resolutions on Palestine in 1947 showed the First and Second Worlds combining against the main members[4] of the nascent Arab–Asian group (the Third World). The November 1947 General Assembly partition resolution recommended the division of Palestine into two states (55% for the Jews with under a third of the population and 45% for the Palestinians with over two-thirds of the population). Jerusalem was to be a *corpus separatum* under a special international regime. Those voting against (a microcosm of the non-aligned to be) were Afghanistan, Cuba, Egypt, Greece, India, Iran, Iraq, Lebanon, Pakistan, Saudi Arabia, Syria, Turkey and the Yemen. All later joined the non-aligned with the exception of Greece and Turkey.

Interestingly Egypt, India and Yugoslavia worked together on a number of subjects including Korea in both the General Assembly and Security Council[5] at the UN in the 1940s and early 1950s. All three served together on the Security Council in 1950; they were the only abstainers on a General Assembly resolution of 7 October which obliquely approved the UN action north of the thirty-eighth parallel. The subsequent Asian, Arab and African 1955 conference at Bandung covered economic cooperation; cultural cooperation; human rights and self-determination (the Arab–Asian group had ensured that the right of self-determination was inserted into the draft of human rights covenant in 1951); and problems of dependent people and international peace and cooperation. The conference has become mythical even though its principles do not entirely agree. It gave self-confidence to its participants and remains (highly) influential.

The first non-aligned summit – Belgrade, September 1961

These developments helped provide the impetus for the convening of the first non-aligned summit. In his opening speech[6] President Tito noted the need for representatives of the non-aligned countries 'to examine on the highest level, in a more detailed manner and in greater numbers, the dangerous international situation and to take, in this connection, co-ordinated action, primarily through the United Nations, in order to find a way out of the present situation and to prevent the outbreak of a new military conflict' (between the United States and the Soviet Union – the Soviet Union had just resumed nuclear testing). The participants discussed the international situation in terms of consolidation and strengthening of international peace and security including the role and composition of the United Nations (they succeeded in expanding the Security Council in the early 1960s), problems of unequal economic development and improvement of international economic and technical cooperation. The non-aligned realised then, as now, that they could best pursue their joint interests through a multilateral UN although they do operate outside the UN when necessary.

The South African cause had always been one of the two major regional planks of the movement (the other is Palestine). The 25 heads of state or government stated that they

> resolutely condemn the policy of *apartheid* practised by the Union of South Africa, and demand the immediate abandonment of that policy. They further declare that the policy of racial discrimination anywhere in the world constitutes a grave violation of the Charter of the United Nations and the Universal Declaration of Human Rights.[7]

The Belgrade Declaration encapsulated the first collective view of the non-aligned on major global issues (which were normally dealt with through the UN). It, like the UN, deals with all major global issues and remains a focal point for its members as they continue to try to find ways of changing certain Western policies on, for instance, self-determination and humanitarian intervention just as they tried to change certain Eastern policies (on, for instance, nuclear testing by the Soviet Union) until the end of the Cold War. Non-aligned activity helped them to achieve certain of these goals.

Internal conflict within the movement, 1965–1979

After the first two summits (the second was in Cairo in 1964) and the sponsorship of a conference on economic development in 1962 which led to the formation of the G77 in 1964, the impetus behind the movement slowed as the Indonesians and Algerians tried to create a more radical organisation. The project failed. Tito then stepped in by convening an extraordinary non-aligned meeting in Belgrade in 1969 which led to the 1970 Lusaka Summit which concentrated on economic development and African problems.

The next summit was held in September 1973 at Algiers. The 75 countries agreed a series of economic demands including a UN Special Session on Development. They also came out against hegemony, a formula which implied distancing the movement from the Soviet Union. A Coordinating Bureau was also set up. The OPEC countries to the annoyance of many other non-aligned countries had raised oil prices following the Arab–Israeli war of October 1973. President Boumedienne's subsequent call for a Sixth Special Session on raw materials and development was due in part to his concern to prevent a wedge being driven between the oil producers and other developing countries by allowing some discussion of energy issues at the UN. The following 1976 Summit at Colombo called upon states to desist from cooperation with the Pretoria regime and to cooperate with the UN in its efforts to eradicate apartheid.

Western fears about the ability of the Cubans to dominate the 1979 Summit and to move the movement away from its traditional determination not to be associated with either bloc turned out to be mistaken. The Cubans lost out on the 'natural allies' thesis, on the Economic Declaration (which was completely rewritten by the Algerians), and on the insertion of non-aligned principles into the Declaration by a number of moderates including the Yugoslavs and Indians. The Cubans were able to ensure the Cambodian seat remained empty but they then found that they were not able to get sufficient votes at the UN to give them a seat on the Security Council. The majority of the non-aligned also voted for or abstained on the General Assembly resolution at an Emergency Special Session in January 1980 which implicitly criticised the Soviet Union for its invasion of a non-aligned country, Afghanistan.

Moderates maintain control over the movement, 1981–1998

The subsequent paralysis of the movement was resolved by the Indians who hosted a Foreign Ministers Meeting in New Delhi in 1981: this agreed the texts on Afghanistan and Cambodia which were implicitly critical of both the Soviet Union and Vietnam. The Indians went on to host the next non-aligned summit in New Delhi in 1983 after it became clear (in 1982) that Iraq would not be able to be a summit host because of the Iran/Iraq war. Under the Indian Chair the movement concentrated on economic questions including debt as well as new issues of the Iran/Iraq war and Antarctica. Harare was deliberately chosen to be the site of the next summit at the Foreign Ministers Meeting in Luanda (1985) in order to focus world attention on Southern Africa.

The Harare Summit (1986) was dominated by economic questions and showed the unwillingness of the Front Line States to impose mandatory sanctions on South Africa without Western support. The Conference also issued a special Declaration on Southern Africa, and an appeal on Namibian independence, as well as setting up the Africa Fund to help the Front Line States and a Standing Ministerial Committee for Economic Cooperation to evolve strategies for future cooperation. At the subsequent non-aligned Foreign Ministers Meeting in Nicosia in September 1988, Ministers called for a UN Special Session on apartheid and welcomed the quadripartite discussions between Angola, Cuba, South Africa and the United States on Angola and Namibia.

The non-aligned had great difficulty in finding a suitable chair for the next summit; the Yugoslavs finally agreed to take it. At Belgrade (September 1989 – two months before the Berlin Wall fell) the Yugoslavs, reacting to the ending of the Cold War, emphasised the interdependence of foreign policy and domestic issues, particularly those dealing with economic questions, as the world became a global village. The driving force behind the concern to modernise the movement (i.e., taking a less confrontational and more cooperative global approach) came from the Yugoslavs with their main allies, Algeria, Egypt and India as well as the silent majority. As one involved Yugoslav noted in 1992[8]

> A more flexible attitude was ... taken vis-à-vis the United States and the West ... in the realisation that no major task or goals of the Movement ... can be solved without establishing a dialogue and cooperation with the centres of political, economic and military might in the notorious triangle Europe–USA–Japan.

Issues of human rights and environment were dragged up the agenda as was political pluralism two years later at the Accra Foreign Ministers Meeting in 1991. Ministers at Accra also decided not to change the name of the movement because it could still be non-aligned to the one remaining bloc.

The non-aligned remained concerned about humanitarian intervention particularly after the invasion and annexation of Kuwait by Iraq (both non-aligned members) in August 1990 as well as at the beginning of the break-up of Yugoslavia in 1991.The Indonesians at the Jakarta Summit (1992) found the movement hugely divided on the future of Yugoslavia. Many black African states promoting Yugoslav territorial integrity and its historical role within the non-aligned were opposed by states belonging to the Organisation of the Islamic Conference (OIC) concerned about the treatment of Bosnian Muslims. Indonesia continued to press the case for South–South and South–North economic cooperation and to try and establish a G7/non-aligned dialogue through its relationship with Japan.

The 1994 Foreign Ministers Meeting at Cairo celebrated South Africa joining the non-aligned. The following low key Cartagena Summit (October 1995) in its short Call from Colombia put economic growth and the eradication of poverty at the forefront of the global agenda. Globalisation and interdependence had mainly benefited industrialised countries and made problems in the areas of both environmental degradation and illicit drugs. The non-aligned pledged themselves to promote the revitalisation and democratisation of the UN and to restructure the Bretton Woods institutions. They continued to have differences on the question of Security Council reform though they acknowledged the need for unity. The Summit 'marked a consolidation of the non-aligned role in the post-Cold-War world as well as emphasizing the continuing dominant role of the moderate mainstream (countries such as Egypt and Indonesia)'.[9]

The Non-Aligned System

The number of non-aligned countries has grown since their first Heads of State Summit at Belgrade in 1961 which had 25 members. It reached 116 at their thirteenth summit at Kuala Lumpur in February 2003. Non-aligned conferences are often held in late August/early September so that countries can discuss the range of subjects that they will face and introduce at the forthcoming UN General Assembly and in the Security Council. They strongly support multilateralism since their regional and global influence would be less if they could not normally work through the UN. Their summits usually move at three-year intervals from Latin America, to Africa and then Asia; the next will be in Havana in 2006. The forthcoming chair produces the first draft of the summit documents a few weeks before the summit begins and amendments from other countries then begin to be submitted. Most of the subjects discussed are dealt with by the Political and Economic Committees which are set up at the beginning of each summit. The actual summit at head of state and government level is preceded by meetings of senior officials followed by foreign ministers. Heads of state normally make speeches or circulate them; some are fascinating.

The summits are part of a system. Meetings are held at foreign minister level about two years after each summit as well as yearly meetings at ministerial level at the UN in New York in late September/early October. The G77, most of whose members are non-aligned, normally meets there at the same time. The Non-aligned Coordinating Bureau in New York and other similar bodies in Geneva, Nairobi and Vienna often meet to discuss new challenges.

A number of countries, the most important of which is China,[10] since 1992, now play a role as Observers in the movement (this means that they have access to most of each summit and could, if all agreed, become members of the movement). Other major Observers include Brazil and Mexico as well as bodies like the African Union, the Arab League, the OIC and the UN. Guests of the movement cannot become NAM members since they are members of Great Power alliances. Like the Observers, they also have some access during a summit. Guests include the UN permanent members, France and the United Kingdom, besides Russia and the United States together with representatives of organisations such as the International Committee of the Red Cross (ICRC), the G8 and the Commonwealth Secretariat.

The non-aligned have always worked to some extent through regional groupings similar to those now in operation at the UN, except in the case of Europe. A few liberation movements such as the ANC (African National Congress) and PAC (Pan-African Congress) were represented (at past meetings). Palestine has been a member since the end of 1988; the PLO (Palestine Liberation Organisation) had been a member since 1975. There have been occasional meetings of other groupings (e.g., Mediterranean members). However the non-aligned have never, deliberately, been exclusively regional in their decision-making. This has helped certain members of regional groups (e.g., the Palestine Liberation Organisation) who have not always been given total regional support. They have, therefore, had to rely on help from other groups which has been more consistent overall. Egypt too has sometimes found it easier to work in the non-aligned as it is part of the African regional group at the UN which is composed of all members of the African continent. These members supported it at Havana in 1979 when many Arab countries wanted to expel it from the movement because of Camp David.

Nevertheless it works closely with its Arab counterparts both within Africa and in the Middle East as well as in the OIC and Arab League. The non-aligned share much of the same membership as the larger G77[11] founded in 1964. This deals almost exclusively with economic issues, works in the context of UNCTAD and is based on UN regional groupings. A Joint Coordinating Committee (JCC) of both bodies has been in operation since 1994. New ideas have usually moved from the non-aligned to the G77 rather than vice versa.

The Durban Non-Aligned Summit, 1998[12]

The internal complexities of the 1992 non-aligned Jakarta Summit had been played out by the time of the low key 1995 Summit at Cartagena. South Africa fitted in well politically with the moderate mainstream of the non-aligned. Its major, new, political problem was nuclear testing by India and Pakistan. And, as already noted, the Yugoslavs had got many members to agree in 1989 that no major goals of the Movement could be resolved without establishing a dialogue and cooperation with Europe, the United States and Japan. Luckily South Africa could produce the first draft of its declaration fairly easily as the internal tensions within the movement on Yugoslavia had dissipated and external tensions were not as great as they were to become after 9/11.

There were, however, many different views on coping with globalisation. Taylor argues that the ANC Government had recognised that there was 'no alternative' to globalisation and therefore adopted neoliberal economic policies and abandoned many of the ANC's traditional policies.[13] Many other members of the non-aligned, as will be seen below, questioned aspects of neoliberal policies.

The Summit Chair, whatever the world circumstances, needs to realise that the summit at the level of heads of state is the only such occasion within the normal three-year period of each summit at the level of heads of state. It has often set the tone for the ensuing years of the chair and some of the language can be particularly important. The presence of President Mandela provided a draw at Durban. It was a great pity that the computerised registration system was not successful and that media attendance was less extensive than usual.

Economic issues

Economic issues are always one important chapter in non-aligned declarations.[14] The final Durban economic chapter dealt *inter alia* with the new context of international economic cooperation; agenda for development; international trade and commodities; financial, investment and monetary issues; external debt; industrialisation; food and agriculture; environment and development; science and technology; information and communication; South–South cooperation; and the critical economic situation in Africa. The participants made the point about the marginalisation of a large number of non-aligned countries under the impact of globalisation and liberalisation and the widening inequalities between rich and poor as well as reaffirming the importance of establishing an open and non-discriminatory system of economic relations.

In an unprecedented move, South Africa also used one afternoon of the proceedings at foreign minister level to discuss the conclusions of the ad hoc Panel of Economists which had been set up at the instigation of Sri Lanka at the 1997 Foreign Ministers Meeting (New Delhi) 'to assess the current international economic situation from the perspective of developing countries and to identify and analyse major issues of concern to them and to assist in developing a positive agenda of the South'.[15] The Panel was headed by Dr Corea of Sri Lanka, a former President of UNCTAD with a number of non-aligned economists.

The report noted that the end of the Cold War had begun a new era in which 'the political and economic ideologies of the major market economies gained a new ascendancy' with policy prescriptions of liberalisation, deregulation, privatisation and monetary-fiscal discipline. 'Almost exclusive emphasis on the role of unfettered markets' had 'displaced key principles that underpinned earlier multilateral discussions and negotiations'. Developing countries should have, but had not, developed an agenda of their own 'to promote their key interests during the negotiating processes promoting liberalization and globalization'. They now had to adapt this process to their own situation and development needs and to work out what actions would enhance their cohesion and effectiveness on the international scene. Their impact in multilateral negotiations still derived from the strength of numbers. Their unity and cohesion remained the source of their strength. Issues on the agenda had to include:

1. the governance of the global economy;
2. the monetary and financial environment for development;
3. international trade and trade-related issues;
4. the widening science and technology gap; and
5. developing and applying the agenda – developing countries needed to consider how joint approaches and policies should be formulated.

The round table discussion[16] was moderated by the South African Minister of Trade and Industry, Alec Erwin, then President of UNCTAD IX. Dr Corea argued that the key issues of concern to developing countries could be merged into a single though varied platform. Indonesia hoped the conference would revive an earlier proposal to organise an international conference on money and finance.

New global negotiations should be based on genuine interdependence, mutuality of interests, common benefits and shared responsibility. India called for a practical agenda of the South. South Africa stated the need to develop South–South economic linkages as well as engagement with the North. Egypt suggested that the chair should consult with the Coordinating Bureau in New York to continue the needed technical and political work. They thought that the new and imaginative protectionist measures taken by the North could be seen as a clear indication that developing countries had become a competitive strength in the world market.

Malaysia noted that all governments should work together to forge a set of acceptable universal norms with regard to currency trading. This provided a lesson in understanding unfettered globalisation. Malaysia believed in the intensification of South–South cooperation and spoke highly of the usefulness of bilateral payment regimes with certain ASEAN (Association of South-East Asian Nations) and South American countries. Strong partnership was important within government and with the private sector. Self-help programmes based on Southern experience should be developed. The movement should remember that Southern resistance to Northern attempts to introduce some non-tariff barriers had been successful during the negotiations on the establishment of the WTO in Marrakech (1994) 'because we were strongly united. ... If lessons could be learned from the experience in Marrakech, it is that by being together, working together, co-operating and demonstrating a very strong commitment to what is of interest to us, we can succeed'. Iran called for a group of friends of the chair to help create a real place for NAM in international economic negotiations. South Africa ended by suggesting that the chair should be mandated to move forward in a consultative process with NAM members to develop and strengthen the research networks proposed by the panel.

Political issues

The Durban Declaration's chapter on global issues reviewed the international situation; the role of the non-aligned; North–South Dialogue; agenda for peace; restructuring the UN; peacekeeping; the UN financial situation; disarmament and international security; terrorism; and international law. The non-aligned expressed concern about intervention in their internal affairs under various pretexts as well as in the use of sanctions. The movement must be active in international negotiations with strong concerted positions. They emphasised the importance of consulting with the G8 and shared concern at the weakening of the role and functioning of the General Assembly. They decided to convene a working group to prepare (by mid-1999) a complete Plan of Action for the movement.

They emphasised their gross under-representation on the Security Council and stated that its expansion must be determined on the basis of principles of equitable geographical distribution and sovereign equality of states. Peace required states to respect and protect the rule of law. They called for an international summit conference under the auspices of the UN to formulate a joint response to terrorism.

The second chapter analysing the international situation concentrated on Palestine and the Middle East; security and cooperation in the Mediterranean; Libya; Somalia; the Chagos Archipelago; Iraq; and Cuba. On Palestine they marked the fiftieth anniversary of the dispossession of the Palestinian people, and reiterated their support for their inalienable rights including their right to return to their homeland and the right to have their own independent state with Jerusalem as its capital. They demanded the withdrawal of Israel, the occupying power, from Arab occupied territories and condemned further steps taken on Jerusalem.

The final chapter on social issues covered *inter alia* social development; poverty eradication; health; education; labour; population; international migration; racism; advancement of women; children; youth; transnational crime; and international drug control. The heads of state reaffirmed that human rights were universal, indivisible, interdependent and interrelated; that the international community must treat human rights globally in a fair and equal manner and that the significance of national and regional particularities and various historical, cultural and religious backgrounds must be respected. They considered it essential to make a distinction between humanitarian action and UN peacekeeping and peace enforcement operations, as well as operational activities for development.

As is now usual the non-aligned also put out a four-page document entitled the Durban Declaration for the New Millennium[17]. This drew attention to their endurance of 'centuries of colonialism, oppression, aggression, exploitation and neglect' and that NAM principles remained valid. The movement was striving to be an 'open, democratic and a forward looking group of nations' facing threats such as drugs, AIDS, transnational crime, famine, terrorism and environmental degradation. The developed world, in particular, was afflicted by exaggerated ethnicity, chauvinism and xenophobia. International relations must be transformed 'so as to eradicate aggression, racism, the use of force, unilateral coercive measures and unfair economic practices, foreign occupation and xenophobia in order to achieve a world of peace, justice and dignity for all'. It should be based on the purposes and principles of the UN Charter and the sovereign equality of nations.

Globalisation needed to be channelled not just by large and powerful nations but South–South cooperation was also central. 'We must address the financing of development, capital flows and their stabilisation, resource mobilisation and trade restrictions faced by developing countries' as well as debt relief and eradication of poverty. To achieve this the Security Council, World Bank and IMF needed to be democratised.

> We recognize that human rights and democracy do not ... automatically bring a better world. They require an environment of peace and development, respect for sovereignty, territorial integrity, and non-interference in the internal affairs of States. Socio-economic rights, including the right to development, are inextricably part of real human rights.

Summit politics

The new and difficult issue of the Indian and Pakistani nuclear tests in May 1998 caused great problems. Eventually a sentence was added to the section on disarmament and international security stating 'They [the non-aligned] noted the complexities arising from nuclear tests in South Asia, which underlined the need to work even harder to achieve their disarmament objectives including the elimination of nuclear weapons' as well as reiterating 'the need for bilateral dialogue'. There was also a reference in the section on South-East Asia to the importance of the coming into force of the treaty on the South-East Asia Nuclear-Weapons-Free Zone. All nuclear-weapons states were encouraged to extend their support and cooperation by acceding to the protocol of the Treaty. Non-Aligned states who were party to the Non-Proliferation Treaty (NPT) regretted the lack of a substantive result from a meeting of the Second Preparatory Committee 'due to the insistence of one delegation to support the nuclear policies of a non-party to the NPT'. They also called for an open-ended standing committee to follow up recommendations concerning the implementation of the NPT Treaty at its 2000 review conference.

Many commented on the important role played by the Iranians including President Khatami then Chair of the OIC. Iran was made chairman of the important Political Committee which had, of course, to deal with South Asian nuclear proliferation. The Iranians also pushed their idea of a dialogue between cultures and civilisations which later that year was designated to be the UN Year for 2001 by the General Assembly (A/53/22). Interestingly President Kabila of the Democratic Republic of the Congo attended the Summit. Reuters noted this enabled Mandela and Mugabe to resolve differences on the DRC and to open the door to a settlement.

President Mandela

President Mandela gave lustre to the non-aligned as he both opened and closed the Summit. In opening he referred to the principles of collective self-reliance and mutual cooperation needed in Africa. South Africa hoped both to strengthen the movement and to contribute to its renewal. His vision included

> respect for democracy and human rights, peace and stability in our own countries and regions, good governance and a principled opposition to corruption and the abuse of power, people-centred processes of development and the provision of a better life for all our peoples, the genuine independence of all countries and genuinely mutually beneficial co-operation among the nations of the world.

'The achievement of our goals' he noted 'depends critically on the collective interests of the developing countries being effectively addressed'. And, as he said in his final speech, the non-aligned was committed to a practical programme 'ensuring that the development agenda of the Southern countries finds a proper place in world politics and the world economy' which meant *inter alia* the re-direction of the UN and other multilateral organisations.[18]

South Africa as Non-Aligned Chair: September 1998–February 2003

South Africa continued as chair for nearly four and a half years rather than the usual three because of problems about who should host the next summit. President Mbeki stated in April 2002 that South Africa had had two goals after becoming chair: 'increased co-operation among countries of the South and enhanced dialogue with the North'.[19] He went on to suggest, perhaps correctly, that they and the movement managed to make the North more open to Southern economic concerns. The South Africans also seem to have managed well in dealing with the normal, prolonged and complex duties of the chair. Both are discussed below.

Non-aligned foreign ministers meeting at Cartagena, April 2000

The non-aligned normally meet once at a foreign minister level during a country's role as the chair.[20] The Cartagena Final Document provided few surprises. It stated that 'Cold War era legacies such as foreign military bases, the use or threat of use of force, pressure, interference in internal affairs and sanctions inconsistent with international law' continued to militate against establishing a system of fair and equitable international relations. It was also concerned to help prepare for the 2001 conference on the proliferation of small arms. The movement went on to adopt the Plan of Action (decided on in 1998) to achieve maximum utilisation of its mechanisms; it had been agreed by the Bureau in August 1999.

On economic questions the non-aligned stressed their commitment to South–South while noting that problems of poverty and social injustice were still being aggravated. They welcomed the G8 Cologne debt initiative of 1999 and the UN decision to convene a conference on financing for development. They stated that all member states must participate effectively at the forthcoming millennium summit. Their separate declaration agreed with the JCC that two subtopics (peace, security and disarmament, and development and poverty eradication) should underline the overall theme – the role of the UN in the twenty-first century.

The G77 Summit at Havana, April 2000

Many of the delegates then flew straight to Cuba to attend the first Group of 77 South Summit for Heads of State and Government. The G77 rededicated themselves to their basic principles and objectives in the Summit Declaration.[21] They continued to be committed to a global system, based on democracy in decision-making and full respect for the principles of international law and the Charter of the United Nations. They noted the problems posed by globalisation and liberalisation and the need to redress the imbalances in WTO Agreements. Developed countries were called upon to implement fully, special and differential treatment for developing countries while G77 countries should coordinate their priorities and negotiating strategies to promote their common interests. They stressed the persistent critical economic situation in Africa which was exacerbated by debt, low savings and investment, declining levels of overseas development aid and insufficient levels of FDI besides pointing to the spread of HIV/AIDS.

The detailed Havana Programme of Action discussed the need to make globalisation more beneficial; to revitalise the UN system in promoting development and international cooperation in the South; and to stimulate South–South trade and investment. On North–South issues the G77 suggested that a new North–South partnership should be developed to promote consensus on key issues of international economic relations and development. Their last section tackled the need to adopt a more structured arrangement for managing the affairs of the Group.

The G8 and the millennium summit, July–September 2000

As always there were a number of outcomes related to these and other conferences in relation to the G8. The NAM troika had met the foreign ministers of the G8 at Cologne in 1999.[22] The NAM troika at senior official level participated for the first time in the preparation for the annual meeting between the NAM troika Foreign Ministers and the chair of the G77 and G8 Foreign Ministers, which took place in Japan in July 2000.[23] The G8 also invited the Thai Foreign Minister then UNCTAD President. A further North/South meeting at heads of state or government level was also held in Tokyo on the eve of Okinawa Summit (2000). Presidents Mbeki and Bouteflika came with an Organisation of African Unity (OAU) Summit mandate on Africa's debt problem while President Obasanjo of Nigeria represented the G77. He and President Mbeki conveyed the outcome of the Havana South Summit to the G8. This was the first G8 Summit to focus on the agenda of the South and the needs of developing countries. These meetings were followed by the UN Millennium Declaration (GAR 55/2 of 8 September 2000) covering values and principles; peace, security and disarmament; development and poverty eradication (these two were the principles advocated at the 2000 Cartagena meeting); protecting our common environment; human rights; democracy and good governance; protecting the vulnerable; meeting the special needs of Africa; and strengthening the United Nations. Non-aligned Foreign Ministers Meeting in New York in September 2000 stated that they considered that the Millennium Summit outcome was 'an important contribution towards renewing and strengthening the mandate of the United Nations to meet the challenges of the new century'.[24] The UN Secretary-General produced a road map towards its implementation in September 2001 (A/56/326).

Ministerial meeting of the coordinating bureau, Durban, April 2002

This meeting[25] was held in Durban to commemorate the fortieth anniversary of the non-aligned movement (September 1961) and to prepare for the next summit. By then it was clear that neither Bangladesh nor Jordan were able to host the forthcoming summit. Malaysia offered to be the host after consultations within the Asian Region. In his opening speech, President Mbeki noted the non-aligned commitment to peace and disarmament within a global development strategy, self-determination, and poverty eradication including economic equity.

As already stated President Mbeki referred to South Africa's two goals as chair: increased cooperation among Southern countries and enhanced dialogue with the North. He suggested that pressure on the North had helped focus its attention on priority issues in the South, at the G8 Okinawa Summit (2000), and the subsequent Millennium Summit which acknowledged poverty eradication as a global priority. These events 'witnessed the beginning of an important paradigm shift in the relationship between North and South. The outcome of the Millennium Summit is the clearest indication yet that it is possible to cultivate the political will, both in the North and the South, to enable us to engage the development issues as equal partners'.

He noted the non-aligned contribution to the formation of the African Union from the OAU and the formulation of the New Partnership for Africa's Development (NEPAD) and stated that the non-aligned needed to prepare for forthcoming conferences by strengthening their unity and methodology and enhancing their partnership with the G77 and China. It was clear that the interaction and synchronisation of ideas between NAM and the G77 and China through the JCC in New York had proved to be 'highly effective in helping to determine the agenda and outcomes of the Millennium Summit'. The challenge ahead for the NAM was 'to find ways and means to strengthen our capacity for united action'. NAM mechanisms like the JCC and troika needed to be strengthened. 'Continuously, we have to emphasise the need for us to plan and act collectively merging national interests with the greater good of all countries of the South ... our own debates and discussions must lead to actual global action to advance the needs of the billions of people that we lead.'

The final document was, as usual, based on previous non-aligned documentation. It noted that regional bodies were bound by Article VIII of the UN Charter and rejected the term 'axis of evil' to target countries under the pretext of combating terrorism. Ministers voiced concern over the loss of seats of experts from non-aligned countries in certain treaty bodies and suggested that the Security Council should make greater use of the World Court as a source of advisory opinions. They expressed outrage at the atrocities committed by the Israeli occupying forces especially since the assault on Palestinian cities and the Palestinian Authority of March 2002 and welcomed the fact that the first summit of the African Union would take place in South Africa in July. They noted the outcome of the presidential elections in Zimbabwe as an expression of the will of the people and remained concerned over the lack of implementation of the outcomes of major UN conferences and summits, due mainly to the lack of political will and to the failure of the developed countries to fulfil their commitments for new and additional resources.

Other activities, September 1998–February 2003

South Africa as chair gave a report of the activities of the movement during its chair to the Kuala Lumpur Summit in February 2003.[26] It noted that the South African Mission to the UN had put out a statement on 14 September 2001 condemning the terrorist attacks (on 9/11) and recalling the section on terrorism in the 1998 Durban Declaration. This had showed that there continued to be a need for a strong non-aligned working for an international order characterised by an absence of want, fear and intolerance based on peace, justice, equality, democracy and full respect for the principles enshrined in the UN Charter and international law in a world dominated by a few powerful and rich countries.

The report suggested that high level meetings useful to the South after Cartagena (2000) were the South Summit; the Millennium Summit; the Doha Ministerial round of WTO trade negotiations; the Finance for Development Conference; and the World Summit on Sustainable Development. The non-aligned needed solidarity and unity to ensure that the interests and aspirations of the South formed an integral part of the agendas of such conferences. These would be usefully followed up by the UN Secretary-General's Roadmap for the Millennium Declaration, the Monterey Consensus and the Johannesburg Plan of Action. The report also drew attention to the Zimbali Group which had come together to reflect on the revitalisation, weaknesses and strengths of the movement.

The report went on to note the achievements of the main NAM Working Groups and Committees, including the Working Group on Disarmament chaired by Indonesia which presented a working paper[27] to the April–May 2000 review conference in New York. Others were the Working Group on Peacekeeping chaired by Jordan; the Sixth Committee Group (on legal questions) chaired by Zimbabwe; the Restructuring the Security Council Group chaired by Egypt; and the Group on Human Rights. The Commission on Human Rights passed a resolution in 1999 on globalisation and its impact on the full enjoyment of all human rights.

The long-standing committee on Palestine was also busy. The Coordinating Bureau gave support to the Arab League in January 1999 for the resumption of the Tenth Emergency Special General Assembly on Palestine. The caucus of non-aligned states on the Security Council was party to a ministerial meeting on Palestine and the peace process at Pretoria in May 2001, attended by the Egyptian and Jordanian Foreign Ministers and President Arafat. The caucus also met to discuss Palestine in December 2001. The US subsequently vetoed a draft Egyptian/ Tunisian resolution encouraging the establishment of a monitoring mechanism. The NAM caucus was very active in negotiating the adoption of SC resolutions 1397 and 1402 respectively of, March and April 2002, on the need to resume negotiations and to express grave concern at the deterioration of the situation. South Africa as non-aligned Chair and the Arab League again asked for the reconvention of the tenth Special Session in August 2002. As many would agree denial of a truly just solution to the Palestine crisis 'is a guarantee that long term instability in the Middle East will prevail'.[28]

The chair of the Coordinating Bureau met regularly with members of the non-aligned Security Council caucus while the NAM troika of ambassadors received mandates from the Bureau to take action for the non-aligned. In July 2000 they put out a statement expressing non-aligned concern at United States intention to prohibit US[29] assistance or debt relief to Zimbabwe. Other problems discussed included Kosovo; the dangers of humanitarian intervention; the status of the Federal Republic of Yugoslavia; and the 1996 Cartagena Document on Methodology. South Africa helped ensure non-aligned cohesion in Geneva and Nairobi. They were also engaged at various levels with Libya on Lockerbie, Iraq and the problem of sanctions.

South–South cooperation was pursued with vigour. The non-aligned continued to work together within the WHO (World Health Organisation), to develop a precise economic agenda based on the work of the Panel of Economists and to discuss this cooperation at the OIC. The JCC of the NAM and G77 met in New York to work on issues of concern such as approaches to the G8. Meanwhile North–South interaction continued with the G8 meetings in Genoa (2001) and Kananaskis (2002) while the NAM troika and the chair of the G77 also held informal consultations on UN reform with the EU troika in October 2002.

Conclusion

This chapter has deliberately concentrated on showing the global range of the problems that face the non-aligned and the way they deal with them in the UN and beyond. They have recognised, as President Mandela noted in his opening speech to the Durban Summit, that the achievement of their goals means that their collective interests must be addressed. The challenge as President Mbeki stated in April 2002 was, and remains, to find 'ways and means to strengthen our capacity for united action'. It will be interesting to see whether he was right in suggesting that 'the outcome of the Millennium Summit is the clearest indication yet that it is possible to cultivate the political will, both in the North and the South, to enable us to engage the development issues as equal partners'. He did not mention their achievement of South/South issues.

The South African Government seems to have had the diplomatic capacity to help, as chair, keep the non-aligned movement and its commitment to multilateralism going even in the problematic circumstances that followed the terrorist attacks on the United States on 9/11(11 September 2001). President Mbeki in his speech[30] to the Kuala Lumpur Summit (February 2003) argued that the movement was 'relevant to the problems that confront all humanity during the post-Cold War period'. The moderate mainstream of the non-aligned with whom they have worked closely and which last swung into action during the 1979 Havana Summit would probably agree. But as in the past the movement has often found it difficult but not impossible to move on to appropriate action. Non-aligned talking and action can be and has been influential. South Africa has certainly benefited from being the chair of the non-aligned. It has been a learning experience and a good introduction to global diplomacy and the global community. However its role as chair was not always easy as it was inexperienced in diplomacy and the non-aligned. The current holder of the chair, the Malaysians, have successfully attempted to 'balance Western influence, enhance ... national power, assert Asian identity and dignity, and build coalitions with other developing nations, while pursuing a partnership with the developed West'.[31] They remain more likely to be a more influential chair in the medium term.

Annexure – The 114 Non-Aligned Members in 1998

Afghanistan, Algeria, Angola, Bahamas, Bahrain, Bangladesh, Barbados, Belarus, Belize, Benin, Bhutan, Bolivia, Botswana, Brunei, Burkina, Burundi, Cambodia, Cameroon, Cape Verde, Central African Republic, Chad, Chile, Colombia, Comoros, Congo, Cote d'Ivoire, Cuba, Cyprus, Dominican Republic. Djibouti, Ecuador, Egypt, Equatorial Guinea, Eritrea, Ethiopia, Gabon, Gambia, Ghana, Grenada, Guatemala, Guinea, Guinea-Bissau, Guyana, Honduras, India, Indonesia, Iran, Iraq, Jamaica, Jordan, Kenya, Kuwait, Laos, Lebanon, Lesotho, Liberia, Libya, Madagascar, Malawi, Malaysia, Maldives, Mali, Malta, Mauritania, Mauritius, Mongolia, Morocco, Mozambique, Myanmar, Namibia, Nepal, Nicaragua, Niger, Nigeria, North Korea, Oman, Pakistan, Palestine, Panama, Papua New Guinea, Peru, Philippines, Qatar, Rwanda, Sao Tome and Principe, Saudi Arabia, Senegal, Seychelles, Sierra Leone, Singapore, Somalia, South Africa, Sri Lanka, St Lucia, Sudan, Suriname, Swaziland, Syria, Tanzania, Thailand, Togo, Trinidad and Tobago, Tunisia, Turkmenistan, Uganda, United Arab Emirates, Uzbekistan, Vanuatu, Venezuela, Vietnam, Yemen, Zaire, Zambia, Zimbabwe.

Notes

1. For more information see Morphet, S., 'Three Non-Aligned Summits Harare 1986; Belgrade 1989 and Jakarta 1992' in David H. Dunn (ed.), *Diplomacy at the Highest Level: The Evolution of International Summitry* (London: Macmillan, 1996), and Morphet, S., 'The Non-Aligned in 'The New World Order': The Jakarta Summit, September 1992', *International Relations*, XI:4 (1993) pp. 359–80.
2. See Taylor, I., *Stuck in Middle GEAR, South Africa's Post Apartheid Foreign Relations*, (Westport: Praeger 2001), p. 143, and Morphet, S., 'States Groups in the United Nations', in Taylor, P. and Groom, A. J. R. (eds), *The United Nations at the Millennium The Principal Organs* (New York, Continuum International, 2000). The annual reports on the Movement by Professor Willetts in the Annual Register of World Events are also very useful.
3. See Morphet, S., 'Multilateralism and the Non-Aligned Movement: What is the Global South Doing and Where Is It Going?', *Global Governance*, 10 (October–December 2004) pp. 517–37.
4. For a discussion on the pressure on certain voters see Anderson, P., 'Scurrying Towards Bethlehem', *New Left Review*, 10 (July–August 2001) pp. 5–30. See also

Khalidi, W., 'Revisiting the UNGA Partition Resolution', *Journal of Palestine Studies*, 27:1 (1997) pp. 5–21.

5. See Morphet, 'States Groups', pp. 224–33.
6. See, *Conference of Heads of State or Government of Non-Aligned Countries, Belgrade, September 1–6, 1961* (Belgrade, Jugoslavija Publishing House) p.16.
7. See Belgrade Conference Proceedings, pp. 272–3.
8. Dr Petkovic, R. 'The Non-Aligned in Jakarta', *Belgrade Review of International Affairs*, 1007–8 (1992) p. 7–8.
9. See Morphet, S., 'The Non-Aligned and Their 11th Summit at Cartagena, October 1995', *The Round Table*, 85 (1996), p. 461.
10. China, in the view of most non-aligned is too influential to become a non-aligned member. But it is well able to pursue non-aligned interests as a permanent member of the Security Council as well as to use non-aligned support. It was able to become an Observer in the movement because India which opposed its application, had lost influence in the non-aligned on account of the break up of the Soviet Union.
11. The Group of 77's website is www.g77.org/main/geninfo
12. The 114 non-aligned members in 1998 are given in the Annexure.
13. See Taylor, *Stuck in Middle Gear*, pp. 5–6.
14. The documents for the September 1988 Summit are available on the South African Foreign Ministry website – www.nam.gov.za/background. The Durban documents were put out by the UN – A/53/667 and S/1998/1071 (13 November 1988).
15. See 'Elements for an Agenda of the South', Report of the Ad Hoc Panel of Economists to the XII NAM Summit, Durban, South Africa, 1998, available on www.nam.gov.za/documentation/elemagenda.htm, Accessed 30 January 2005.
16. Transcript of Round Table Discussion of the Report by the Ad Hoc Panel of Economists of 30 June 1998, entitled 'Elements for an Agenda of the South', available on www.nam.gov.za/documentation/southelements:htm
17. In the Summit documents see note 14.
18. The opening speech is in the Summit documents see note 14 and www.nam.gov.za/xiisummit/manclose.htm. The closing speech is in the Summit documents.
19. Speech to opening session of the Ministerial Meeting of the Coordinating Bureau to Commemorate the 40th Anniversary of NAM, in Durban. Available on the South African website – see note 14.
20. In the Summit documents see note 14.
21. In the Summit documents see note 14.
22. See 'Report of the Outgoing Chair on the Activities of the Non-Aligned Movement during is full term as Chair, September 1998 – February 2003', available on the Malaysian Government website, www.mfa.gov.my/namkl, Accessed 30 January 2005.
23. See 'Report of the Chair on the Activities of the Non-Aligned Movement, Ministerial Meeting, Millennium Assembly, New York, September 2000' on the South African NAM website – see note 14.
24. In the South African website, see note 14.
25. In the South African website, see note 14.
26. On the South African and Malaysian websites, see notes 14 and 21.

27. See www.basicint.org/nuclear/NPT/2000revcon/wp_nam.htm
28. See Morphet on multilateralism, note 3, p. 531.
29. See Morphet on multilateralism, note 3, p. 531.
30. See www.nam2003.com/events/newnam2003
31. See Morphet on multilateralism, note 3, p. 533.

4
Post-Apartheid South Africa and the European Union
Integration over Development?
Stephen R. Hurt

From the very beginning of the post-apartheid era, the South African government was keen to formalise its relationship with the European Union (EU).[1] In 1995 the EU was South Africa's biggest trade partner and the most significant source of foreign investment. The importance of South Africa to the EU is of course much more limited. In 2002 South Africa accounted for just 1.6 per cent of EU imports and 1.3 per cent of its total exports.[2] The relationship that Pretoria has forged with the EU is therefore significant in the way it defines the integration of South Africa into the global economy. This chapter locates EU–South Africa relations within a critical understanding of South Africa's domestic political economy. In doing so it argues that South Africa has prioritised a neoliberal approach to integration within the global economy over the developmental needs of the poor black majority.

An appreciation of the political nature of the negotiations is also vital to an understanding of the relationship that has been forged with the EU. The new government in South Africa was faced with the task of bargaining with a powerful trading bloc that has years of experience of conducting trade negotiations, both within the multilateral context and on a bilateral basis. The timing of the negotiations, which took place during the first few years of the post-apartheid era, exacerbated this inequality as issues related to the transition and reconciliation dominated the immediate focus of the post-apartheid government.

The foundations for the negotiation of a long-term agreement between South Africa and the EU were agreed on 10 October 1994 when a Cooperation Agreement was signed between the two parties. The aims of future negotiations were made explicitly clear from the beginning; it was hoped that the development of such an agreement would 'encourage the smooth and gradual integration of South Africa into the world economy'.[3]

Negotiations of the Trade, Development and Cooperation Agreement (TDCA) formally began on 30 June 1995, after EU member states had agreed upon the negotiating directives to be adopted by the European Commission. These negotiations were concluded in October 1999 and the TDCA became operational on 1 January 2000. It includes two main areas of cooperation. The first and most significant is the creation of a Free Trade Area (FTA) between the EU and South Africa. In addition the EU provides development assistance. It is the negotiation and potential impacts of the TDCA that form the central focus of this chapter. In analysing the negotiations and implementation of the TDCA, it becomes clear how the multilateral environment, especially the World Trade Organization (WTO) in this case, has a significant impact on the detail and direction of South Africa's relationship with the EU.

Integration as a priority?

The South African government views the TDCA as a key driver in the further integration of post-apartheid South Africa into the world economy.[4] This is reflected by the comments of one senior figure in the South African government. Minister of Trade and Industry, Alec Erwin suggested that the TDCA would benefit South Africa in both assisting the necessary restructuring of the economy and by opening markets, which will increase productivity levels and the stimulation of exports.[5] Hence it is clear that in its relations with the EU, the South African government was in broad acceptance of the neoliberalism that dominates the world's multilateral institutions. Unlike in other multilateral bodies, discussed elsewhere in this volume, South Africa in acting on its own has no chance to form alliances with other Southern elites. Consequently, its ability to adopt even a reformist position is compromised.

South Africa cannot avoid engagement with the global economy; given the contemporary nature of world politics, autarky is not a viable option. However, it is the *nature* of this integration, and the *importance* attached to it, which is open for debate. Those progressive forces that argue that South Africa should engage with the global economy in a strategic fashion, whereby the state would adopt an active industrial policy and redistributive measures to counter the negative impacts of liberalisation, are currently marginalised within this debate.[6]

The concerns of the Congress of South African Trade Unions (COSATU), for example, appear to have had little impact on the nature of the agreement.[7] In fact Bilal and Laporte suggest that in general 'the trade unions ... did not contribute in any substantive way to shaping the trade agreement'.[8]

In contrast, a number of dominant forces within South Africa support the view that building stronger ties with the EU, at the expense of the region, are in South Africa's 'national interest'. As Balefi Tsie suggests,

This neo-liberal position is favoured by the five conglomerates which dominate the South African economy, the white establishment in the top echelons on the public sector, South African finance capital in general and their external allies in the form of IFIs.[9]

The dominance of such a view has been reflected domestically in the development of macroeconomic policy within South Africa. The shift from the Reconstruction and Development Programme (RDP) to the Growth, Employment and Redistribution Strategy (GEAR) has been well documented.[10] The GEAR document was little removed from the type of neoliberal proposals found in numerous structural adjustment programmes, which have been promoted by the International Monetary Fund (IMF) and World Bank throughout much of the developing world. Hence, the GEAR strategy sees the role of the state being limited to providing an enabling environment, with the ambitious targets for jobs and growth to be almost wholly dependent on the performance of the private sector. The proposal of the GEAR document was that a strategy that pushed non-gold exports and private sector investment would 'provide sufficient impetus for GDP growth to climb to the targeted six per cent by the year 2000'.[11]

The EU–South Africa TDCA is also symptomatic of the shift in development policy away from aid and towards trade. Rather than see a dichotomy between trade and development, the dominant view in both Pretoria and the EU at present is that the two are complementary in a normative sense. Hence, a source from the European Commission has suggested that in the medium-term it would be in South Africa's interests to build a purely trade-based arrangement with the EU.[12] There are a few signs that questions are beginning to be raised over this approach. A recent report by the United Nations Conference on Trade and Development (UNCTAD) demonstrates that the link between increased trade and poverty alleviation is empirically suspect in a number of developing countries.[13]

Historical background

The EU considered its strategy towards its relationship with South Africa in the post-apartheid era as being aimed at cementing the political reform that had provided the focus of its relationship dating back to 1977. In this section a brief summary of the historical background to the relationship between the EU and post-apartheid South Africa is provided to put more recent developments into context.

The origin of a European policy towards South Africa was strongly influenced by the UK's accession to the EU in 1973. Gaston Thom, as President of the Council of Ministers, made the first EU statement regarding South Africa on 23 February 1976, condemning the policy of apartheid.[14] The twin aims of EU policy were the removal of apartheid and the promotion of economic independence for South Africa's neighbours, which was to be achieved through direct assistance to the Southern African Development Coordination Conference (SADCC).

In July 1977 the first EU foreign policy initiative was implemented. This was prompted by the actions taken by the South African government in response to the Soweto uprisings of 1976. Prior to this the EU had only a peripheral interest in South Africa and considered it part of Britain's 'foreign policy sphere'.[15] The policy was a code of conduct for European firms operating in South Africa and was an adaptation of an existing UK code of practice.[16] The aim was to reconcile the difficulties between the political rhetoric of opposition to apartheid, whilst justifying the continuing levels of EU–South Africa trade and investment. The code had limited success and was seen as the lowest common denominator of EU opinion. The policy reflected the diversity of levels of economic interest within EU member states. The UK and West Germany had the most significant economic links with South Africa and they made it difficult for the EU to arrive at a common position.[17] In contrast, Denmark, Ireland and The Netherlands were much more critical of the apartheid system and campaigned for an enforceable code.[18] Hence the code was flexible enough to be interpreted in a number of different ways to suit various European states and was voluntary, meaning that EU firms had no legally binding obligation to follow its provisions.[19] For example, one of the most essential requirements of the code was the removal of racial segregation within the workplace, yet 11 German and 18 British companies failed to achieve this.[20]

Civil unrest within South Africa and the declaration of a state of emergency in 1985 by the apartheid regime did lead to a renewal and strengthening of the EU's policy. Until this point the code of conduct had remained the central feature of its approach. Under the Special Programme that came into operation from this point until 1994, the EU adopted a twofold approach. First, new measures were adopted that included a limited number of sanctions that prevented Krugerrands and certain iron and steel products being imported from South Africa, and a decision was also taken to discourage any new direct investment in South Africa.[21] Second, support was given to civil society organisations involved in non-violent struggle against apartheid.[22]

Of central importance for the development of EU–South Africa relations after the end of apartheid is the fact that the various policies that the EU implemented during the 1970s and 1980s failed to alter the extensive economic links between Europe and South Africa. In 1992 and 1993 the EU accounted for just over 40 per cent of all exports to South Africa and was also a major recipient of South African exports.[23]

Trade

The FTA forms the central pillar of post-apartheid South Africa's relations with the EU. It was the first FTA to be negotiated after the conclusion of the Uruguay Round of the General Agreement on Tariffs and Trade (GATT) and the subsequent creation of the WTO. The priority of South Africa's integration into the global economy appears to take precedence over the developmental nature of the FTA. The technical nature of much of the negotiations was reflected in the fact that the Department of Trade and Industry (DTI) and not the Department of Foreign Affairs (DFA) led the negotiations with the EU. It has been suggested that this has increased tensions between the two departments.[24]

The main beneficiaries of the FTA are likely to be export-oriented capital within South Africa, whether it is domestic or internationally sourced. Despite claims to the contrary, the development that will follow may be limited. Even if a very narrow view of development such as Gross Domestic Product (GDP) is considered, it has been estimated that South Africa will increase its real GDP by only 0.44 per cent.[25] It is debatable whether this will translate into a wider conception of development, which takes into account health, education and jobs.

Initially the South African government requested that it should be granted a five-year transitional membership period of the EU's non-reciprocal trade relationship with the African, Caribbean and Pacific States (ACP).[26] This request was made in 1994 and reflects the nature of government policy-making during the early part of the post-apartheid era, when policies were formulated that had more than a rhetorical desire to reflect the interests of the poor black majority. This could be seen as an attempt to placate potential 'leftist' critics of the idea of a FTA. In reality the domestic debate within South Africa had little impact on the nature of the agreement. As Bertelsmann-Scott suggests, despite the widespread discussion within South Africa and the influence of the National Economic Development and Labour Council (NEDLAC) on the final mandate, the constraints of international norms and multilateral governance meant 'the outcome of the negotiations was to a large extent a foregone conclusion'.[27]

The EU responded to this argument with a number of reasons as to why South Africa could not be accorded membership of the Lomé Convention. First, they suggested that a special relationship was needed to reflect the fact that South Africa's economy has many features that resemble a developed country. One might wish to question the claim that South Africa can readily be classed as a developed country. Both South Africa's GDP per capita and its human development index are lower than a number of ACP countries.[28] Moreover, with hindsight this can be seen as quite ironic. The renegotiation of the EU–ACP relationship that resulted in the Cotonou Agreement led to the adoption of an approach very similar to that which had been only deemed relevant to a *developed* country such as South Africa.[29]

Second, it was argued that if South Africa enjoyed the full trade benefits of the Lomé Convention the potential benefits for the other ACP states would be compromised. In 1995 South Africa's exports to the EU totalled €7.8 billion, whereas the total for the other seventy ACP states for the same year was only €19.9 billion.[30]

Third, the EU argued that the inclusion of South Africa within Lomé would increase the likelihood of a challenge within the WTO to the non-reciprocal nature of the trade relationship between EU and ACP states. It was claimed there were two likely sources of complaint: either other developing countries that were not members of the ACP group, or countries who felt they were of a similar level of development to South Africa. A source in the European Commission recently suggested that this argument was overplayed at the time and that given the overwhelming international support South Africa enjoyed in the first few years of the post-apartheid era, it was in fact very unlikely that any WTO member state would have challenged their full membership of Lomé.[31] Finally, the potential threat to some sectors of the European economy, in particular the agricultural and textile sectors, was put forward as a reason for the refusal of South Africa's full membership of Lomé.

Rather than viewing this as a serious attempt to pursue a more developmental relationship with the EU, it was suggested by the then head of the South African negotiating team, Elias Links, that the case for full Lomé membership was never taken that seriously. Rather it was an attempt to try and highlight some of the developmental needs of South Africa as a way of trying to influence the FTA negotiations.[32] Organised business within South Africa was also quick to highlight that full membership of the Lomé Convention might contradict the neoliberal macroeconomic strategy being adopted by the South African government. The South African Foreign Trade Organisation and the South African Chamber of Business both expressed concerns. In particular, they argued that by labelling itself as one of a number of developing African countries, South Africa would be sending the wrong signals to the global market.[33] It was argued in the business press in South Africa that full membership of the EU–ACP relationship 'could hamper South Africa's access to capital markets and make foreign investors question the country's risk rating'.[34]

The discussions over South Africa's membership of the Lomé Convention were then de-linked from the main negotiations. In June 1998 South Africa became a qualified member of the agreement. The main qualification being that South Africa was not party to the non-reciprocal trade preferences granted to other ACP states. In addition to this the special trade protocols for the stabilisation of export earnings and resources from the European Development Fund (EDF) were not included. This allows the TDCA to dominate the relationship between the EU and South Africa.

The approach adopted in the FTA is that the EU, as the more highly developed partner, conceded that the agreement should adhere to the principles of asymmetry and differentiation. To be compatible with WTO rules regarding the negotiation of a FTA, substantially all trade between the two parties should be included. This was interpreted as 90 per cent of the actual trade between the two parties, with the asymmetry reflected in the fact that by the end of the adjustment periods 95 per cent of South African exports will enter the EU duty-free, whilst only 86 per cent of EU exports will gain tariff free access to South Africa.[35] The differentiation refers to the timing of tariff reductions on both sides. The EU committed itself to reduce all tariffs within ten years with much of the adjustment occurring in the first few years of this period. South Africa is granted an extra two years to complete its adjustment and much of its trade liberalisation will occur towards the end of this period.

This expressed concern with South Africa's needs was tempered by the power of the agricultural constituency within Europe. This lobbying was particularly prevalent in France and the Mediterranean states, where concern was expressed about the impact of agricultural exports from South Africa. These European states also had lower levels of overall trade with South Africa and therefore had less to gain from the FTA.[36] The restrictive nature of the negotiating mandate given to the European Commission was further enhanced by the influence of Germany, both in terms of its influential role in agriculture within the EU and – as it was also rumoured – with German industrial investors' fears of the impact of increased competition on their South African affiliates.[37]

Another part of the developmental nature of the FTA is supposed to lie in the generous rules of origin.[38] The rules of origin in the TDCA are similar to those found in other agreements between the EU and third parties. However, there are some notable differences. First, there is bilateral cumulation, which means that materials from either the EU or South Africa are counted in assessing origin. Second, inputs from other ACP states are allowed as long as their value is less than the value added in South Africa itself. Southern African Customs Union (SACU) members have an additional benefit where full cumulation is allowed as long as the final stage of processing takes place within South Africa.[39] The significance of rules of origin is questionable. Within the SADC region there is a huge informal trade regime and rules of origin are unlikely to be enforced with any great efficiency.[40]

In summary, the FTA is officially portrayed as a developmental trade relationship that will address the needs of South Africa whilst providing mutual benefits for all sides. This section has highlighted how the aspects tailored towards development within the FTA are limited. The major justification is the asymmetrical nature of the FTA. Nevertheless, once the 12 years of liberalisation are concluded, apart from the slight differentiation, South Africa will be trading with the EU on an even playing field. The claims to partnership within the FTA fail to account for the highly unequal nature of the negotiations and the needs of the majority of South African citizens. Reflecting on the experience of negotiations with the EU, Davies concluded that they 'involve hard bargaining, in which professed concerns to promote development and greater equity in trade relations with developing countries are often swamped'.[41]

Development assistance

The second arm of the EU–South Africa TDCA is development assistance. This is very much of secondary importance in comparison to the FTA. It should be acknowledged that parts of this funding have been focused directly on the needs of the poor majority and the legacies of apartheid.

The EU provides development assistance to South Africa through the European Programme for Reconstruction and Development (EPRD). The impact of the EPRD is augmented by loans made by the European Development Bank (EDB). The EDB has made loans averaging €120 million per year. This makes the EU the most significant provider of development assistance within South Africa. Nevertheless, these funds only represent about 1.5 per cent of the annual budget of the South African government.[42] This makes any possible impact of the EPRD fairly negligible.

It is the case that for the period 1995–2001 well over half of the commitments made in the EPRD framework were in support of programme areas designed to directly support the needs of the poor. A summary of the breakdown of commitments within the EPRD (see Table 4.1) shows that the four areas that are most focused towards the needs of the poor (human resources development, health, water and sanitation, local economic development) accounted for 66 per cent of the €847 million in commitments. Good governance and human rights is another area to be welcomed. However, past experience of how the EU has interpreted these concepts in its relations with ACP states suggests that a limited liberal interpretation is to be expected, which often lacks a genuine commitment to democratisation beyond polyarchy.[43]

However, EPRD funding should not be seen as wholly positive. The decisions over the priorities for the use of EPRD funds are taken in a

Table 4.1   EPRD commitments by sector, 1995–2001

Sector	Commitments (€)	Percentage of total commitments
Human resource development	154,556,000	18.26
Health	113,965,444	13.46
Water and sanitation	108,480,000	12.81
Local economic development	182,100,000	21.51
Private sector development	95,072,000	11.23
Good governance and human rights	149,408,000	17.65
Regional cooperation	16,580,100	1.96
Technical assistance	26,405,796	3.12
Total	846,567,340	100

Source: European Commission (2003).

joint approach between the two parties. This claim to 'partnership' in EU development assistance has been widely criticised in relation to the ACP states.[44] However, in the case of South Africa there is arguably more substance to this claim to equality in decision-making and it could be argued that a genuine 'partnership' is in place.[45] This consensual decision-making process has been reflected in the complementarity between the focus of the EPRD and the South African government's macroeconomic strategy. Between 1995 and 1996 the EPRD was focused on supporting the aims of the ANC's RDP, whereas from 1997 onwards the emphasis of EU development assistance has shifted towards the priorities of the GEAR strategy.[46]

The substantial role played by the South African government in both co-funding and planning the programmes funded from the EPRD has served to further marginalise the voice of progressive forces within civil society. The focus on democracy assistance, whilst not based on enforced political conditionalities from the EU, has enabled the ANC to entrench the dominance of those groups broadly supportive of its neoliberal development strategy. Fioramonti has raised such concerns over the ANC's partnership in EU democracy assistance by suggesting that 'important actors which are not welcomed by the ANC government could be excluded from getting financing or hindered during their activities'.[47] Moreover, much of the support that goes to civil society has not resulted in the needs of the poor majority being addressed. It is often urban-based think-tanks such as the Institute for Democracy in South Africa that receive funds from the EPRD, and many of these have limited claims to represent the needs of the poor.

Other aspects

Sources at the European Commission have emphasised the growing importance of political dialogue within the TDCA.[48] The Cooperation Council was established to facilitate such dialogue between the South African government, the European Commission and representatives of EU member states. This forum meets annually to discuss issues of common concern to all parties. However, dialogue only occurs between official representatives and there is therefore continued marginalisation of progressive forces. The fourth and most recent meeting took place in November 2004. The South African delegation was led by Foreign Affairs Minister, Nkosazana Dlamini Zuma, whilst the EU representation was headed by Agnes Van Ardenne who is the Dutch Minister of Development and Cooperation.

A number of separate agreements were also included in the TDCA. A science and technology agreement was signed in 1997. Furthermore a separate wines and spirits accord was signed on 28 January 2002. The issue of wines and spirits caused much tension during the negotiations and, at times, threatened the very conclusion of the overall FTA. Central to the dispute was the use of terms that indicate a source of origin such as 'port' and 'sherry'. Within the WTO, the EU has led the way in trying to instigate a register of geographical indications as part of the agreement on Trade-Related Intellectual Property Rights (TRIPS). This has proved difficult and in response the EU appears to have decided to 'bypass the TRIPS agreement and protect geographical indications through bilateral treaties where, through its market power, it can force smaller trading countries to protect a range of names'.[49] This is precisely what happened within the TDCA between the EU and South Africa. During the negotiations concerns were raised over the terms 'port' and 'sherry' and then 'grappa' and 'ouzo'. In the end South Africa agreed to phase out the use of these terms in an effort to reach agreement in this area.

At the time of writing, the negotiations over a fisheries accord have been suspended under pressure from the Spanish government over its desire for fishing rights within South African waters. In fact it appears that no resolution of this particular agreement is likely in the foreseeable future. This is one particular area where the South African negotiators have stood firm. In part this may reflect the fact that in this sector any agreement to open up South African waters is perceived as being against the wishes of all interested parties (small-scale fishermen, large fishing companies, trade unions and government representatives).[50] The petty nature of both these disputes led Barber to conclude that 'the enthusiasm that had greeted South Africa's political miracle was lost amidst the noise of clashing economic interests'.[51]

The implications of the TDCA

Much of the analysis of the agreement between the EU and South Africa takes a rather simplistic view of the possible consequences of the agreement. With regard to the FTA there has been debate over the possible economic impacts for both the South African economy and the wider regional economy. This approach adopts a very narrow conception of the process of development and often assumes that there is a coherent 'national interest' within South Africa.

The immediate impact of the FTA appears to have boosted trade between the two parties. There was significant growth in both South African exports to the EU and imports from the EU entering the South African market (see Table 4.2). Whether these trade statistics can be attributable purely to the impact of the FTA is debatable. The early part of this period also saw a substantial decline in the value of the Rand, which by making exports comparatively cheaper could have helped to increase South Africa's trade balance.

Despite the various claims made about the developmental nature of the FTA between South African and the EU, this is essentially an agreement that will secure the EU's economic interests within South Africa. Whilst export-oriented sections of South African capital will gain by improved access to the European market, these gains are likely to be limited given the restrictions on certain agricultural goods. The agreement might help in attracting both domestic and foreign investment in industries where South Africa could provide an export platform for entry to the EU market.[52] However, the access afforded to EU exporters may threaten domestic industry. Despite the asymmetry and differentiation included in the FTA, by 2012 the resulting trade liberalisation will mean the EU will have vastly improved access to the South African market than was previously the case.

Debate over the type of relationship that South Africa should develop with the EU did take place during the negotiating period. Representatives of organised South African labour have expressed concerns over the TDCA and, in particular, the FTA. The link between tariff reductions, increased exports and job creation has been criticised. COSATU, for instance, argued that

A key problem with this approach is that scarce resources are mobilised into competitive, export-oriented, usually capital-intensive industries, while the resourcing of more labour-intensive forms of benefication and industrial activity is neglected.[53]

Table 4.2   Trade between the European Union and South Africa, 1999–2002

	1999	2000	2001	2002
South African exports to the EU (€ billion)	10.7	14.4	16.0	15.6
Index (1990 = 100)	180	243	270	263
EU exports to South Africa	9.4	11.7	12.5	12.4
Index (1990 = 100)	238	285	305	304

Source: Eurostat Trade Statistics.

Part of the reason for the protracted nature of the negotiations was the time that the South African government took to consult various domestic policy elites over its response to the initial negotiating mandate adopted by the EU.[54] A South African representative in Brussels claimed that the most significant discussions took place within NEDLAC.[55] However, one commentator has suggested that in reality NEDLAC had little significant influence over the direction of the negotiations with the EU, and that 'the overriding impression of NEDLAC's influence over the negotiations has been one of business dominance'.[56]

The FTA element of the agreement between the EU and South Africa is wholly consistent with the strategy of the South African government in its attempts at increasing the country's reintegration into the world economy in the post-apartheid era. In the implementation of its Uruguay Round commitments, the South African government chose to signal its faith in liberalisation by moving faster than it was required to on some areas of tariff reductions. Furthermore, the South African government demonstrated its commitment to a deepening of integration within the global economy through its liberalisation of exchange and capital controls.

In the early years of the post-apartheid era there was a special emphasis placed on the Southern African region within foreign policy statements. Nelson Mandela, for instance, suggested that 'Southern Africa commands a special priority in our foreign policy'.[57] Indeed the dominant view within the ANC was that 'South Africa could not remain 'an island of prosperity in a sea of poverty'.[58] However, such a concern for their regional neighbours did not appear to be given a high priority in South Africa's negotiations with the EU. The existence of the SACU, which includes not only South Africa, but also Botswana, Lesotho, Namibia and Swaziland (BLNS), means that the FTA is a *de facto* agreement with SACU and not just South Africa. Despite this, the BLNS states were not seriously consulted during the negotiations. The EU financed the only impact study that was conducted on their behalf after a request was made by the BLNS states in January 1998.[59] One of the aspects that this study focused on was the potential loss of revenue for the BLNS states. The common external tariff and revenue-sharing formula within the SACU provides these states with a significant part of their annual budgets. As trade liberalisation within the TDCA takes place this source of revenue will be affected. The impact study estimated that the drop in income could be between 5 and 15 per cent.[60]

Sectors of the BLNS economies are also under threat from duty-free exports from the EU. It has been estimated that in the private sector alone as many as 12,000 jobs could be lost as a result of the FTA.[61] Within the wider region there is also the potential, due to rather porous border controls, for EU exports to reach the wider SADC market. In general it appears that since the Democratic Republic of Congo became a member of SADC in 1997, South Africa's desire to promote the interests of SADC have been overtaken on two fronts: first, in its negotiations with the EU, and second in the shift towards a continental-wide project and the development of the New Partnership for Africa's Development (NEPAD).

Conclusions

This chapter has sought to highlight how post-apartheid South Africa's relationship with the EU can be seen as in keeping with the ANC government's multilateral diplomacy. Relations with the EU are to be seen as evidence of the government's attempts to become an active participant and supporter of the multilateral system.[62] The TDCA indicates a clear acceptance by both sides of the suitability of a neoliberal basis to South Africa's development strategy.

In its dealings with the EU, the South African government has been less able to adopt the 'reformist' posture that it has adopted in other multilateral fora.[63] In part this stems from the lack of manoeuvre provided in a relationship where it is working as a singular Southern state with what were formerly 15 and is now 25 European states. It is only by working in tandem with other Southern states at the multilateral level that South Africa is in a position to effect any significant changes.

Rather than reflecting a harmony of interests between states, South Africa's relationship with the EU contributes to the reproduction of hegemonic norms within the current world order. The FTA between the EU and South Africa reflects the pressures for increased liberalisation within the global trade system. South Africa, for its part, appears to have fully adhered to this process in accepting a reciprocal relationship with its largest trading partner. As one analysis has put it, 'such an important trade agreement further demonstrates that South Africa is deeply embedded in global networks that are Western-dominated, capitalist and neoliberal'.[64]

The EU–South Africa negotiations reflect the prioritisation given by the ANC-led government to integration into the world economy. This is consistent with its macroeconomic strategy, detailed in the GEAR document in 1996, where the attraction of investment and the promotion of exports are seen as vital elements in the stimulation of economic growth. This is a strategy that ultimately privileges the interests of a nascent historical bloc within South Africa, based around externally oriented capital. This historic bloc is composed of elite fractions within the ANC, the emerging black African bourgeoisie, and 'specific fractions of capital (centrally, banking and financial institutions) and ... large corporations'.[65] The launch of negotiations on 2 June 2003 towards a FTA between the United States and SACU merely reinforces South Africa's broad acceptance of the tenets of neoliberalism and the trends outlined in this chapter.

As other chapters in this book have highlighted, at times the South African government has adopted a critical rhetoric towards the North and neoliberal globalisation. However, it could be argued that this 'reformist' stance is only taken to meet the needs of the intended audience. The official portrayal of the TDCA with the EU has been one of mutual benefit and partnership. Yet, when speaking to intellectuals back in 1999 at an African Renaissance event, Thabo Mbeki made some very critical comments about the experience of negotiating with the EU. 'Stripped of all pretence', Mbeki argued,

> what has raised the question whether the agreement can be signed today or not, is the reality that many among the developed countries of the North have lost all sense of the noble idea of human solidarity. What seems to predominate is the question, in its narrowest and most naked meaning – what is in it for me! – [A]nd all this with absolutely no apology, and no sense of shame.[66]

Two of the most significant challenges that South Africa faces in the consolidation of its democratic future are the high levels of inequality and the need to create jobs. Upon finalisation of the agreement, EU Commissioner for Development, Poul Nielson, argued that the TDCA provided 'the necessary basis for promoting prosperity and fighting poverty with respect for democratic principles and fundamental human rights'.[67] However, the arguments of this chapter suggest that the relationship that has been forged with the EU is likely to exacerbate rather than solve these problems.

Acknowledgement

I would like to thank Oxford Brookes University for financial support from the University Research Fund to enable my most recent research trip to Brussels.

Notes

1. I use EU throughout this chapter to represent both the European Union and the organisation, pre-Maastricht Treaty, officially referred to as the European Community.
2. Eurostat, 2003.
3. European Commission, *The European Union and South Africa: Building a Framework for Long-Term Cooperation* (Brussels: European Commission, 1995) p. 26.
4. Lee, M. C., 'The European Union – South Africa Free Trade Agreement: In Whose Interest?', *Journal of Contemporary African Studies*, 20:1 (2002) p. 81.
5. Erwin, A., 'Preface' in T. Bertelsmann-Scott, G. Mills and E. Sidiropoulos (eds), *The EU-SA Agreement: South Africa, Southern Africa and the European Union* (Johannesburg: SAIIA, 2000) p. vii.
6. For an excellent overview of the debate over the limits to economic policy-making in post-apartheid South Africa see Koelble, T. A., 'Economic Policy in the Post-colony: South Africa between Keynesian Remedies and Neoliberal Pain', *New Political Economy*, 9:1 (2004) pp. 57–78.
7. COSATU presented its views on the agreement to a joint sitting of Parliamentary Committees on 26 October 1999. The details can be found at www.cosatu.org.za/docs/1999/eutrade.htm
8. Bilal, S. and Laporte, G., 'How did David prepare to talk to Goliath? South Africa's experience of trade negotiating with the EU', European Centre for Development Policy Management Discussion Paper, No. 53 (2004), p. 15.
9. Tsie, B., 'International Political Economy and Southern Africa' in P. Vale, L. A. Swatuk and B. Oden (eds), *Theory, Change and Southern Africa's Future* (Basingstoke: Palgrave, 2001) p. 142.
10. See for example, Williams, P. and Taylor, I., 'Neoliberalism and the Political Economy of the 'New' South Africa', *New Political Economy*, 5:1 (2000) pp. 21–40 and Bond, P., *Elite Transition: From Apartheid to Neoliberalism in South Africa* (London: Pluto, 2000).
11. Department of Finance, *Growth, Employment and Redistribution: A Macroeconomic Strategy* (Pretoria: Department of Finance, 1996) p. 6.
12. Author's interview (Brussels, 26 May 2004).
13. UNCTAD, *The Least Developed Countries Report, 2004* (New York, UNCTAD, 2004).
14. Holland, M., *The European Community and South Africa: European Political Co-operation Under Strain* (London: Pinter, 1988) p. 31.
15. Holland, M., *European Union Common Foreign Policy: From EPC to CFSP Joint Action and South Africa* (Basingstoke: Macmillan, 1995) p. 33.
16. Holland, M., 'The European Community and South Africa: Economic Reality or Political Rhetoric?', *Political Studies*, 33:3 (1985) p. 411.
17. Perry, B., 'Rhetoric or Reality? EU Policy towards South Africa, 1977–2000', (European Development Policy Study Group Discussion Paper, No. 19, 2000) p. 2.
18. Holland, *European Union Common Foreign Policy*, p. 37.
19. Holland, 'The European Community and South Africa', p. 411.
20. Holland, *European Union Common Foreign Policy*, pp. 38–9.

116   *Stephen R. Hurt*

21. Holland, M., 'Disinvestment, Sanctions and the European Community's Code of Conduct in South Africa', *African Affairs*, 88:353 (1989) p. 530.
22. Lee, M. C., *The Political Economy of Regionalism in Southern Africa* (London: Lynne Rienner, 2003) p. 208.
23. Guelke, A., 'The European Union: A Most Important Trading Partner?' in G. Mills, A. Begg and A. van Nieuwkerk (eds), *South Africa in the Global Economy* (Johannesburg: SAIIA, 1995) pp. 89–90.
24. Alden, C. and le Pere, G., *South Africa's Post-Apartheid Foreign Policy – from Reconciliation to Revival?* (Oxford: Oxford University Press, 2003) p. 16.
25. Lee, 'The European Union – South Africa Free Trade Agreement', p. 92.
26. The South African government asked for membership of the general trade provisions of the Lomé Convention, but not the separate protocols for specific products and the scheme for the stabilisation of export revenue. See ibid., p. 86.
27. Bertelsmann-Scott, T., 'The Democratization of Trade Policy – The SA-EU Trade, Development, and Cooperation Agreement', in N. Philip and J. van der Westhuizen (eds), *Democratizing Foreign Policy? Lessons from South Africa* (Oxford: Lexington Books, 2004) p. 130.
28. For details on the comparison of Human Development Indices see Hurt, S. R., 'A Case of Economic Pragmatism? The European Union's Trade and Development Agreement with South Africa', *International Relations*, 15:3 (2000) p. 71.
29. For more detail on the Cotonou Agreement see Hurt, S. R., 'Co-operation and coercion? The Cotonou Agreement between the European Union and ACP states and the end of the Lomé Convention', *Third World Quarterly*, 24:1 (2003) pp. 161–76.
30. European Commission, *The European Union and South Africa*, p. 6.
31. Author's interview (Brussels, 26 May 2004).
32. Author's interview with Dr. Elias Links (Brussels, 25 November 1997).
33. Hurt, 'A Case of Economic Pragmatism?', p. 72.
34. 'Now Comes the Horse-Trading', *Financial Mail* (Johannesburg), 18 August 1995.
35. Lee, 'The European Union – South Africa Free Trade Agreement', p. 87.
36. Hurt, 'A Case of Economic Pragmatism?', p. 75.
37. Stevens, C., 'Trade with Developing Countries: Banana Skins and Turf Wars', in H. Wallace and W. Wallace (eds), *Policy-Making in the European Union* (Oxford: Oxford University Press, 2000) p. 421.
38. European Commission, *Partners in Progress: The EU/South Africa Trade Development and Cooperation Agreement for the 21st Century* (Brussels: European Commission, 1999) pp. 12–13.
39. Ibid., p. 11.
40. Lee, 'The European Union – South Africa Free Trade Agreement', p. 98.
41. Davies, R., 'Forging a New Relationship with the EU' in T. Bertelsmann-Scott, G. Mills and E. Sidiropoulos (eds), *The EU-SA Agreement: South Africa, Southern Africa and the European Union* (Johannesburg: SAIIA, 2000) p. 11.
42. Author's interview (Brussels, 27 May 2004).
43. Hurt, 'Co-operation and Coercion?', p. 171.
44. See, for example, Hurt, 'Co-operation and coercion?'; Raffer, K., 'Cotonou: Slowly Undoing Lomé's Concept of Partnership' (European Development

Policy Study Group Discussion Paper, No. 21, 2001); and Van de Walle, N., 'Aid's Crisis of Legitimacy: Current Proposals and Future Prospects', *African Affairs*, 98:392 (1999) pp. 337–52.

45. Author's interview (Brussels, 27 May 2004).
46. Fioramonti, L., 'The European Union Promoting Democracy in South Africa: Strengths and Weaknesses' (European Development Policy Study Group Discussion Paper, No. 30, 2004) p. 6.
47. Ibid., p. 11.
48. Author's interview (Brussels, 26 May 2004).
49. Craven, E. and Mather, C., 'Geographical indications and the South Africa-European Union free trade agreement', *Area*, 33:3 (2001) p. 318.
50. 'South Africa in Dangerous Waters with EU', *Mail and Guardian* (Johannesburg), 29 January 1999.
51. Barber, J., *Mandela's World: The International Dimension of South Africa's Political Revolution 1990–1999* (Oxford: James Currey, 2004) p. 164.
52. Davies, 'Forging a New Relationship with the EU', p. 10.
53. COSATU, 'Shaping South Africa's Future Trade Relations with the European Union: COSATU's Concerns' in T. Bertelsmann-Scott, G. Mills and E. Sidiropoulos (eds), *The EU-SA Agreement: South Africa, Southern Africa and the European Union* (Johannesburg: SAIIA, 2000) p. 111.
54. Hurt, 'A Case of Economic Pragmatism?', p. 70.
55. Author's interview with Thabo Thage (Brussels, 27 May 2004).
56. Bertelsmann-Scott, 'The Democratization of Trade Policy', p. 127.
57. Mandela, N., 'South Africa's Future Foreign Policy', *Foreign Affairs*, 72:5 (1993) p. 90.
58. Alden and le Pere, *South Africa's Post-Apartheid Foreign Policy*, p. 13.
59. Lester, A., Nel, E. and Binns, T., *South Africa, Past, Present and Future: Gold at the End of the Rainbow?* (Harlow: Longman, 2000) p. 294.
60. Hurt, 'A Case of Economic Pragmatism?', p. 78.
61. Lee, 'The European Union – South Africa Free Trade Agreement', p. 97.
62. Author's interview with Thabo Thage (Brussels, 27 May 2004).
63. See Taylor, I., *Stuck in Middle GEAR: South Africa's Post-Apartheid Foreign Relations* (London: Praeger, 2001) for a demonstration of how this reformist stance has been adopted in a number of different multilateral organisations.
64. Lester, *et al.*, *South Africa, Past, Present and Future*, p. 294.
65. Marais, H., *South Africa: Limits to Change: The Political Economy of Transition* (London: Zed Books, 2001) p. 234.
66. Cited in Bond, P., 'Thabo Mbeki and NEPAD: Breaking or shining the chains of global apartheid?' in S. Jacobs and R. Calland (eds), *Thabo Mbeki's World: The politics and ideology of the South African president* (Pietermaritzburg: University of Natal Press, 2002) pp. 56–7.
67. European Commission, *Partners in Progress*, p. 4.

5
South Africa in Africa: The Dilemmas of Multilateralism

James Hamill

South African foreign policy has been informed by, shaped by and ultimately defined by a robust commitment to multilateralism in the post-1994 era. Whilst – at least with regard to Africa – former President Nelson Mandela was prone to honouring that commitment more in the breach than in the observance, his successor's African approach has been anchored in an impeccable, indeed at times overly rigid, attachment to the norms and practices of multilateralism.[1] Thabo Mbeki's commitment to multilateralism is also imbued with a strong pan-Africanist flavour. This is characteristic of his politics in general as domestic political discourse under Mbeki has become more aggressively racialised. While Mbeki's more assertive Africanism rests rather uneasily alongside the African National Congress's (ANC's) non-racial traditions, it is designed to advertise and bolster the country's African credentials and to secure its unconditional acceptance within the continent's institutions.

With their strong emphasis on the rediscovery by Africans of their dignity and self-esteem, Mbeki's speeches carry within them strong echoes of Steve Biko and the politics of Black Consciousness, an ideological tradition which ANC members have traditionally gravitated from rather than towards. That said, the development of a more Africanist hue to South African politics has helped facilitate South Africa's integration in Africa after a period in which, fairly or unfairly, it was perceived by important sectors of continental opinion as essentially a Western state in its political and economic outlook and a proxy for Western interests. For a period of time, post-apartheid South Africa had been seen by some as a state *in* Africa but not one truly *of* Africa.[2]

Yet in seeking to reverse such perceptions, and advance South Africa as a serious player on the continent, Mbeki's diplomacy faces a number of challenges. The African renaissance rhetoric and Mbeki's own rhetoric have raised expectations about South Africa's precise role in translating the renaissance aspiration into political and economic reality. South Africa, with its 'economic and political clout' and 'moral capital', is considered by many commentators to be the 'indispensable nation', the only one that can realistically 'step on the plate and lead the continent out of the abyss'.[3] The sheer persistence of Mbeki's renaissance rhetoric since 1996–1997, and the implication in those speeches of a pivotal role for South Africa in leading that renaissance, has created expectations within Africa and in the wider international community of what South Africa can do on Africa's behalf. Yet these expectations threaten to restrict Pretoria's room for political manoeuvre and to narrow rather than broaden its strategic options. Having 'introduced and popularised'[4] the renaissance concept, and given that on his visits to the US and Britain in May 2000 his own entourage were projecting him as 'the standard-bearer of Africa and the developing world',[5] Mbeki can hardly retreat from his obligations without exposing himself to ridicule. This is dangerous as Mbeki's interventions have already ensured that South Africa is now expected to 'respond unequivocally to every crisis in Africa' – a potentially onerous undertaking.[6]

However, at least three factors are likely to concentrate the mind of the South African government as it seeks to formulate an African policy, one that can possibly scale down the overall level of expectation. The first is the danger of continental overstretch. The South African government will be acutely aware that it risks becoming overextended if it attempts to play the role of mediator, conflict resolver, peacekeeper, peace enforcer and all round continental fire fighter (see also Chapter 9). Africa remains a continent 'plagued with civil uprisings, military coups, corrupt leadership, maladministration and territorial conflicts',[7] and 'mere repetition doesn't make an African renaissance a reality'.[8]

The second and related factor inhibiting an extensive South African role in Africa is the country's congested domestic agenda. Mbeki has been consistently appreciative of the notion that foreign policy grows out of, and should help sustain, the domestic agenda of economic reconstruction. However, the challenge of addressing the socio-economic backlogs bequeathed by apartheid is of such magnitude that the government will be aware that a preoccupation with securing an African renaissance – particularly involvement in the minutiae of Africa's numerous conflicts – is likely to frustrate and possibly even undermine the achievement of a *South African* renaissance.

Finally, there is at least a danger that if South Africa becomes deeply embroiled in the continent's myriad conflicts, its interventions may be resented *and* ineffective, particularly if Pretoria chooses to intervene in conflicts where its grasp of the issues is weak. South Africa may lack the intellectual resources and leverage required for successful peacemaking and mediation beyond its own immediate neighbourhood, and even within that neighbourhood success is hardly guaranteed as its experience in Angola, in the DRC (at least pre-2002) and Zimbabwe has demonstrated, confirming the wisdom of Graham Evans's observation that an African renaissance is 'deceptively easy to articulate but very difficult to implement.'[9]

Consequently, South Africa urgently required a formula which would allow it to meet its African obligations without becoming bogged down in a potential quagmire of conflict. Two considerations will certainly inform South Africa's policy. First, there is an explicit recognition that South Africa has incurred a debt of honour to Africa for the support and solidarity it received during the struggle against apartheid and a degree of reciprocity for this can be expected to feature in the policy-making process, *at least at some level.* Cabinet minister Kader Asmal made the government's position clear in 1995 when he noted:

> There is not a corner of the vast continent where our people were not received with affection and fraternal support. Our integration into the affairs of the continent, as a result will be a joyous homecoming, because we are of the same flesh. Not surprisingly, therefore, we believe that all the policies of our country should reflect the interests of the entire African continent.[10]

Second, South African officials, acting in a spirit of enlightened self-interest, have always recognised that the country cannot flourish as an island of prosperity in a wider African sea of poverty, stagnation and conflict. It is understood that such conditions will eventually have a detrimental impact upon South Africa's own well-being, whether through increased refugee flows, a further influx of economic migrants or by frustrating the ability of the South African business sector to expand northwards. Moreover, 'bad neighbourhood syndrome' is a distinct negative for any country seeking to attract foreign direct investment. This has been a central plank of government policy since 1996. As Mbeki stated in 2002:

> It is very directly in the interests of South Africa that there should be development in the rest of the continent. I don't think that you can

have sustainable, successful development in this country if the rest of the continent is in flames.[11]

So the task for South Africa has been to work out how it might play an African role commensurate with the country's size and status without becoming hopelessly overextended. Here it is felt that multilateralism – an active and full participation in the continent's various multilateral structures – offers a creative response to this policy dilemma. South Africa will continue to vigorously commit itself to the African renaissance project but, crucially, it will see its own activity as part of a much wider process which stresses *African* rather than *South African* ownership of that project, with South Africa pooling its efforts with others in a variety of inter-governmental settings – 'an active participant with other Africans', to quote Mbeki.[12] This is the very essence of multilateralism and, in view of the suspicions generated by South African power and by that state's previous capacity for unilateralism, it is also a position rooted in an irrefutable logic: the African renaissance is achievable only through an immense collective effort embracing action from governments, both national and provincial, regional and sub-regional structures, non-governmental organisations, as well as a raft of civil society initiatives. To borrow a phrase from an earlier era, although it may now be deployed with more progressive intent, this effectively amounts to a 'total strategy' to move the continent forward. South Africa, however, can make an important contribution within these various multilateral settings in a number of ways.

Pretoria and the continent

In Africa beyond the SADC zone, South Africa is relatively well equipped to play a supporting role in a range of renaissance-related enterprises. These might be grouped loosely under the following headings: negotiations, mediation and conflict resolution; deepening democratisation; Africa's advocate; and building African security.

Negotiations, mediation and conflict resolution

By placing its own experience *of* and expertise *in* negotiations at the disposal of other African states, South Africa can help facilitate conflict resolution processes throughout the continent. It is important, however, that South Africans should proceed cautiously in the pursuit of that objective. For one thing, it is vital that they should not believe their own publicity by succumbing to the sentimental notion that the outcome of their own transition enjoys a universal application and provides an inspirational example to those in other divided societies. In fact, the protagonists in many conflict-ridden societies may well be repelled by the strong majoritarian thrust of the 1994 outcome. That said, the original thinking which created the space for transition (the subterranean 'talks about talks' pre-negotiation phase), the conduct of the negotiations themselves and the actual mechanics of transition in South Africa – in short, the *process* of change – all contain many useful lessons from which others can learn. This assumes, of course, that the political will actually exists to kick-start a negotiation process and to overcome visceral ethnic, racial or religious animosities, something that no external power can generate.[13] Moreover, South Africa must be sensitive to realities on the ground and must avoid overestimating its influence and diplomatic capacity in particular conflict situations. In particular, Pretoria needs to show a much greater appreciation of the changing dynamics of regional conflict and insecurity and to recognise that many of the continent's wars – the DRC is only the most obvious among recent examples – may well prove unresponsive to the diplomatic therapy on offer. Such conflicts are being ruthlessly exploited by the protagonists, both local warlords and their external sponsors, as an opportunity to maximise their own commercial interests and to establish private networks of accumulation free from all political and ethical constraint.[14] Any exercise in attempted conflict resolution which remains rooted in the orthodox and theoretically rational assumption that ceasefires, mediation, and governments of national unity are automatically beneficial for all sides, risks foundering when confronted by those not easily persuaded of the virtues of negotiation and compromise.

It is also worth pointing out that diplomatic settlements rooted in South African style compromise and power-sharing arrangements may not always provide an appropriate response to particular conflicts. As the United Nations has learned through the report of the Brahimi Panel in August 2000, a studious neutrality in conflict situations can amount to a 'complicity with evil' as some armed factions have such a record of abuse – Uganda's Lord's Resistance Army being a current example – that they need to be militarily defeated rather than diplomatically accommodated.[15]

Deepening democratisation

South Africa can also play an important role within the AU, the SADC, and the NEPAD by deepening the continent's commitment to democratic change consistent with the sentiments articulated in Mbeki's speeches. This will entail action on a number of fronts including helping to design *effective* peer review mechanisms to entrench good democratic practice; a commitment on the part of African multilateral bodies to act not only against unconstitutional coups, but also against the authoritarian practices of *formally elected* governments; and, finally, to correct the impression that elections are synonymous with democracy. The current fixation with elections on the continent as the ultimate barometer of democratic progress is giving rise to the phenomenon of the steered or 'managed election', a process in which style invariably triumphs over democratic substance as incumbent regimes frequently seek to manipulate their control of the media and the machinery of state with a view to closing down rather than opening up the space available to opposition forces. The 2002 Presidential Election in Zimbabwe offers the most egregious example in recent times, although the presidential polls in Rwanda (August 2003) and Cameroon (October 2004) also merit closer scrutiny in this regard.[16]

The task for Africa is to address this democratic deficit by moving beyond such minimalist forms of 'illiberal democracy'.[17] A wider, more inclusive democratic infrastructure needs to be put in place, one which *might* embrace techniques such as power-sharing and devolved government, but which *must* embrace a free press, the judiciary, independent state institutions, a Bill of Rights and the creation of space for a vibrant civil society, with elections being treated as a necessary *but hardly a sufficient* condition for democratic consolidation. As Heather Deegan has noted:

> Elections are a milestone on the road to democracy and should not be viewed as a means of anointing existing political elites and dominant parties, which can only encourage complacency at best, corruption at worst.[18]

Multilateralism may prove to be a barrier to this more thoroughgoing democratisation process *or* a mechanism for its realisation, depending upon the balance of forces within multilateral organisations between authoritarian and democratic camps and the precise interpretations to which multilateralism is subject in practice.

Africa's advocate

Mbeki is now Africa's 'strongest and most eloquent voice in world politics'[19] and during his presidency South Africa has emerged as perhaps the leading 'Southern' campaigner for a democratised system of global governance. This approach has progressed on two levels. First, Mbeki has consistently challenged the existing distribution of power within global multilateral organisations, calling for a programme of structural reform, which would allow much greater weight to be given to Africa's voice within the Bretton Woods institutions, the World Trade Organisation (WTO) (see Chapter 2) and the United Nations family.[20] Mbeki argues, with justification, that as the decisions emanating from these various bodies invariably have a universal application, the institutions themselves require a legitimacy which can only be acquired by addressing the absence of equitable forms of representation within them. As Evans has observed, South Africa committed itself to 'amending the institutional, legal and economic regimes which were created by the north and which serve to sustain its global dominance'.[21] The key word here is the commitment to *amending* rather than to *replacing* those regimes to allow for the creation of the much-vaunted 'level playing field' and to facilitate a meaningful African input.

Second, Mbeki has sought to exploit the country's position within global multilateral institutions to draw upon the reservoir of goodwill towards South Africa with a view to placing African poverty and under-development at the head of the global agenda and to effect changes in specific areas. These would include the level of African indebtedness, the need for 'fair trade', a significant increase in development aid which has been radically scaled back since the 1990s, and the channelling of greater levels of investment to Africa (the continent is at the bottom of global league tables on virtually all socio-economic indicators and currently attracts less than 1 per cent of global FDI).[22] In a May 2000 address at Georgetown University in Washington, for example, Mbeki exhorted the West to take 'urgent and extraordinary steps' to address Africa's 'oceans of entrenched poverty', including investment on the scale of Europe's post-war Marshall Plan to help stimulate recovery. He urged a 'similar passionate response' towards African want as was demonstrated by the West during the 1999 Kosovo crisis.[23] The message was repeated at the opening of the World Summit on Sustainable Development in Johannesburg in August 2002, when Mbeki lamented the new 'global apartheid' and declared:

A global human society based on poverty for many and prosperity for a few, characterised by islands of wealth surrounded by seas of poverty, is unsustainable. It is as though we are determined to regress to the most primitive condition of existence in the animal world, of survival of the fittest. It is as though we have decided to spurn what the human intellect tells us, that the survival of the fittest only presages the destruction of all humanity.[24]

Ultimately Mbeki's campaign will be judged against its ability to transform global institutions, to place Africa's concerns at the top of the international agenda, and to produce a massively increased flow of resources to the continent for the alleviation of poverty and for long-term reconstruction. Thus far, at least, he can claim a measure of success in exploiting his easy access to the high table of international politics to help give Africa's condition a new salience in international political discourse. This is evidenced by the prominence of the debate around the NEPAD at the G8 summits in Genoa in 2001, Kananaskis in 2002, Evian in 2003 and Sea Island in 2004,[25] and the coverage given to British Prime Minister Blair's Commission for Africa in 2004.

However, elsewhere the credibility of the Mbeki position is more questionable. The reform or democratisation of international organisations remains a distant and in all likelihood unrealisable objective, as these institutions provide for expressions of raw power, of capability and of access to resources, and it is these power imbalances, rather than the more vague, ephemeral notions of justice, level playing fields and international egalitarianism which will ultimately determine a state's influence within them. Consequently, they reflect the variable distribution of power at the global level, just as surely as the AU and the SADC reflect the balance of power at the regional and sub-regional levels. Moreover, the reform campaign continues to fall victim to a now familiar paradox, namely, that the institutionalised inequality within international organisations, which gave the campaign its initial impetus, has also provided an insurmountable barrier to its realisation. Mbeki's campaign in this area amounts to more than empty posturing and he does seek to provide a conscious and purposeful challenge to powerful and vested interests, one motivated by a genuine concern for economic and social justice at the global level. However, the very remoteness of reform does afford him further opportunities for political theatre, allowing him to make the radical gestures to his constituency (and to a wider 'Southern' audience) which help to partially compensate for his complicity (as his critics would see it) with the fundamental principles underpinning the global system. It is also questionable whether Mbeki's most notable achievement – Africa's enhanced global visibility – can be translated into the flow of resources which are required, particularly in view of the seismic changes triggered by 9/11 in Washington's foreign policy strategies and the all-consuming nature of the 'war on terror'.[26] It is worthwhile noting that Mbeki has already chastised the Bush administration for ignoring the bigger African picture by concentrating its development assistance, contained within the so-called Millennium Challenge Account, on particular African states, normally those able to contribute to the 'war on terror' and/or those with a favourable foreign investment climate.[27]

Finally, Mbeki's contention, even if it is rarely expressed in such candid terms, that the interests of Africa and the global South can be most effectively advanced within the framework of neoliberalism, albeit a reformed or moderated version, and that neoliberalism is capable of delivering ethical and inclusive outcomes based upon *sustainable people-centred development* as opposed to a more narrowly defined *growth* deserves at best much closer scrutiny and, in the view of this writer at least, remains worthy of the deepest scepticism.[28]

Building African security

Creating a new security architecture in Africa is likely to be a complex and laborious process, one which can only be satisfactorily addressed within a multilateral framework given the diverse challenges confronting the continent and the extent to which they transcend state borders. That said, South Africa's military resources and the professionalism of its defence force vis-à-vis the rest of the continent ensure that it must play a prominent role in helping build Africa's capacity for peace operations within those multilateral forums. In the 1994–1997 period, South Africa was predictably cautious about the projection of force beyond its borders due to the legacy of apartheid era cross-border activity, coupled with the ongoing project to create a new integrated defence force. That process was effectively completed in 1997 from which point South Africa has been more willing to contemplate involvement within continental and sub-regional peace operations under a SADC/OAU mandate or at least it was in a much weaker position from which to justify a continuing detachment from such operations.[29] That position was confirmed by the government's *White Paper on South African Participation in International Peace Missions* approved by the Cabinet in 1998 and by Parliament in 1999, which has paved the way for South African participation in peace operations. As suggested above, extensive deployments are likely to be confined to the sub-regional SADC theatre but South Africa is now making an important contribution to the overall continental debate on complex peace operations and some 3000 SANDF personnel are currently deployed in the DRC and Burundi (see also

Chapter 9). In the mid- to late-1990s, the government remained sceptical about the merits of a US-sponsored African Crisis Response Initiative (ACRI) on the rather flimsy basis that it was an external rather than an African initiative and was being promoted by Washington in a paternalistic and cavalier fashion.[30] However, the central premise of the ACRI, namely, that Africans should take the lead in resolving African crises – with extra-continental powers providing logistical, training and financial support – contained an irresistible logic and has since been revived. This time, the fact that it is a more obvious African-driven project has made it more palatable to South African opinion. At its summit meeting in Libya in February 2004, the AU agreed to set up an African Standby Force which will be empowered (at least in theory) to intervene to bring civil wars under control and to prevent or halt genocide.[31]

The aim is to have five sub-regional bases in place by 2005 and a full continental force operational by 2010 with 15,000 AU troops – divided into five brigades – drawn largely from South Africa, Nigeria, Kenya and Egypt. The force will operate under the control of the AU's new 15-member Peace and Security Council, which will also be responsible for establishing reliable continental mechanisms for early warning and preventive diplomacy. External assistance, both financial and training, will continue to be crucial here and at the 2004 G8 summit President Bush spoke of ultimately training some 75,000 African peacekeepers.[32] What South Africa urgently requires in this area, and indeed in a range of other policy areas, is the emergence of a number of effective African partners, a coalition of both the *willing*, the *stable* and ideally the *democratic* with whom it can collaborate to take the continent forward – a concert of African powers in effect. To the states listed above would be added three who have made a significant input to the NEPAD: Ghana, Senegal and Algeria, although it would have to be acknowledged that democratic values are *at best* in a fragile condition in at least four of those: Nigeria, Algeria, Egypt and Kenya.

Thus far in this chapter, the embedding of South African foreign policy within Africa's various multilateral structures has been portrayed as a creative response both to the country's vexed historical relationship with the continent and to a range of contemporary South African foreign policy dilemmas. However, for South African policy-makers to proceed on the basis that multilateralism, particularly in its consensus-based form, provides an unconditional blessing – rather than merely being a useful instrument in particular contexts – would be to underplay the problems that a rigid adherence to this particular foreign policy technique is likely to generate.

Multilateralism and its discontents

The overt commitment to multilateralism in developing South Africa's relations with Africa raises a number of dilemmas, concerns and possible contradictions which the country's official posture fails to acknowledge, but which may nonetheless blight attempts to operationalise this option. I would like to highlight just two examples (among many) of the inherent limitations of multilateralism. These examples will demonstrate the extreme difficulties South Africa will confront if it attempts to confine its policy options to what is acceptable within African multilateral frameworks (particularly in the area of economic policy) and the damage it has already sustained to its Africa policy, and to its own reputation, of attempting to do so in the field of political governance or democratisation.

The multilateralism – hegemony nexus

It would be easy to conclude that multilateralism and hegemony are polar opposites as they are often treated as such in much of the international relations literature, particularly in the discourse before, during and after the 2003 Iraq war.[33] Yet this underestimates the proven capacity of hegemons to utilise multilateral structures as a means of building coalitions and mobilising support on specific issues and for giving momentum to the campaign for the wider diffusion of particular sets of norms and values. In the African context, this form of assertive multilateralism in which South Africa would become *primus inter pares* certainly does not preclude compromise, nor does it exclude the possibility, even the likelihood, of outcomes which fall short of the hegemon's ideals; it is, after all, *multilateralist* as well as being *assertive*. However, on occasions, and across a number of policy areas, there is likely to be an inherent tension between hegemony and the type of consensus-based multilateralism which many of the smaller to medium-sized African states envisage as an ideal – and which South Africa itself favours in many areas – and even with the more assertive model, a stratified multilateralism in effect, in which a certain group of African states – a core leadership group – make the running on issues of security, economics and democratisation. Put simply, multilateralism, whatever its precise form, has tended to be viewed as a positive-sum game, resting upon an assumption that South Africa's interests will automatically converge with those of the rest of the continent, or that such differences as do exist are never so profound that they cannot be accommodated, mediated and ultimately resolved within the continent's various multilateral frameworks. That is a highly dubious assumption, but one that is invariably allowed to stand unchallenged because to concede otherwise would allow a gaping hole to open up in the entire African unity/ renaissance project, even though the very centrality of South Africa generally and Mbeki personally to the future of that project should alert us to significant disparities in strength and capability which are likely to prove problematic.

In most respects, South Africa cannot be considered to be a typically African state in its position vis-à-vis the international system and it is that fact which will complicate any attempt by Pretoria to 'unequivo- cally project itself as an African country', as some have suggested it should.[34] This is not to revisit the tired debate about South Africa's supposedly 'Western' political and economic values, but merely to high- light the stark differences between it and the rest of Africa (and particu- larly the sub-region) in terms of economic power aggregations and their respective assets and capabilities as actors in the international political economy. These differences reflect the obvious contrast in economic size, sophistication, levels of diversification and their integration within the global economy,[35] and they are differences which, at the very least, will complicate the formulation of common policy positions as well as South Africa's ability to 'speak for Africa' in wider international forums beyond a bland, lowest common denominator, rhetoric which airbrushes away such tensions and contradictions.

But such dilemmas are not necessarily confined to the economic sector. South Africa faces intense pressure from the G8 states to lead the continent, and if South Africa accepts the logic of that position it is likely to destroy any commitment to a consensus-based multilateralism and may even place increasing strains on the more assertive multilateral approach in which South Africa works with informal coalitions of other leading African states. Moreover, South Africa's aspiration to assume a middle power profile in international politics will invariably require a freedom of diplomatic manoeuvre and the adoption of positions which, while not overtly insensitive to Africa's best interests, are unlikely to have been endorsed within African forums and, as with most middle power diplomatic interventions, they will be primarily motivated by a desire to promote the national interest over regional community inter- ests in marked contrast to the 'goody two shoes image' which middle powers have acquired.[36] That middle power profile will also entail the further strengthening of partnerships and relationships with extra- continental powers with whom South Africa has been developing com- mon interests, such as India, Brazil and China and others in the G20+ more industrialised 'Southern' states.[37] That, in turn, may complicate its position within Africa where there may not be an automatic coincidence of interests with the smaller African states in particular. Even where common interests can be identified, this emerging Southern power bloc may presume to speak on behalf of a developing world which is held to lack the intellectual expertise and skilled bureaucratic capacity to conduct negotiations in specific areas, such as complex trade negotiations at the WTO,[38] a paternalism which may well be resented and which may generate resistance. Indeed, it is not impossible that, in a neat ironic twist, South Africa's complaints about the distribution of power within global multilateral forums may be reproduced in African forums, with the powerful position of South Africa and certain others drawing increasing criticism.

A useful guide to South African attitudes in this whole area is likely to come in response to the ongoing debate over the restructuring of the UN Security Council. A South African commitment to securing a seat for itself as Africa's *permanent* representative, as opposed to support for a regional African seat with a *rotating* membership, will provide an emphatic confirmation of the primacy of the national over the regional interest and to paternalism over egalitarianism. Mbeki's rather portentous declaration in September 2004 that South Africa 'is ready to serve the people of Africa and the world' by joining the Security Council certainly points in that direction.[39]

Is Multilateralism facilitating or impeding democracy?

In ideal circumstances Africa's multilateral forums will serve as effective vehicles for the expansion and consolidation of democratic values on the continent and that is the position adopted within the official mission statements of the SADC, the AU and the NEPAD. South Africa has certainly been extremely active at the level of ideas in promoting a commitment to democratic norms and practices within African multilateral structures and in securing recognition for democracy as an indispensable resource for African development. This is classic hegemonic behaviour with South Africa leading and shaping the continental debates and ultimately leaving its ideological imprimatur on the continental and sub-regional structures emerging from them. That said, Africa's experience in translating democratic theory into *actual political practice* suggests that South Africa's democratisation campaign has clashed head on with other African imperatives, most notably 'solidarity', 'unity' and 'consensus', and has, in effect, been subordinated to them.[40] South African behaviour in two areas in particular – areas where a bold lead was required from the continent's most powerful democracy to help signal a definitive break with the past – demonstrates that while Pretoria is an admirably robust and assertive multilateralist at an ideological or conceptual level, at the level of implementation of those same ideals it has retreated into a rigidly consensus-based version of multilateralism. In practice, this is producing a form of diplomatic entrapment or immobilisation with South Africa, in what represents a clear regression into pre-NEPAD and pre-AU patterns of behaviour, choosing to elevate an African (regime) consensus and an African (regime) unity as the highest of political ideals to the detriment of African peoples.

The first and clearest example of this is provided by Pretoria's response to the crisis in Zimbabwe since 2000. The failure of South Africa's policy of 'quiet diplomacy' towards the Mugabe regime in Zimbabwe has been extensively debated elsewhere,[41] but by way of illustrating the dangers of a consensus-based multilateralism, a few brief reflections are in order here. 'Quiet diplomacy' and the search for an 'African solution' to the programme of state terror unleashed by ZANU-PF since February 2000 were initially perfectly defensible means of seeking to resolve Zimbabwe's crisis. However, their manifest failure by, *at the very latest*, the fraudulent Zimbabwean presidential election of March 2002 necessitated a policy shift towards a more coercive approach. Instead, South Africa has remained steadfastly committed to an 'African way' of dealing with an African problem. In practice, this has meant paying lip service to national reconciliation in Zimbabwe while effectively kicking the issue into the long grass of African multilateralism and rallying round an embattled authoritarian regime – inertia at best, and an active complicity in Mugabe's authoritarian excesses at worst. That procrastination has been costly, however, and the endorsement by South Africa of the 2002 presidential election as a valid expression of the popular will has been extremely damaging to South Africa's reputation as a force for democracy on the African continent and to the international *gravitas* which the earlier renaissance declarations had earned for Mbeki.

What is required from South Africa here – and it is not a major undertaking for a sub-regional hegemon given the geographical location of the crisis and its own material strength vis-à-vis Zimbabwe – is a serious attempt to lead and to build a progressive African coalition based upon respect for democratic values and the application of strong peer pressure upon those authoritarian elements who are obstructing the advancement of those values. In extremis, this should involve the suspension of unreconstructed authoritarian regimes from membership of regional and sub-regional structures. South Africa's Zimbabwe policy therefore needs to be rooted in, first, a direct and open criticism of Mugabe and the disaster his ZANU-PF regime is visiting upon the country, and second, support for Zimbabwe's suspension from African multilateral structures, before, finally, viewing Zimbabwe's economic dependence as providing South Africa with an opportunity or a lever for change – a policy of coercive diplomacy, in effect. In the event of its leadership failing to attract 'followership' on the issue from the majority of African states (as with Nigeria in 1995), then South Africa, if for no other reason than to protect its own democratic integrity and to avoid sustaining any collateral damage from NEPAD's failure, needs to signal its emphatic rejection of a business as usual approach to a state that has now degenerated into tyranny. Instead, however, the imperatives of maintaining a multilateral position and an 'African consensus' have produced a passive and timorous policy which has steadily evolved over time into outright indulgence *of* and even expressions of support *for* Mugabe. ZANU-PF's authoritarian abuses and its long record of misrule have over time been effectively supplanted as the prism through which Pretoria views the Zimbabwe crisis. In its place, we have witnessed South Africa's enthusiastic endorsement of Mugabe's anti-imperialist, anti-white sloganising and its support for the notion that land redistribution lies at the heart of the crisis.

The second example is South Africa's retreat from the rigorous African Peer Review Mechanism to ensure good governance, transparency, democratisation and human rights, which had initially been envisaged as a cornerstone of the NEPAD project in 2001–2002. The promise of a thoroughgoing process of external peer review has since been watered down to a voluntary 'self-assessment' arrangement, assessments which rulers may 'consider' but are not obliged to act upon. This promises to be a relatively toothless approach and those authoritarian regimes either submitting to or, more likely, choosing to remain outside of this voluntary process, will not face the likelihood of sanctions or indeed punitive measures of any kind from their African peers.[42] Yet it was the prospect of a more exacting peer review process which allowed the NEPAD to be marketed (particularly in the West) as representing a genuine break with the past and its absence (allied to the disappointing African response to events in Zimbabwe) is certain to engender cynicism that this is yet another African plan 'based primarily on rhetoric rather than action'.[43]

South Africa needs to take a proactive position in this debate and to mobilise the broadest possible support for a peer review process which goes well beyond voluntary self-assessment, constructive peer dialogue and a sharing of common experiences, although the latter two are certainly not to be despised. Nor should there be an exclusive reliance upon 'market forces' in which those states failing to accept peer review and to promote good governance receive an indirect censure by attracting significantly less, *if any*, investment and development assistance, thus producing a *de facto* multi-tier Africa. However, the misgivings expressed in the West about this more limited arrangement have prompted a renewed burst of chauvinistic anti-Western rhetoric from Mbeki, with a denunciation of Western governments' pretensions to be 'champions of democracy' in Africa, coupled with the accusation that they have a 'contemptuous prejudice'[44] for Africans; hardly the language of partnership on which the NEPAD was originally founded.

Ultimately, however, these two failures stem from the same problem and they expose the same South African weakness in responding to it. Across the continent the attachment of governing elites to the NEPAD and AU principles of good governance and human rights is demonstrably weak. This contrasts with their undoubted enthusiasm for managed elections and the simultaneous attempt to pass off the introduction of a thin democratic veneer as being synonymous with the substance of representative and accountable government. Africa's elites are still inclined to view democratic government and those mechanisms which might help facilitate it, such as peer review, as a mortal threat to their power and privileges rather than an opportunity, and from their own narrow authoritarian perspective they are doubtless right to do so.[45] South Africa still displays considerable reticence in confronting this issue, a response conditioned or, perhaps more accurately, warped by its own historical experience. However those inhibitions are frustrating the type of assertive South African-led multilateral action or even the 'single minded hegemonic intervention'[46] which might help promote regional stability and foster democratic progress. As Habib and Selinyane tell us, it is that very reticence that is 'compromising its moral standing in the international arena and rendering hollow its calls for [African] reform'.[47]

Thus far, South Africa has demonstrated a willingness to intervene or to apply concentrated pressure on African states only in very specific, narrowly defined, contexts: actual or embryonic military coups, or where authority is seriously challenged and the government has retained only partial control (see the Mandela–Zuma mediation in Burundi), or, again, where sovereign authority has effectively collapsed across large parts of the country leaving in its place a patchwork of warring fiefdoms (see Mbeki's promotion of the Inter-Congolese Dialogue in the DRC).[48] Where authoritarian governments are securely entrenched in power – stable tyrannies in effect – South Africa remains not only dogmatically non-interventionist but effectively silent. Mbeki has even been prepared to take refuge under the discredited, fraying canopy of Westphalianism and its accompanying dogmas of state sovereignty and non-interference, which have long provided a convenient pretext for the brutalisation of Africa's peoples and which now serve as a 'powerful hindrance' to the realisation of the democratic ideals of the AU and the NEPAD.[49] To assert, as Mbeki has, that South Africa has no wish to impose its will on other countries,[50] and to argue that a country's citizens rather than outsiders must determine its future, is an attempt to cloak a reactionary and anachronistic approach to sovereignty in a progressive garb, as allowing its own citizens to determine a state's future is the one thing authoritarian regimes are entirely unwilling to concede.[51] It is also a radical departure from Mbeki's previous thinking in this area, which was dismissive of a traditional national sovereignty/non-interference paradigm, one which allowed 'terrible things' to occur within state borders while the continent 'stands paralysed'.[52]

A commitment to remaining within an 'African consensus' may have a superficially progressive appeal, but it leaves no obvious exit route when that consensus is itself based upon an endorsement and protection of authoritarian government and is therefore profoundly undemocratic. Instead of stepping outside of that consensus and using its status as Africa's 'strongest, most democratic and most developed state'[53] to help forge a new more enlightened regional consensus based on a robust defence of democratic principles, South Africa has chosen the well-travelled, if morally bankrupt, route of African (regime-based) populism and pan-Africanist (regime-based) solidarity. Thus, it might be legitimately asked with regard to South Africa's effective abdication of responsibility on both Zimbabwe and NEPAD's peer review mechanisms: whatever happened to Mbeki's 'democratic rage' and to his scorn for 'petty gangsters who would be our governors by theft of elective positions' or to Africa's obligation to 'resist all tyranny [and to] oppose all attempts to deny liberty by resort to demagoguery?'[54] These ideals have either been sacrificed on the altar of a consensus-based but in reality highly reactionary form of multilateralism or they lie buried under an avalanche of pan-Africanist cliché.

Conclusion: Multilateralism and the (over) compensation culture

The preceding discussion suggests that a dogmatic adherence to a consensus-based multilateralism will ultimately prove to be unsustainable in the economic field while in the political arena attempts to make it sustainable will prove unduly constraining by compromising South Africa's own core (or what were previously thought to be its core) foreign policy commitments and its wider standing in the international community. While Pretoria should always strive to secure the widest possible African consensus on political issues, it should certainly not allow this to become a fetish-like attachment to consensus-based multilateralism in all circumstances. After all, a search for an African consensus can never be, or at least *should never be*, an end in itself and is only valuable and defensible if that consensus is motivated by and is constructed around the advancement rather than the obstruction of democratic and progressive values.

The evidence to date is that African multilateral organisations have not served as forums within which South Africa is able to help drive forward a democratisation process by persuading, pressuring and cajoling African states into observing standards of good governance. Instead, the reverse is happening. In the interests of maintaining consensus, South Africa appears to be retreating from a vigorous defence of democratic principles, a policy which, is once again, prioritising the interests of the continent's elites at the expense of its peoples and is reducing the founding principles of these various regional and sub-regional organisations to so much political ephemera.

South Africa requires a more dexterous and imaginative African policy, one built upon the politics of flexible response and one which is sufficiently nuanced, adaptable and appreciative of African realities to accommodate a range of policy approaches: assertive multilateralism at the head of a coalition – helping to create a bandwagon effect – while in those areas where South Africa has less leverage and knowledge (normally beyond the sub-region) it might defer to, and support the work of, other African states (*if, but only if*, those states are helping to advance democratic government). However, there should also be a willingness to act unilaterally where required – particularly if the defence of democratic principles is at stake, an area where South Africa's voice, in Habib and Selinyane's phrase, must be more than 'one among the many'.[55] This would be coupled with a candid recognition that South African and African interests do not automatically converge in all circumstances. The strong South African commitment to a particular definition of multilateralism contains a strong 'motherhood and apple pie' element, as though it is an accepted truth that multilateralism is an absolute good (and hegemony an absolute bad), whereas in the current African context it is increasingly a mechanism for avoiding rather than resolving problems, particularly those posed by the persistence of authoritarian rule on the continent. South Africa has recognised the potential of this brand of consensus-based multilateralism to help erase the memory of the country's unacceptable past, but, equally, it needs to acknowledge its more malign capacity to frustrate attempts to build a democratic African future.

The 'exaggerated sensitivity and restraint'[56] shown towards African (regime) opinion which has characterised recent South African diplomacy – and the laboured parading of the country's African credentials at almost every opportunity, though most notably in its responses to the Zimbabwe and the HIV/AIDS crises – provides a perfect example of a foreign policy trapped in a culture of overcompensation for the apartheid past and for the supposed shortcomings of the more recent (Mandela era) past.[57] It is also in danger of producing a potentially dangerous foreign policy paradox: a *hegemon* incapable of *hegemony*.

More disturbingly, however, it is helping to transform the content as well as the style of South Africa's African diplomacy. On both the domestic and external fronts, the past four years have witnessed a steady gravitation on Mbeki's part towards a more insular, at times aggressively anti-Western, and increasingly racialised model of Africanism, one steeped in traditional continental notions of victimhood.[58] This playing to the African gallery may succeed in drawing plaudits from fellow leaders, but it is all very far removed from the outward looking, inclusive, and progressive project for the continent articulated in the earlier renaissance speeches of Africa's philosopher king. It also demonstrates the abject folly of allowing South African policy to be locked into a straitjacket of 'pan-Africanist political correctness'[59] through a rigid attachment to a consensus-based multilateralism. In short, the regional leader needs to shed its inhibitions and to rediscover the simple virtues of leadership and the principles of democracy which that leadership should exist to serve.

Notes

1. See Taylor, I., *Stuck in Middle GEAR: South Africa's Post-Apartheid Foreign Relations* (Westport, CT: Praeger, 2001); and Nel, P., Taylor I. and van der Westhuizen, J. (eds), *South Africa's Multilateral Diplomacy and Global Change: The Limits of Reform* (Aldershot: Ashgate, 2001).
2. An attitude typified by the infamous remark of the former Nigerian Foreign Minister, Walter Ofonagoro, that Mandela was 'the Black president of a White state'. See Vale, P. and Maseko, S., 'South Africa and the African renaissance', *International Affairs*, 74:2 (1998) p. 273.
3. An anonymous if 'influential newspaper columnist' cited in Lodge, T., *Politics in South Africa: From Mandela To Mbeki* (Oxford: James Currey, 2002) p. 229.

4. Gerrit Olivier, 'Is Thabo Mbeki Africa's saviour?', *International Affairs*, 79:4 (2003) p. 826.
5. Gumede, W. M., 'Battling on behalf of Africa and the South', *Financial Mail*, 26 May 2000.
6. Ibid. On the expectations of a more proactive South African role in Africa as a result of Mbeki's statements and the post-Somalia reluctance of the US to be actively engaged, see Taylor, I. and Williams, P., 'South African foreign policy and the Great Lakes Crisis: From African Renaissance to *vagabondage politique*', *African Affairs*, 100:399 (2001) p. 266.
7. Olivier, 'Is Thabo Mbeki', p. 827. On the intractability of African conflict and the obstacles standing in the way of any grand transformative agendas for the continent see J. E. Spence 'South Africa's Foreign Policy: Vision and Reality' in Elizabeth Sidiropoulos (ed.), *Apartheid Past, Renaissance Future: South African Foreign Policy 1994–2004* (Johannesburg: South African Institute of International Affairs, 2004).
8. Gaye, A., 'What African Renaissance?' *Newsweek*, 15 June 1998.
9. Evans, G., 'The End of the Rainbow', *The World Today*, 55:1 (1999) p. 12.
10. Asmal, K., 'South Africa in Africa: A South African Perspective' in Adebayo Adedeji (ed.), *South Africa and Africa: Within or Apart?* (London: Zed Books, 1995) p. 31.
11. Cited in 'South African Business Moves North', *International Herald Tribune* (New York, 19 February 2002).
12. 'The African Renaissance and the World', Speech by Deputy President Thabo Mbeki at the United Nations University, 9 April 1998.
13. This theme is given more extensive treatment in Hamill, J., 'A Disguised Surrender? South Africa's Negotiated Settlement and the Politics of Conflict Resolution', *Diplomacy and Statecraft*, 14:3 (2003) esp. pp. 19–26.
14. For the most extensive treatment of this new malignant phenomenon see Taylor and Williams, 'South African foreign policy'.
15. On the Brahimi Commission see 'UN tries to curb peace disasters', *Guardian* (London, 9 September 2000).
16. On Rwanda, see 'Rwanda: presidential elections', *Keesing's Record of World Events*, 49:7/8 (July–August 2003) pp. 45544. On the many imperfections of the Cameroon poll, see 'Cameroon votes for leader', *BBC News*, 11 October 2004.
17. For a wider discussion of the concept, see Zakaria, F., 'The Rise of Illiberal Democracy', *Foreign Affairs*, 76:6 (1997) pp. 22–43.
18. Deegan, H., 'Voting More Often', *The World Today*, 60 (April 2004) p. 23. Of course an obvious problem in this respect is that whilst the 1999 and 2004 elections in South Africa have been impeccably conducted, they too have effectively served to anoint 'existing political elites and dominant parties'. This may make Pretoria less than critical of similar trends elsewhere, particularly where such elites have their roots in liberation politics and where democratic standards have been much less rigorous, Zimbabwe being an obvious case in point.
19. Olivier, 'Is Thabo Mbeki', p. 816.
20. See 'Mbeki says UN needs revamping', *Business Day*, 21 September 1999.
21. Evans, 'The End of the Rainbow', p. 71.

22. Ahead of the 2004 G-8 Summit, Mbeki called upon the US to assist the continent as a whole, rather than specifically targeted states. See 'Help the Whole of Africa, Says Mbeki', *Mail and Guardian* (Johannesburg) 10 June 2004. Mbeki views fair trade, increased investment and developmental assistance as the *quid pro quo* for the reforms in economic policy and good government required by the NEPAD.
23. See 'Mbeki urges rich nations to help Africa', *Mail and Guardian* (Johannesburg, 24 May 2000) and 'Batting on behalf of Africa and the South', *Financial Mail* (Johannesburg, 26 May 2000). On South Africa's wider role in attempting to stimulate investment in Africa, see 'OECD launches African investment initiative' *Sunday Times* (Johannesburg, 19 November 2003).
24. Cited in 'End Seas of Poverty, Says Mbeki', *Independent* (London, 27 August 2002).
25. See Attwood, J. B., and Lyman, P., 'G-8 Partnership with Africa: Relevant To All', *The World Today*, 60:6 (2004) pp.26–7.
26. This debate will ultimately turn upon US interpretations of the 'war on terrorism' and whether it is defined in narrowly militaristic terms or is sufficiently nuanced to accommodate a broader developmental agenda. The latter offers Africa some hope of engaging US interest whereas the former offers little beyond security cooperation with a few strategically positioned states, those with substantial oil reserves or large Muslim populations. For further discussion, see Lyman, P. N. and Morrison, S. J., 'The Terrorist Threat in Africa', *Foreign Affairs*, 83:1 (2004) pp. 75–86.
27. 'Help the Whole of Africa, Says Mbeki', *Mail and Guardian* (Johannesburg, 10 June 2004).
28. See Taylor, *Stuck in Middle GEAR*.
29. On the development of South African thinking on its involvement in peace operations in Africa, see Malan, M., 'Keeping the Peace in Africa: A Renaissance Role for South Africa?' *Indicator South Africa* (Winter 1998). Malan argues in favour of a strong peace role to raise South Africa's diplomatic profile and to help stabilise the continent.
30. On the hostile South African reception for the US ACRI see 'SA joins with Nigeria to slam Clinton's crisis force policy', *SouthScan*, 13:5 (6 March 1998) – another indication that the image of South Africa as a US proxy in Africa has a very flimsy factual basis. On the ACRI project as a whole see Omach, P., 'The African Crisis Response Initiative: Domestic Politics and Convergence of National Interests', *African Affairs*, 99:394 (2000) pp. 73–95.
31. 'Africa sets up intervention force', *Financial Times* (London, 1 March 2004) and 'An African Peacekeeping Force: How to Put the House in Order', *The Economist* (13 March 2004).
32. 'Peacekeeping in Africa: Into the Breach', *The Economist* (19 June 2004).
33. See, for example, Soares, J. C. B., 'United Nations and Global Security: Yes to Multilateralism', *The World Today*, 60:8/9 (2004) pp. 26–7.
34. Alden, C.and le Pere, G. *South Africa's Post-Apartheid Foreign Policy – from Reconciliation to Revival?* (Oxford: Oxford University Press for International Institute of Strategic Studies, 2003) p. 69.
35. Ibid., pp. 56–7. For example, South Africa has 6 per cent of sub-Saharan Africa's population but accounts for 44 per cent of its GDP and 42 per cent of total exports. See Ahwireng-Obeng, F. and McGowan, P. J., 'Partner or

Hegemon? South Africa in Africa' in Jim Broderick *et al* (eds), *South Africa's Foreign Policy: Dilemmas of a New Democracy* (London: Palgrave, 2001), p. 63.
36. See Hamill, J. and Lee, D., 'A Middle Power Paradox? South African Diplomacy in the Post-Apartheid Era' *International Relations*, 15:3 (2001) p. 48.
37. See Taylor, I., 'South Africa, the G20, the G20+ and the IBSA Dialogue Forum: Implications for Future Global Governance', UN University conference, Buenos Aires, Argentina, 19–21 May 2004.
38. See 'The Rise of the New Power Bloc', *Mail and Guardian* (Johannesburg, 16 July 2003).
39. See 'Room at the Top Table?', *The Economist*, 2 October 2004.
40. For discussion of this phenomenon with regard to the SADC see Alden and le Pere, *South Africa's*, p. 54.
41. See for example Taylor, I., 'Africa's leaders and the crisis in Zimbabwe', *Contemporary Review*, 280:1637 (2002); Hamill, J., 'South Africa and Zimbabwe: A Little Local Difficulty', *The World Today*, 57:6 (2001) pp. 11–13; James Hamill, 'African Development: Despots or Aid?', *The World Today*, 58:6 (2002) pp. 17–19; and Ian Taylor 'The New Partnership for Africa's Development and the Zimbabwe Elections: Implications and Prospects for the Future', *African Affairs*, 101:404 (2002) pp. 403–412.
42. See Ian Taylor 'Is NEPAD Just a Toothless Blueprint?', *Zimbabwe Independent* (Harare, 8 November 2002).
43. Ian Taylor, 'The failure of the New Economic Partnership for Africa's Development', *Contemporary Review*, 282:1648 (2003) p. 285.
44. Ibid., 284.
45. For a fuller treatment of the entirely rational hostility of African elites to democracy and good governance, see Ian Taylor 'NEPAD ignores the fundamental politics of Africa', *Contemporary Review*, 285:1662 (2004) pp. 29–32.
46. Adam Habib and Nthakeng Selinyane, 'South Africa's Foreign Policy and a Realistic Vision of an African Century', in Sidiropoulos (ed.), *Apartheid Past*, pp. 57–8.
47. Ibid., p. 50.
48. On South Africa's diplomatic interventions in the DRC and Burundi, see 'Come, let's be friends', *The Economist*, 10 May 2003; 'Mbeki: the midwife of the DRC peace deal', *Mail and Guardian* (Johannesburg, 17 December 2002).
49. Elizabeth Sidiropoulos and Tim Hughes 'Between Democrtaic Governance and Sovereignty: The Challenge of South Africa's Africa Policy', in Siridopolous (ed.), *Apartheid Past*, p. 64.
50. 'Come, let's be friends', *The Economist*, 10 May 2003. On the same theme see Habib and Selinyane, 'South Africa's foreign policy', p. 56 note 10.
51. Siridopoulos and Hughes, 'Between Democratic Governance', p. 64.
52. Ibid., p. 66.
53. Olivier, 'Is Thabo Mbeki', 823.
54. Mbeki cited in ibid., 817. The contradictions between democratic rhetoric and multilateral consensus politics are also explored in Alden and le Pere, *South Africa's*, p. 54, and with regard to Zimbabwe in Iden Wetherell, 'What happened to principles?', *Mail and Guardian*, (Johannesburg, 4 October 2002).
55. Habib and Selinyane, 'South Africa's foreign policy', p. 55.
56. Spence, 'South Africa's foreign policy', p. 46.

57. I say 'supposed' because I would argue that Mandela's attempt to ostracise the Nigerian regime in 1995 was entirely the correct policy, but one foiled by a botched implementation and another depressing display of African regime solidarity. It is also worth noting at this point the deficiencies of an 'Africanism' which manages to ignore the fact that the principal victims of both Mugabe's misrule and the HIV/AIDS pandemic are in fact black Africans.

58. Explanations for this lapse into an aggressive Africanism may also be viewed through an overcompensation prism, as Mbeki attempts to demonstrate his bona fides as an African leader and to live down the previous reputation he had acquired as a distinctly un-African Anglophile. See for example the profile of him 'Out of nowhere', *Observer* (London, 23 May 1999).

59. Olivier, 'Is Thabo Mbeki', p. 817.

6
Dilemmas in South Africa's Regional Strategy
Political and Economic Relations in SADC

Mzukisi Qobo

South Africa's sub-regional strategies have evolved through different phases since the country achieved democracy in 1994 and the sub-regional dimension has since been an important preoccupation in Pretoria's post-apartheid foreign policy. This has witnessed South Africa playing an active role in the Southern African Development Community's (SADC) integration process and, at the official level, projecting an image of an equal partner rather than an aggressive hegemon, which was a hallmark of the apartheid regime's regional strategy. Of course there are divergent views on the precise nature of South Africa's approach towards the region: is it a hegemon or a partner,[1] or has Pretoria used SADC as an organisational cloak to advance its own interests.[2] Other commentators have argued that South Africa should play the role of a 'pivotal state' in the region, arguing that the country should not shy away from playing a visible leadership or even hegemonic role in the region.[3]

As background, SADC was established in 1992 when it was transformed from the Southern Africa Development Coordinating Conference (SADCC)[4] to a so-called integrating community: SADC. SADC's predecessor was largely politically driven and donor-funded, with its agenda revolving around political-security considerations and infrastructural development, all ostensibly in opposition to apartheid South Africa. South Africa joined SADC on 29 August 1994. There is no doubt that this accession was something of a seismic shift in regional relations and has subsequently served to shape the content and direction of political and economic relations within Southern Africa. The elements underpinning South Africa's sub-regional strategy and how to best conceptualise the nature of this strategy will be examined below. One thing that is clear though is that Southern Africa, specifically the SADC (including the Southern African Customs Union, SACU) region has pride of place in South Africa's political and economic strategy.[5]

But how this has played itself out has not been as clear-cut as some of South Africa's official pronouncements claim. Consequently, this chapter locates the tensions that lie at the core of South Africa's sub-regional strategy within a historically and structurally pre-determined 'hegemonic' role on the one hand and impulses that claim to seek to disentangle the country from hegemonic expectations and perceptions on the other. I contend that the essence of South Africa's sub-regional strategy is the establishment of a multilateral security regime that narrows the scope for instability and maximises the potential for South Africa's economic interests in the sub-region, including trade and investment opportunities. Thus, the two dimensions – security relations and political economy – in South Africa's sub-regional strategy are inextricably inter-related; both serve an objective that is crucial to South Africa's long-term interests.

Regarding political economy, South Africa's trade and investment penetration of the region will be analysed, particularly the anxieties underlying the negotiations for a SADC Free Trade Area (FTA) and the negative perceptions of South Africa arising from its conduct in these negotiations. Currently, the SADC FTA negotiations are one of the central pillars of SADC's cooperation and integration process, yet at the same time it has brought to the surface considerable areas of tension between South Africa and SACU countries[6] on the one hand and non-SACU SADC countries on the other. Importantly, the negotiations and Pretoria's conduct has revealed specific economic interests embedded in South Africa's economic strategy for the region.

Similarly, security relations in the region have been subject to intense power rivalries and a distinct lack of inter-subjective norms that are necessary to create a solid basis for cooperation. The discussion of the security dimension in this chapter will critically examine the Organ of Politics, Defence and Security (OPDS), particularly the power rivalries between South Africa and Zimbabwe over the political management of the OPDS, as well as the deployment, in a fractured manner, of armies from Southern African countries in the Democratic Republic of Congo (DRC) war.

The balancing act: South Africa in Southern Africa

It is evident that South Africa has developed a strong inclination towards downplaying its hegemonic role within the region. This is precisely so given the seemingly unassailable structural dominance South Africa has in the Southern Africa region, supported by an array of material capabilities, including military power. Its economy (with a GDP three times the size of all the SADC countries combined) and a relatively well-developed infrastructural platform makes, in aggregate terms, South Africa far more advanced than its neighbours in the region.

Given such dominance in the region it would be understandable to interpret some of its behaviour as displays of hegemonic attitudes, even ambitions. Certainly, South Africa's behaviour in the region, especially regarding its trade relations, can be linked to both the influence of its domestic capital on state strategies as well as influence by the trade unions; the neo-mercantilist character of South Africa's regional trade policy (discussed below) also gives the flavour of a hegemonic actor out for what it can get. The use of aggregate measurement in according hegemonic status to South Africa has characterised some of the literature on South Africa's relations with its neighbouring countries in the region.[7] Consider for example, Ahwireng-Obeng and McGowan's question: 'Can the new South Africa be a partner focusing on the mutually beneficial development of the region because it is recognized that South Africa cannot long endure as an island of prosperity in a regional sea of misery?'[8] In their work they contrast two examples of regional leadership. One relates to the notion of a 'partnership' and the other to a selfish regional hegemon. Their emphasis is on material capabilities possessed by the 'hegemon' and how it uses these in its relationship with its partners.

However, this chapter contends that South Africa has had to be remarkably sensitive to charges that its policies are hegemonic or have designs on regional leadership, even if this is actually the case, de facto. Instead, Pretoria seeks to cast itself as a benevolent actor in the region, perhaps at worst a first amongst equals, but no more so. Such a role is less imposing and does not carry the negative connotations attached to an outright hegemonic role yet it is extraordinarily difficult to pull off successfully, as I shall show. Hegemony is an uncomfortable concept, 'because of its overtones of force, threat, pressure'[9] and this is no more so than in Southern Africa where for historical reasons post-apartheid South Africa cannot openly claim a hegemonic role proper.

Past hegemonic designs have generated deeply negative perceptions of South Africa, even after apartheid has been vanquished. In effect, political barriers between the country and the rest of the region still exist, in spite of official pronouncements to the contrary. Breaking down these walls have been among the most daunting challenges facing post-apartheid South Africa. Any sign pointing towards plans aimed at reconstituting hegemonic relations would not be politically tenable and would be disastrous to regional relations and harmony. Indeed, Davies notes that 'the new South African government has sought to be an active participant in regional affairs, but it has been anxious not to be seen to be dominating the region'.[10]

Because of these factors, I argue that Pretoria is currently seeking to advance a strategy that at all times attempts to be outwardly benevolent and non-threatening, avoiding the charge that it sees itself as the regional leader, even if in reality the leadership element in South Africa's relations with the region often comes to the fore in practical terms. To stress such diplomatic imagery is not to deny the de facto leadership role that the country is playing regionally or the fact that it is in a structurally dominant position in relation to other countries in the region. Rather I contend that the aggregate position of the country relative to the others in Southern Africa is an unavoidable given, yet it does not mean that South Africa can be simply characterised as an untrammelled regional hegemon, insensitive to the opinions of the region, however lesser they may be vis-à-vis Pretoria's material power.

Indeed, I suggest that in regard to its regional relations, South Africa fits the image of a keen multilateralist rather than an unreconstituted unilateralist. At the global level, as this volume's Introduction contends, multilateralism stands to benefit South Africa. But at the local, regional level it is not immediately obvious, if one adopts the Realist perspective of Ahwireng-Obeng and McGowan, why Pretoria should care too much about multilateral diplomacy given its material preponderance? The answer can be found quite early on in the new government's tenure. In the Reconstruction and Development Programme (RDP) of 1994, the ANC made the following assertions:

> In the long run, sustainable development in South Africa requires sustainable reconstruction and development in Southern Africa as a whole. Otherwise, the region will face continued high unemployment and underemployment, leading to labour migration and brain drain to more industrialised areas.[11]

Indeed, Pretoria quite clearly appears to see South Africa's destiny as being intricately bound with the political and economic character of the region; its economic interests have to be balanced – at least in part – with the developmental needs of the region. This attitude has informed the new ANC government that came into power in April 1994. Yet, despite South Africa's progressive pronouncements and the ANC's historical ties with various Southern African states, its realignment to regional politics and economic relations has faced intractable hurdles. In particular, South Africa's structural dominance and political clout has been disconcerting for established regional Big Men such as Robert Mugabe.

At the same time, South Africa's participation in the region, cast as it is in 'developmental' language, has a hard-edged selfishness to it all, even if this is camouflaged by the public imagery of a 'partner'. Taylor observes an activist approach by the South African state in facilitating South African capital's penetration of the region. He notes for example a range of business interests from mining in Zambia and DRC, South African Breweries in Zambia and Zimbabwe, and rail infrastructural development to the retail sector.[12] In a similar vein, Daniel, Naidoo and Naidu have noted that 'peace in Angola and the prospects of peace in the Democratic Republic of Congo (DRC) will open up massive opportunities for South African capital so that one can anticipate that Africa's share of South Africa's overall export trade will continue to climb'.[13] South Africa's foreign affairs spokesperson recently made remarks confirming this view stating that the DRC holds 'enormous economic potential for South Africa's private sector in general and the mining sector in particular'.[14] These remarks were made during a state visit by President Mbeki to the DRC, accompanied by a delegation of South African businessmen, including 20 senior executives. This political mission was sealed with a cooperation pact to set up joint ventures in mining. Under this pact a South African black economic empowerment company – Mvelaphanda[15] – with interests in mining, signed a Memoranda of Understanding (MoU) with the DRC government. This guarantees investments, over the next ten years, covering processing of gold tailings, copper and cobalt mining, road building and property acquisition.[16] In addition, South Africa and the DRC signed a bilateral agreement worth US$10 billion covering defence and security, the economy and finance, and agricultural and infrastructural development.[17] This expresses clear linkages between a state's interests in enhancing political relations and stability on the one hand and the logic of specific economic interests in society on the other. However, as much as these developments have the net effect of developing the regional infrastructure and contributing to growth and development across Southern Africa, they have also fed into negative perceptions about South Africa's dominance in the region and the alleged recolonisation of Southern Africa, this time by Pretoria.

Such perceptions are extremely hard to counter and, indeed, are somewhat unfair. If South African capital prefers external, that is, non-African, sites of investment, then Pretoria is accused of embarking on an 'investment strike' and accusations of treachery towards the continent are bandied about. If on the other hand South African capital *does* invest regionally, then it is accused of trampling on local economies and ruining the regional industrial and manufacturing base (ignoring the fact that this base has, in most countries in Southern Africa, been disastrously run down since independence). That is why I see South Africa's diplomacy in the region being one guided by and bound by an intricate balancing act, one that makes few friends in the short term, though it is arguably correct in the long term. To provide evidence for this assertion, I look now at how South Africa has approached its trade relations in the SADC region, specifically with regard to the SADC Trade Protocol, effective as of September 2000.

South Africa–SADC trade relations: SADC Protocol on trade negotiations

The signing of the SADC Protocol for Trade in 1996 brought trade integration to the centre of SADC's long-term economic agenda. The Protocol, which covers a range of 39 trade-related articles, lays out a framework for the establishment of a Free Trade Area in SADC eight years after the Protocol comes into force. This finally came into effect in 2000 when all members, with the exception of the DRC, Angola and the Seychelles, ratified it. SADC's ambition to implement a Free Trade Area by 2008 for most products and by 2012 for all products 'represents the cornerstone of the SADC agenda to open up the region'.[18] According to the Protocol, it is expected that by 2008 over 85 per cent of SADC trade will be duty-free. The remaining tariffs on 'sensitive' products, for example, dairy products, wheat, sugar, cotton, fabric, leather footwear and vehicles, will be removed over the period 2008–2012.

Finalising the FTA and developing a framework for its implementation took several rounds of negotiations. Much of the negotiations for the SADC FTA were characterised by the dominance of South Africa's mercantilist interests. South Africa initially drove a hard bargain in ways that are akin to the manner in which developed countries negotiate with developing countries, betraying its hard-edged interests uncamouflaged by the imagery of partnership and sensitivity. With regards to modalities for tariff reduction for clothing and textiles, South Africa tabled a double-stage transformation rule similar to that contained in its Trade and Development Cooperation Agreement (TDCA) with the European Union (see Chapter 4). However, this would have seriously disadvantaged the least-developed SADC members, who lack the industrial capacity necessary to add value before exporting their products, as required in terms of the original provisions.

Overall, the SADC FTA negotiations were fraught with tensions and disagreements. Central to these disagreements were rules of origin. Negotiations were also uneasy on issues related to modalities for tariff reduction and tariff structure, customs cooperation and trade facilitation, and the standardisation of customs certification and procedures.[19] In so far as the rules of origin were concerned, the sectors included were industrial products, textiles and clothing, and the milling industry. Coincidentally, or not as the case may be, all these were of considerable importance to South Africa and generally regarded as sensitive sectors.

The textiles and clothing negotiations were initially tense and difficult. This was because of South Africa's initial proposal for the adoption of a double-stage transformation rule for the export of textile and clothing material within the region. However, as mentioned above, most countries in the region did not have the industrial capacity to achieve significant transformation before exporting their textile and clothing products within SADC – they could only manage to export on a single-stage basis. In contrast, South African negotiators (and SACU countries it should be noted) were concerned about the implications of liberal rules of origin, as their own domestic industries could be flooded by foreign imports transhipped via low-tariff countries within SADC.

Rules of origin are used to determine whether goods can be regarded as originating from outside or within the FTA. SADC rules of origin were initially flexible, set at 35 per cent of the local content or value addition. These were later altered at the insistence of South Africa and other SACU member countries which, for mainly protectionist reasons, argued for complex and much tighter rules.

Unlike in a customs union where there is a common external tariff, in an FTA it becomes important to verify the originating status of goods as individual countries are allowed to negotiate preferential trade agreements with third parties and also have latitude to set individual tariffs against non-members. It is on the back of this seemingly innocuous instrument of rules of origin that mercantilist interests gain a foothold. It is difficult to argue against these when they are presented, as South Africa does, as they are intended to ensure substantial transformation and, by implication, to achieve industrial development of lesser-developed SADC countries. But, there is always the suspicion that these are made unnecessarily complex and restrictive in order to protect domestic labour and capital, even if this is disadvantageous to non-SACU SADC exports, particularly to the South African market.

Yet, given the diversity of South Africa's productive structure and its economic strength, it was likely that its negotiating strategy would be strongly assertive and aimed at placating domestic pressures. Put bluntly, the moral sentiment of uplifting the region is easily shipwrecked on the rocks of selfish economic interests. As Helpman argues, 'quite often countries design their trade policies in a way that yields to pressure from special interest groups, and trade negotiations at the international arena respond similarly'.[20] South Africa's approach was no different – its nego-tiating position was articulated to benefit its domestic interests. It was much later in the negotiations that South Africa relaxed its requirement for double transformation on textile and clothing and offered the least developed members a special arrangement based on single-stage trans-formation. However, it would not relent on the product-specific rules of origin.

Four years later, it is unclear how far trade integration has progressed in SADC. There is a general sense that, while the political rhetoric emphasises progress, the reality on the ground suggests that the process has run aground. Much of the blame for limited progress is directed towards South Africa's protectionism, in particular the restrictive, product-specific rules of origin. In this sense the balancing act vis-à-vis regional trade has not worked and Pretoria is viewed in a negative light by many of the region's states.

Certainly, given the existing regional economic asymmetries there is general apprehension about how costs and benefits are distributed amongst various actors across Southern Africa. This has been a serious test of South Africa's regional strategy and has brought to the surface a crucial dilemma faced by South Africa between pursuing progressive, 'developmental' relations with its 'partners' on the one hand and opening opportunities for its domestic capital interests on the other. Two points need making here. First, it is somewhat unrealistic, if not unreasonable, to expect South African capital to be somehow instructed by Pretoria to be developmentally inclined. As Asante contends, 'no government can be expected to justify its participation in a grouping to its people by saying that their interests should legitimately be sacrificed to those of the group as a whole'.[21] Certainly, there have never been any calls for Zimbabwean capital (when it existed) to be aimed at 'uplifting' the region, and so why this call should be aimed at South Africa's entrepreneurs is somewhat unclear. Second, and more controversially, the spectre of South African capital hovering over the region provides a convenient alibi for the failure by regional elites to promote national development, now that apartheid has gone. In the past colonialism, neo-colonialism, commodity prices and, latterly, 'globalisation' have been used to excuse policy failures. There is now the palpable danger that 'South African expansion' will be – and is – used by regional elites as an alibi for the slowing down – even running down – of their own economies. And given the longstanding resentment against South African aggression during apartheid as well as the perceived 'arrogance' of the new South Africa, we are likely to see such sentiments come to the fore, probably in inverse relationship to how badly performing any given economy in the region is doing. Such tensions in the area of trade and commerce are also mirrored in the political and security domain. This is an area to which the next section will now turn.

The Organ of Politics, Defence and Security: Balancing the unbalanced

The significance of security in SADC cannot be overemphasised given the plethora of crises in most parts of Africa. Historically, the region was affected by the interplay of Cold War tensions and South Africa's destabilisation agenda. This moulded a particular security agenda among regional actors whose concern was to preserve territorial integrity and ensure protection against external threats. Even after the Cold War had thawed and a new political dispensation was in place in South Africa, hostilities continued to run deep in the region, given that a number of states were mired in civil war.

The conception of security in SADC and in most of Africa is generally informed by the traditional Realist view that regards state survival as supreme and in which the pursuit of power lies at the core of defining relations between states.[22] The notion of 'existential threat' has been the obsession of political actors in the region for many years and moving away from this narrow view remains an important challenge.[23] The thinking behind this approach is reminiscent of the Cold War era. Indeed, one would be forgiven in thinking that the region has been frozen in time with regard to conceptions of security. Yet the definition of security in narrow military, strategic terms has in many respects drawn attention away from a far broader agenda in the SADC region: economic resource mobilisation, cross-border drug trafficking, environmental threats, migration, health concerns and so on. The OPDS was established in 1996, officially replacing the Front-Line States. In carving a space of influence for himself as he lost the crown of regional leader to Mandela, Robert Mugabe of Zimbabwe insisted on taking the lead over the newly-formed Organ. Yet during this time, Mandela assumed the chair of SADC. Whilst the OPDS operated at summit, ministerial and technical levels, and functioned independently of other SADC structures, its chair was supposed to rotate annually and serve on a Troika basis.[24] The existence of two, potentially rival summits in SADC created a situation that was bound to unravel the pretence of post-apartheid regional unity. And in fact the tensions between Mandela and Mugabe were sharply brought to light soon after the establishment of the OPDS.

In its first few years of existence the Organ lacked a clear direction, and its work was characterised by acrimony and discord. The first signs of fragility were evident in 1996 when SADC refused to endorse Mandela's criticism of human rights violations in Nigeria.[25] Given the undemocratic nature of many SADC regimes, this was to be expected. However, Mandela also protested at the manner in which the Organ functioned and the way Mugabe ran it as his personal fiefdom and threatened to resign if it remained truncated from the SADC body.[26]

As part of this tension, from the outset, South Africa had favoured a less militaristic approach to regional security, whose focus would be on conflict avoidance, management and resolution. Mugabe instead favoured a strong military-based idea of security, one that in effect guaranteed military security only for the elites of the region. In essence, the lack of inter-subjective principles, norms and rules that foster greater levels of trust and commitment to deeper forms of regional cooperation was glaringly evident, with the democratic Mandela on the one hand squaring off against the tyrannical Big Man of Mugabe on the other. Tensions were unavoidable and performing the balancing act inherent in South Africa's regional strategy was virtually impossible if Pretoria was to retain any sense of its democratic, human rights-based diplomacy in the face of Mugabe's provocations.

Although the idea of the Organ was initially a laudable attempt at creating a security regime,[27] the complexity of regional power politics rapidly undermined its effectiveness. The rivalry between South Africa and Zimbabwe did not help build sustainable foundations for a security framework and in fact the Organ agenda dominated SADC and over-shadowed other concerns related to human security, collectively referred to as development security, including water, food, gender issues and health.[28] The weaknesses of the Organ's operating modalities under Mugabe were tested and exposed during the DRC conflict when Laurent Kabila, the DRC's 'President', faced internal and external threats to his rule. Having joined SADC (something which many SADC members have since bitterly regretted), the DRC issue soon rose to prominence and would for a considerable amount of time dominate regional relations.

This conflict demonstrated the difficult choices faced by South Africa in its regional foreign policy and how power rivalries and perceptions in the region shape South Africa's consciousness of its regional approach. The war in the DRC started in 1998 when Uganda and Rwanda sent their armies to help various rebel movements topple Kabila's government, which they had helped put in power the previous year.[29] In response to Kabila's call for aid, Angola, Zimbabwe and Namibia (the so-called SADC allies) deployed troops to the DRC, ostensibly to 'protect' a SADC member against foreign invasion. Yet as one Lesotho government official noted,[30] the DRC was another South African creation in SADC; its application for membership was sponsored by South Africa when Mandela made a persuasive point about the space SADC would have in influencing political developments in the DRC. This was despite the opposition from the majority of SADC countries who had argued that it would not be viable to accept a new member when meaningful integration amongst existing members had not been achieved. Mandela was subsequently proved wrong, although the decision cannot be simply reversed.

Having accepted the DRC into SADC, there was a sense of obligation amongst some SADC countries to come to its defence. This provided the opportunity for Mugabe to use the Organ to intervene in the war in defence of Kabila. This conflict went on for over two years and was temporarily abated when a diplomatic solution was explored, with Zambia assuming the role of a neutral mediator. The process initiated by Zambia culminated in the Lusaka Cease-Fire Agreement in 1999. Later, South Africa was at the centre of facilitating the Inter-Congolese Dialogue which opened in August 2001 in Gaborone, Botswana, with the actual peace deal agreed on 30 July 2002.

However, South Africa's initial opposition to Zimbabwe's stance on the DRC did not bode well with Mugabe or some other SADC leaders. In particular, Pretoria was seen to have challenged Mugabe's self-perceived political standing in the region. Mugabe was handed an ideal opportunity to plug into perceptions of South Africa's hegemonic pretensions, if not arrogance, in the region, something which a number of regional leaders encouraged. It is quite clear that in Zimbabwe at least, various interests have great difficulty in accepting South Africa's larger role in the region.[31] The same is probably true to a greater or lesser degree across the region and has served to confine South Africa's ability to 'deal' with one of the greatest problems in Southern Africa at present: the collapse of Zimbabwe.

The crisis in Zimbabwe and Pretoria's response

Zimbabwe emerged from the maelstrom of the DRC conflict badly weakened, politically and economically. The country had committed huge resources in the conflict and is estimated to have poured in about US$30 million a month, most on the maintenance of a military presence. Coupled with the already teetering economy, this had driven the country into a tailspin. The crisis of confidence in the political administration was revealed by the defeat suffered by Zanu-PF during its proposed constitutional reforms on 12–13 February 2000. This outcome was unprecedented and quite unsettling for the Zanu-PF in general and Mugabe in particular. For the first time in the history of Zimbabwe under Zanu-PF a new opposition in the form of the Movement for Democratic Change emerged and it was evident that this would be a permanent mark in Zimbabwe's political life.[32]

As a result, Mugabe embarked on a populist strategy to expropriate land from white commercial farmers without compensation, ostensibly to redistribute to peasants, war veterans and the urban poor. This was designed to create patronage but badly backfired as it failed to receive legitimate support and rapidly caused the country's economy to implode. The spiralling economic crisis inside Zimbabwe soon threatened human security, with fears of potential spill-over effects that could weaken regional security. In particular it has had a negative effect on Zimbabwe's largest trade partner – South Africa. It is said to have wiped a cumulative 1.3 per cent off South Africa's GDP and cost the wider region's economies about US$2.5 billion since 2000.[33]

Of critical importance, Zimbabwe's crisis tested South Africa's regional de facto leadership position and exposed the remarkable difficulties in performing its delicate balancing act in Southern Africa. The diplomatic acrimony that resulted from South Africa's unhappiness with Zimbabwe's handling of the Organ was still fresh in the minds of South African policy-makers, and any future approach towards Zimbabwe or any other SADC member for that matter would, to a considerable extent, be conditioned by this historical factor. Consequently, South Africa as a regional 'hegemon' faced an uphill task in dealing with Zimbabwe's political crisis. On the one hand there were strong external pressures for South Africa to demonstrate leadership and distance itself from Mugabe's self-created quagmire. On the other hand, for fear of being perceived to be dictating terms to a neighbouring country, thus courting the resentment of other SADC member countries (and possibly thereby losing ground for long-term political influence), South Africa chose a path of least resistance by opting for 'quiet diplomacy'. This however has been widely criticised, particularly outside the region, as unhelpful and abetting Mugabe's reign of terror.[34]

South Africa consistently pointed to the fact that it alone would not be able to solve Zimbabwe's crisis and therefore preferred a multilateral SADC approach (Pretoria was far more reticent to use the Commonwealth as the primary vehicle to deal with Zimbabwe). Unfortunately, SADC was paralysed by indecision and lack of a coherent position amongst its members. Indeed, the fact that the organisation is torn into different factions makes it impossible for it to deal decisively with politically sensitive issues emanating in an individual country's domestic polity. The Zimbabwean situation demonstrated not only SADC's political weaknesses but the limits of South Africa's power in the region and tensions between its structurally defined hegemonic attributes and its attempt to posture a more benevolent role, one inscribed by multilateral commitments.

Furthermore, for Mbeki, the preservation of regional 'solidarity' seems more important than making principled interventions and promoting South Africa's ostensible commitment to democracy. Yet a groundswell of critical voices viewed this 'quiet diplomacy' approach as a tacit support for state-sanctioned repression in Zimbabwe and was seen as unjustifiable in the light of South Africa's own experience with a repressive regime during apartheid years.

Given South Africa's credentials as a strong democracy not only in SADC but on the African continent, as well as its human rights culture, what could possibly explain this conundrum in its foreign policy approach towards Zimbabwe? I suggest that Pretoria is keenly aware of not only performing its tricky balancing act in the region, but also has its eyes on the long term, where South Africa hopes to exercise and influence regional affairs. Although there are no easy solutions for South Africa in the Zimbabwe political situation, I would argue that at the core of Pretoria's policy is the tension between its expressed preference for multilateralism and its regional hegemonic expectations. In short, South Africa is constrained by its hegemonic 'straight-jacket', that is, the expectation that as an economically and politically powerful country it should play a leadership role in the continent and act to preserve stability. Yet, I would also argue that South Africa cannot have it both ways. It cannot on the one hand claim to speak for Africa when it advances the NEPAD to the West – a quite consciously chosen leadership role adopted by Pretoria – whilst on the other hand disclaiming any meaningful role for itself in protecting democracy and human rights in Zimbabwe. This is a major contradiction and one that several commentators have remarked upon.[35]

It could be argued that South Africa's regional strategy is anchored in the principle of multilateralism and that Pretoria would not want to risk regional relations by acting alone. Yet it is quite clear that South Africa would not have been alone in criticising Mugabe; most of the Commonwealth and some other SADC members would have welcomed South Africa speaking out. It is of course noted that Pretoria's economic clout is resented by state elites from other countries in the region and that for historical reasons it is somewhat difficult for South Africa to throw its weight around without courting resentment; that is why Pretoria pursues its balancing act. Yet, with power comes responsibility and it is unavoidable to deduce that South Africa's 'sensitivity' to regional elites (many of whom are undemocratic and illegitimate) trumps the concerns and interests of the ordinary Southern African, not least the ordinary Zimbabwean. Whilst multilateralism requires the use of diplomatic instruments and a consensus-based approach, there are limits to this and multilateralism cannot be seen (or used) as handcuffs binding actors in perpetuity to 'consensus', not least when, as mentioned, the voices making up this consensus are, in some important respects, illegitimate. In short, South Africa's failure to provide effective leadership over Zimbabwe is not only a reflection of how ineffectual SADC is, but also a reflection of the failure of Mbeki's government to take a stand for the human rights of ordinary Zimbabweans. Whilst there clearly are deeper political issues within SADC that make it difficult for South Africa to effectively pursue a clearly differentiated policy towards Zimbabwe, these are, it should be noted, difficulties and not impossibilities.

Certainly, the gravity of the situation in Zimbabwe called for a very clear and bold approach that would have a demonstration effect on the rest of the continent, in particular in the context of commitment to 'good governance' as espoused in NEPAD. South Africa would have done well to speak forthrightly against specific instances of abuse and intensify pressure on Mugabe using both bilateral and multilateral avenues. It is certainly less than clear why South Africa has at times adopted questionable positions, engaging in what amounts to active and sustained support for a tyrant like Mugabe, most recently exposed at the Commonwealth Heads of Government Meeting in Abuja in December 2003, when Mbeki called for the lifting of Harare's suspension from the group even though conditions on the ground hardly warranted such an action. In short, in trying to pursue its regional balancing act of not being seen to be the overt hegemon, South Africa has allowed its regional strategy to cause policy drift, if not shunted it in the unfortunate direction of open support for malgovernance and human rights abuses.

Conclusion

There is a wide scope for South Africa to learn lessons from both the failures and successes of its multilateralism in the region, in particular on issues that have a bearing on regional security. The failure to resolve the crisis in Zimbabwe has undermined SADC's credibility and diminished its political stature in international society. The same might be said about Mbeki. It is important to redeem this if a stable political and security community is to be established and if Mbeki is to be taken seriously in the future. Much needs to be done if the region is to redefine itself away from the tensions of the past and structure new forms of relations based on commitments to a common set of norms, principles, rules and objectives. One of South Africa's challenges is to strongly pursue a distinct foreign policy approach in the region, firmly grounded on democratic principles. It need not and should not seek to preserve 'consensus' and 'balance' at the expense of the normative essence of its foreign policy.

South Africa's regional approach is governed by both political and economic considerations. On the economic level, there are clear material gains to be secured for domestic capital in the regional economy. The interests of these firms play an important role in shaping South Africa's foreign economic thinking, particularly as the regional market is of key importance for export-oriented firms. However, South Africa has to advance the imagery of a strong developmental aspect in favour of less developed regional partners. This is the balancing act that Pretoria must perform if it is to continue playing an instrumental role in regional affairs. South Africa cannot afford to be half hearted about a strong role in the region, but this should not necessarily be constructed in hegemonic terms. As mentioned at the start of the chapter, a role as first among equals, however vacuous this might sound, is perhaps the best that South Africa can play within Southern Africa. It is nonsensical to try and ignore the structural dominance of South Africa within the region or ignore the fact that it will always be the most powerful in terms of material ability. At the same time, whilst South Africa has to always try and portray itself as a committed multilateralist and one infused with a diplomatic spirit aimed at consensus and accord, in realistic terms this is something that will always be compromised by the politics of the region. It cannot be emphasised enough that several of the region's elites are undemocratic, if not illegitimate (such as Dos Santos, Kabila, Mugabe, King Mswati, etc.). Working with such actors will always involve compromise and contradiction. Yet at the same time, the principles that supposedly underpin South Africa's diplomacy, the respect for human rights and a normative commitment to democracy cannot be allowed to be sacrificed on the altar of realpolitik nor be waved away as inconvenient embarrassments when faced with the likes of Mugabe. Performing a principled balancing act with Southern Africa will never be easy for Pretoria, but it would be unforgivable for a democratic South Africa not to at least try.

Acknowledgement

I would like to thank Mills Soko, Laurie Nathan, and Chris Alden for their considered comments made on an earlier draft. The usual disclaimer applies.

Notes

1. See Ahwireng-Obeng, F. andMcGowan, P. J., 'Partner or Hegemon? South Africa in Africa' in Jim Broderick, *et al.* (eds), *South Africa's Foreign Policy: Dilemmas of a New Democracy* (London: Palgrave, 2001).
2. See Lieberman, E., 'Organisational Cloaking in Post-Apartheid Southern Africa: The Southern African Development Community (SADC)', *Transformation: Critical Perspectives on Southern Africa*, 34 (1997) pp. 86–107.
3. See Habib, A. and Selinyane, N., 'South Africa's Foreign Policy and a Realistic Vision of an African Century', in Elizabeth Sidropoulos (eds), *South Africa's Foreign Policy 1994–2004: Africa Past, Renaissance Future* (Johannesburg: SAIIA, 2004).
4. This was launched in 1980 by nine states: Angola, Botswana, Lesotho, Malawi, Swaziland, Tanzania, Zambia and Zimbabwe. Deon Geldenhuys called this group a counter-constellation in his *The Diplomacy of Isolation: South Africa's Foreign Policy Making* (London: Macmillan, 1984) p. 41. Namibia joined after attaining independence in 1990. On 17 August 1992, SADCC was transformed into SADC.
5. SADC is made up of the following countries: Angola, Botswana, Democratic Republic of Congo (joined in 1997), Swaziland, Lesotho, Malawi, Mauritius,

Namibia (joined in 1990), South Africa (joined in 1994), Seychelles, Tanzania, Zambia and Zimbabwe. Seychelles subsequently left the organisation as of 2004.

6. These countries are made up of South Africa and what is called the BLNS states – Botswana, Lesotho, Namibia and Swaziland. South Africa is in a customs union which dates back to 1910 with these countries. As such, this is a closely-knitted integrating area falling under South Africa's economic dominance. The SACU Agreement establishing this customs union has been renegotiated over different phases of its existence, with the new SACU Agreement signed in 2002.
7. See Obeng and McGowan, 'Partner or Hegemon?'.
8. Ibid., p. 13.
9. Kindleberger, 'Hierarchy', p. 841.
10. Rob Davies, 'Building a New Relationship in Southern Africa', in Bjorn Hettne, Andras Inotai and Osvaldo Sunkel (eds), *Globalism and The New Regionalism* (London: Macmillan, 1999) p. 267.
11. *Reconstruction and Development Programme* (Johannesburg: Umanyano Publications, 1994) p. 119.
12. Taylor, I., 'Good Governance or Good for Business: South Africa's regionalist project and the African Renaissance' in Shaun Breslin *et al.* (eds.), *New Regionalisms in the Global Political Economy* (London: Routledge, 2004) p. 191.
13. Daniel, J., *et al.*, 'South African Expansion into Africa: Can the leopard change its spots?' in *South African Labour Bulletin*, 27:5 (2003) p. 15.
14. Ronnie Mamoepa cited in *BBC Africa Service*, 14 January 2004.
15. Mvelaphanda is a black economic empowerment company headed by a high profile businessman with strong ANC ties, Tokyo Sexwale. Its major interests are in minerals.
16. See, 'South Africa overtakes Zimbabwe in the DRC scramble', *Zimbabwe Independent*, 24 January 2004.
17. *BBC Africa Service*, 14 January 2004; 'OTAL Market Report', February 2004, www.otal.com
18. SADC Discussion Paper, 'Proposal on Fast-Tracking on SADC Trade Protocol Implementation'. A paper prepared by the SADC Secretariat, Gaborone, 29 January 2001.
19. *South African Year Book 2003/2004* (Pretoria: Government Printers, 2003) p. 317.
20. Helpman, A., 'Politics and Trade Policy' in R. E. Baldwin, *et al.* (eds), *Market Integration, Regionalism and the Global Economy* (Cambridge: Cambridge University Press, 1999) p. 106.
21. Asante, S. K. B., *Regionalism and Africa's Development*, (Macmillan: London, 1999), p. 69.
22. See Dunne, T. and Schmidt, B. 'Realism' in John Baylis and Steve Smith (eds), *The Globalization of World Politics* (Oxford: Oxford University Press, Second edition, 2001) p. 152; Brown, C., *Understanding International Relations* (London: Palgrave) pp. 87–105; and Leysens and Thompson, 'Emancipating the Dead?', p. 53.
23. Buzan, B., *et al.*, *Security: A New Framework for Analysis* (Boulder: Lynne Rienner, 1998) p. 21. Note that securitisation is often invoked by state representatives to justify using whatever means necessary to block a particular threat.

24. The expectation was that the chair would act in consultation with the incoming and outgoing chair. This principle is still preserved in the restructured Organ for Politics, Defence and Security. This provides a degree of guarantee for accountability.
25. Leysens and Thompson, 'Emancipating the Dead?', p. 58.
26. Ibid., p. 59.
27. Buzan, *et al., Security*, p. 12, define a security regime as where states still treat each other as potential threats but have made reassurance arrangements to reduce the security dilemma among them. This is contrasted with conflict formation characterised by fear and rivalry, and pluralistic security community in which states no longer expect or prepare to use force in their relations with each other.
28. See, du Pisani, A., 'New Sites of Governance: Regimes and the Future of Southern Africa' in Vale, *et al.* (eds), *Theory, Change and Southern Africa's Future*, p. 212; and Thompson, L., 'Feminist Theory and Security Studies in Southern Africa: Yet Another Faddish Trend?' in Vale, *et al.* (eds), *Theory, Change and Southern Africa's Future*, p. 258.
29. The two main rebel movements: Rally for Congolese Democracy (RCD) and the Movement for the Liberation of Congo (MLC). The MLC is led by Jean-Pierre Bemba and backed by Uganda. The RCD split into two factions: RCD-Goma is based on the northeast and led by Emile Ilunga, and backed by Rwanda; and the RCD-ML is led by the original leader of the RCD, Ernest Wamba dia Wamba, backed by Uganda. For a useful overview of the war see Clark, J. F. (ed.), *The African Stakes in the Congo War* (New York: Palgrave, 2002).
30. Confidential interview, Geneva, 27 May 2004.
31. Oden, B., 'South African Benevolent Hegemony in Southern Africa: Impasse or High Way?' in Vale, *et al.* (eds.), *Theory, Change and Southern Africa's Future*, p. 184.
32. Chan, S. and Primorac, R., 'The Imagination of Land and the Reality of Seizure: Zimbabwe's Complex Reinventions', *Journal of International Affairs*, 57:2 (2004) p. 70.
33. 'Zimbabwe cost region $2.5bn', *Financial Times*, 21 May 2003.
34. See Taylor, I. and Williams, P., 'The Limits of Engagement: British Foreign Policy and the Crisis in Zimbabwe', *International Affairs*, 78:3 (2002) pp. 547–66; Taylor, I., 'The New Partnership for Africa's Development and the Zimbabwe Elections: Implications and Prospects for the Future', *African Affairs*, 101:404 (2002) pp. 403–12; and Alden, C. and Schoeman, M., 'The Hegemon that Wasn't: South Africa's Foreign Policy towards Zimbabwe', *Strategic Review for Southern Africa*, 25:1 (2003) pp. 1–28.
35. See Taylor, 'The New Partnership for Africa's Development', 2002.

7
South Africa and the Nuclear Non-Proliferation Treaty

Ian Taylor

Acting through multilateral institutions, the post-apartheid government in South Africa has attempted over the past ten years to posture a 'new' foreign policy. However, closer inspection of this erstwhile novel foreign policy indicates that Pretoria rarely if ever questions the basic underpinnings of the global order. Instead, by pursuing its diplomacy through multilateral bodies and acting within the perceived constraints operating at the structural level, the South African government exploits the space afforded to the country for playing a technical role in smoothing out the global order. As such, South Africa is often seen as a valuable member of the 'international community', particularly as Pretoria is often perceived as *the* voice of Africa.

By pursuing an energetic foreign policy, the South African government at once seeks to placate domestic critics, who demand an activist and transformative stance, whilst retaining the confidence of the dominant economic and political powers and 'the market'. This has, as suggested, been primarily operationalised within multilateral fora. Indeed, the importance of multilateralism for South Africa was recognised early on, with commentators noting that within the South African diplomatic context 'multilateral coalition building among state and nonstate actors is becoming increasingly important in a world groping for the reestablishment of order'.[1]

As part of this development, Pretoria has assumed the form of a 'middlepowermanship' role, which has taken on 'a commitment to orderliness and security on interstate relations and to facilitating ... orderly change in the world system'.[2] In short, this has meant that South Africa approaches multilateralism from a technical perspective (or 'problem-solving' approach). Critics note that in large part this fails to address the structural inequalities in the global political economy and leaves alone the huge power imbalances that mark out contemporary international relations. By doing so, the government in Pretoria presupposes that the fundamental underpinnings of the system are not subject to major transformation and that actions must thus be limited to problem solving and reformism. Hence though Pretoria's multilateralist activity is in parts aiming to 'improve' the world, *it is reformist within the limits set for it by the dominant global actors.* In short, South Africa's foreign policy takes its cue from positions taken by the dominant global actors, and although independent flourishes are not entirely absent, Pretoria's diplomacy is well within the bounds of 'acceptability'. Indeed, the new South Africa has adopted an overall stance that is veritably keen to iron out problems affecting the global order, one that 'is intent on modifying the worst aspects of the ongoing global capitalist order, without getting rid of it altogether'.[3] By order it is meant 'the [common] sense of the way things usually happen' – not 'orderliness' or the lack of upheaval in global affairs.[4] This overall pattern in Pretoria's multilateralism can be illustrated with reference to South Africa's diplomacy surrounding the Treaty on the Non-Proliferation of Nuclear Weapons (NPT), a subject we now turn to.

Nuclear proliferation and global politics

The issue of nuclear proliferation has been one of the key issues in international politics in the post-1945 era.[5] Efforts to control the process stem from the start of the Cold War through such initiatives as the Baruch Plan of 1946, which proposed to set up an international body to monitor nuclear production. Being the first nuclear power, the United States was keen to make use of an international institutional approach, primarily through the foundation of the International Atomic Energy Agency (IAEA) in the 1950s. At the same time, the US encouraged horizontal dissemination by collaborating with London's own nuclear programme (which has always been largely dependent on the US). However, vertical proliferation increased dramatically with the invention of the hydrogen bomb, tactical weaponry and advanced testing procedures, and the problem of a nuclear arms race came increasingly to dominate international politics. Following the detonation of China's first nuclear weapon in 1964, the world was faced with a build-up of nuclear weapons outside the remit (and control) of the Superpowers and their Cold War allies. This development came after the Cuban Missile Crisis of 1962, which had, many believed, brought the world to the brink of nuclear war. A cohesive international management of nuclear weaponry *and* a systematic attempt to control their proliferation had thus become a matter of urgency by the 1960s. Concern to stop 'irresponsible' parties gaining such weaponry was integral to such impulses.

International efforts to control the proliferation of nuclear weaponry were initially based around secrecy (shattered by successful Soviet espionage coups); proposals regarding a single international monitoring agency; attempts to ban all nuclear weapons tests; and through trying to limit access to critical materials and technologies.[6] However, by 1968 the control of the future spread of nuclear weaponry was seen to lay in a treaty regime (negotiated between 1961 and 1968) that would demand:

- that states in possession of nuclear weapons do not assist others to acquire the same;
- that states not already in possession of nuclear weapons do not attempt to acquire them;
- that facilities in non-nuclear weapon states capable of producing fissionable materials that could be converted to weapon usage be subject to monitoring from the IAEA;
- that cooperation on nuclear matters be restricted to the peaceful application of atomic power; and
- that the results of peaceful explosive testing be shared with non-nuclear weapon states.[7]

Originally opened for signature on 1 July 1968 and coming into force on 5 March 1970, the NPT has become the most widely observed arms control covenant in diplomatic history and is the only global legal instrument which commits non-nuclear weapon states to refrain from acquiring nuclear weapons. As part of the regime, there are certain conditions ostensibly underpinning this Treaty, notably that the nuclear weapon states (NWS) will proceed towards disarmament whilst providing economic aid to develop civilian nuclear technologies.[8]

There are currently 187 signatories to the NPT; that is, virtually all the nations of the world with the notable exception of Brazil (which instead signed the Treaty of Tlataloco, the South American nuclear-free zone treaty), Cuba, and the three de facto but undeclared nuclear states, namely India, Israel and Pakistan.

The NPT aimed to create a prohibition against the further proliferation of nuclear weaponry and by doing so it transformed the acquirement of such weapons from a status symbol to something that is either officially denied or downplayed in most instances. Ultimately, it has also motivated a number of states such as Argentina, Brazil and Sweden, as well as post-Soviet republics such as the Ukraine, Belarus and Kazakhstan to give up their nuclear programmes.

According to the NPT, the five 'nuclear weapon states' are France, the People's Republic of China, Russia, the United Kingdom and the United States of America. These are the states that had manufactured and exploded nuclear devices prior to 1 January 1967. All other states are defined as non-nuclear weapon states (NNWS). This definition includes those states now known to possess nuclear weaponry or the potential to build such material, such as India, Israel, North Korea and Pakistan. Here it should be pointed out that there is a distinction between those states such as Iraq, Iran and North Korea who signed the NPT but then reneged on their commitments and the three states who simply have not signed the NPT: India, Israel and Pakistan. Interestingly, it is not the last three who have been denounced by Washington as 'rogue states'.

The distinction between official nuclear and non-nuclear states (however redundant) is twinned with a second basic assumption, namely that military and civilian usage of nuclear technology can be visibly demarcated. The fact that the nuclear powers take great pains to restrict the export of 'delicate' nuclear technologies as well as the well-known anxiety over the smuggling of uranium out of the former Soviet Union by criminal networks[9] show that this assumptive premise of the Treaty is not shared by the key signatories.

However, for the purpose of this chapter, the key problem with the NPT according to its critics is its effective monopolisation of the right of the existing NWS to manufacture weaponry and possess them whilst the NNWS are prohibited not only from manufacturing such armaments but also from possessing them. This in itself, in part, sprang from the major (i.e., nuclear) powers having a shared interest in halting proliferation 'since it [made] global politics more complicated than ever before'.[10] This reality has remained problematic for the Treaty and has provoked heated debate on the matter. India in particular has consistently held the position that it is hypocritical for the nuclear powers, already happily in possession of the desired weaponry, to dictate that other nations cannot have them, calling the NPT an 'unfair and discriminatory treaty' that in its current shape is 'simply unacceptable'.[11]

This being so, under Article X of the original NPT, 25 years after its entry into force a conference was to be convened to discuss whether the Treaty would continue as it was or be extended. It was that proviso that set the scene for the NPT Renewal Conference in New York from 17 April to 12 May 1995 and which provided a platform for some early South African multilateral diplomacy.

NPT Renewal Conference

The Renewal Conference came at a time of increasing anxiety over nuclear proliferation and tension with aspirant nuclear powers. In March 1993 Pyongyang threatened to withdraw from the NPT, citing national security considerations, and refused permission for routine monitoring of its nuclear sites.[12] At the same time, Pakistan announced in November of that year that it would not roll back its nuclear programme in the face of the perceived threat from another de facto nuclear power, India. Also, following the end of the Gulf War, deep suspicion was levelled at Iraq's nuclear programme by Washington and its allies. This international tension over nuclear weaponry was compounded by the break-up of the Soviet Union, which saw 30 per cent of its nuclear arsenal stranded in the newly independent republics of Belarus, Kazakhstan and Ukraine.[13] Importantly, this was the first Review Conference after the end of the Cold War. Thus as the Conference convened, participants were faced with not only what to do with those states suspected of possessing nuclear weapons (or aspiring to do so), but also with new states in possession of large portions of the former Soviet Union's stockpile. Furthermore, the question of nuclear weapons testing, which had failed to be resolved at the last NPT Review and Extension Conference in 1990, was also on the agenda.[14]

The most controversial question was the issue of the future duration of the NPT, as Article X required that 25 years after the Treaty had entered into force a conference should be held to resolve whether the NPT should continue in force indefinitely or should be extended for fixed periods. Some NNWS wanted the Treaty extended for a fixed period (lasting 25 years) after which the NPT's duration would again be discussed. This stance was seen as a way to continue influence over the NWS vis-à-vis nuclear disarmament. In other words, if the NWS were not seen to be acting in accordance with their responsibilities and be slow in actively moving towards disarmament, the NNWS would have the opportunity of not renewing the NPT. This would instantly throw the whole regime into question. On the other side, the NWS were in favour of an indefinite extension of the Treaty. It was in these circumstances that Pretoria was to move to smooth out potential problems.

South Africa and nuclear weapons

Pretoria began a nuclear weapons programme in 1970 when the South African Atomic Energy Corporation (AEC) embarked on a government-sponsored construction of a clandestine plant for the enrichment of uranium.[15] This programme may be seen as a natural outcome of the assumptions that provided a framework for South Africa's security policies, particularly with regard to its external security.[16] Although interest in creating a nuclear capability had been expressed in the early 1970s (a test site being built in the Kalahari in 1974), it was the geopolitical developments following the Lisbon coup of 1974 and the involvement of Soviet and Cuban troops in Angola that spurred Pretoria to adopt a 'total national strategy' aimed at combating the perceived threat from Moscow. South Africa's nuclear programme was part of this.

At this juncture it should be pointed out that Pretoria did not hope to compete with Moscow in the creation of its own nuclear arsenal. The policy objective was to coerce the West (in particular Washington) into providing a 'nuclear guarantee' to offset Moscow's ostensible threat.[17] By effectively encouraging nuclear proliferation in a flash-point strategic region, Pretoria aimed to force the United States' hand into offering to provide a security umbrella against alleged Soviet machinations. Later, as pressure on Pretoria increased and incremental sanctions began to bite, the South African administration began to vaguely hint that its nuclear capability would enter the equation somehow.[18] This deterrence by uncertainty was akin to Israel's longstanding stance being implicit and deliberately ambiguous regarding its nuclear status – of having the 'bomb in the basement'.[19] In other words, Pretoria's bomb had little military utility but was perceived by policy-makers as possessing potentially plenty of political use. Such posturing however was more a sign of the times in an embattled South Africa, than a measured policy vis-à-vis Pretoria's nuclear custody.

With the active assistance of Israel, South Africa constructed its first atomic device in 1977, but this was aborted after it was apparently discovered by a Soviet spy satellite.[20] Two years later and at the behest of the then head of government, P. W. Botha, responsibility for the manufacture of nuclear weaponry was passed over from the AEC to Armscor, the parastatal arms manufacturer. That same year, South Africa conducted a secret nuclear test in the southern Indian Ocean. Between 1981 and 1989 Armscor constructed six nuclear weapons and was finalising a seventh when Botha resigned in 1989.

Under Botha's successor, F. W. de Klerk, the programme was shut down in November 1989 and all seven devices ordered to be destroyed.

A reappraisal of Pretoria's nuclear weapons policy was undertaken. By the time de Klerk took over office, South Africa's external security status had improved with the movement towards Namibian independence and the withdrawal of the Cuban presence in Angola following the December 1988 agreement. The year 1987 had seen South Africa offer to negotiate vis-à-vis the NPT, probably linked to both the threatened suspension of Pretoria from the IAEA and/or posturing over Angola and a comprehensive regional settlement, than it did with any change of heart within the securocrat-run administration. Yet at the same time, Moscow's preoccupation with its own domestic restructuring meant that its interest in southern Africa was now minimal; the *rooi gevaar* was no more and the rationale behind Pretoria's nuclear policy disappeared. Cost and the wish to prevent an ANC-led government taking possession of nuclear weapons have also been suggested as motivating factors propelling Pretoria to give up its nuclear weaponry.[21] Indeed, it should be noted that at the beginning of 1990, Washington – supported by the United Kingdom and Israel – sent Pretoria a robust 'hostile nation warning' demanding that South Africa roll back its nuclear weapons programme.[22] After all, 'With the prospect of the ANC taking power, the U.S., the UK and Israel did not want to see the programme's assets or secrets being sold to adversaries in the Middle East or elsewhere.'[23]

On 10 July 1991, South Africa acceded to the NPT and in September of that year Pretoria agreed to accept the monitoring of the IAEA. Since that date South Africa has been fully committed to a non-nuclear policy and has supported the concept of a nuclear-free Africa (the Treaty of Pelindaba) endorsed by the Organization of African Unity (now African Union) and within the framework of the NPT.

With regard to the NPT, South Africa's stance has been evolutionary. At an ANC-convened conference on the 'Nuclear Policy of the Democratic South Africa' in 1994, three proposals were advanced as the Movement's position on the NPT: first, that it would *not* push for a limited extension as this would undermine the non-proliferation regime; second, that it would *not* support an indefinite/permanent extension without a serious alteration of the non-proliferation regime – in particular addressing disarmament by the five nuclear powers; third, that Pretoria should adopt a principled position of supporting a 15-year fixed extension period.[24] Why elements within the ANC adopted such policy prescriptions was informed by the perceived unequal nature of the NPT.

Indeed, although the most widely observed arms control covenant in diplomatic history, the ANC's initial stance seemed to be influenced by the notion that the NPT acted as a legitimising device in favour of the five NWS. It is true that legitimisation is effectively based on possession and dating, that is, 'who got there first'. States are legitimised on the basis that they manufactured and exploded nuclear devices prior to 1 January 1967. Thus the ANC at first argued that the NPT underpinned a 'balance of power' heavily in favour of the industrialised world and one at the expense of the developing world. Whether this actually mattered was a moot point, but perception is everything and the NPT was perceived by elements within the ANC as being a Treaty that somehow enshrined global domination – reflecting a somewhat limited understanding of the relationship between nuclear weapons and political power and the idea that possession of a nuclear bomb immediately made one a global player of import.

The South African government's initial stance, displayed at the third preparatory meeting (PrepCom), was to extend hesitant support for a fixed extension – a position close to the official stance of the Non-Aligned Movement (NAM). At the PrepCom meeting, South Africa 'call[ed] on State parties to comply with all the provisions of the treaty, whether they relate to non-proliferation, disarmament or peaceful uses'.[25] In other words, it appeared that the Review was seen as a window of opportunity to move the world towards concrete steps regarding nuclear disarmament. An indefinite extension of the NPT was seen as the antithesis of such sentiments by a number of NNWS. As the *New York Times* (New York) reported on 12 May 1995:

> Malaysia's delegate to the present conference, Hassiny bin Agam, reflected the view of a number of other developing nations when he said the treaty provided a carte blanche to the nuclear powers. [And]... could be interpreted as 'justifying nuclear weapons states for eternity'.

It was this background that set the scenario for the NPT Review and Extension Conference in New York from 17 April to 12 May 1995.

The NPT Review and Extension Conference

Prior to the NPT Review, the world's leading nuclear power – the United States – made it clear that it favoured an 'indefinite extension of the NPT without conditions'.[26] Such a posture was opposed by the NAM, which saw any indefinite extension as an implicit recognition of the perpetuation of the existence of nuclear weapon powers.[27] This opposition also sprang from the belief that an indefinite expansion of the NPT would effectively eliminate pressure on those states already in possession of nuclear capability to make any type of meaningful assurances regarding disarmament. This would then send a powerful signal to threshold states or those not 'officially' recognised by the Treaty as nuclear powers to press on with their own nuclear weaponry programmes.[28]

The potential for discord between those pressing for limited extension and conditionalities and Washington was thus high. This left South Africa, now under the ANC's control, in a difficult position. As a member of the NAM it would be expected to vote with its allies. This would certainly also gel with previously expressed ANC preferences over the matter. Yet, if Pretoria was to line up alongside those opposed to the US position, it would perhaps weaken the strong linkages then being formed between the new South Africa and the leading global power. This was at a time when the ANC government was embarking on its 'gamble on growth' development strategy, which brought with it a profound sense of vulnerability and a desire not to alienate the leading capitalist power.[29] In desperate need for foreign investment and development assistance, South Africa simply felt that it could not appear to be too much out of step with the dominant powers, particularly Washington.[30] That is not to say that South Africa was from the start aligned with the US position. Initially, it seemed that Pretoria offered tentative backing to a fixed extension duration, a stance close to the official position of the NAM. Indeed, Pretoria's delegate at the third preparatory meeting before the NPT Review asserted that his country 'call[ed] on state parties to comply with all the provisions of the treaty, whether they relate to non-proliferation, disarmament or peaceful uses'.[31]

However, American pressure was swiftly brought to bear on Pretoria. The American ambassador to South Africa, Princeton Lyman, warned the South African leadership what was expected from them in the form of a demarché, warning Pretoria that a contrary vote by South Africa regarding indefinite extensions would damage 'mutual interests' and change Washington's perceptions of South Africa's non-proliferation credentials.[32] 'Certainly, "arm-twisting" occurred: the United States made it clear it wanted countries to vote its way and that it would take those votes into account.'[33] The US Vice-president, Al Gore, personally lobbied the South African Vice-President, Thabo Mbeki, for Pretoria's backing for a non-time-bound extension and President Clinton wrote to Mandela demanding support. Indeed, 'South Africa [was] a special target for lobbying because it [was] perceived to have influence over other Non-Aligned Movement (NAM) and especially African countries'.[34] Interestingly, this pressure was so intense that it nearly backfired and threatened to provoke Pretoria to reverse its position: According to one source, President Clinton was warned by Mandela to 'back off, or else'.[35]

Although the success of this intense pressure was denied by South African diplomats, commentators remarked that Pretoria was 'submitting to extreme pressure exerted by the United States to conform to its desires'[36] and that the adoption of a non-time-bound extension 'crowned months of persuasion, pressure and manoeuvre by [the] US'.[37] For his part, Alfred Nzo, the South African Foreign Minister, admitted that the *realpolitik* of the global order helped move Pretoria's position and acted as a constraint: 'there are certain realities we cannot ignore. [The West] constitute the undeniable economic power base of the world today'.[38] Abdul Minty, Deputy Director-General of the Department of Foreign Affairs, later disingenuously claimed that South Africa might have supported the NAM but – reflecting the weakness of the organisation – there was no official NAM position.[39] Far more likely is American pressure at a time when South Africa was actively trying to reintegrate itself into the global community as a trustworthy partner and site for investment by the West. In other words, adopting a stance so wildly at odds with that favoured by the major powers, particularly the Americans, was quickly dropped from any agenda it may once have been on (i.e., ANC academic conferences). A middle power-type role of consensus-building and legitimisation was thus adopted by Pretoria in support of the nuclear order favoured by the dominant powers.

Pretoria hence used its 'moral suasion' to act as a 'bridge-builder' between the developed and developing world in defending the line favoured by the US. Having been the first country to roll back its nuclear weapon status and also sign the NPT in 1991,[40] and having just emerged as a democratic state, the euphoria surrounding South Africa's re-emergence on the world stage was a useful factor in pushing a particular stance vis-à-vis nuclear weaponry, particularly as Pretoria's position earned considerable kudos in both the West and the developing world.[41] As sources have later claimed, 'no one else had ... the prestige ... to bridge the gap between the nuclear haves and have-nots',[42] and 'South Africa's new morality meant that it could be used to bring on board other states to the United States' position'.[43]

However, as a member of the NAM, most observers expected 'that South Africa would support some form of long-term but limited extension',[44] and indeed 'mindful of Mandela's stature and his potential influence over Third World countries, the United States had worried that South Africa might not support an indefinite extension'.[45] South Africa's role in facilitating an eventual broad base of support or 'middle ground' for an indefinite extension is thus of profound significance when looking at post-apartheid foreign policy, especially as South Africa's then Foreign Minister regarded the Review as 'clearly one of South Africa's successful efforts' in its diplomacy.[46] Yet at the Review conference,

> [South Africa] endorsed some of the NWS' arguments, i.e. rejecting the linking of permanent extension to conclusion of the CTBT [Comprehensive Nuclear Test Ban Treaty], other nuclear disarmament measures or a time-bound framework for disarmament, thereby adopting a narrow interpretation of Article VI. At the plenary session of the conference, South Africa's Minister for Foreign Affairs, Alfred Nzo, stated that it supported, in principle, indefinite extension 'without any preconditions or linkage to other nuclear disarmament measures such as CTBT'. South Africa also endorsed the NWS' argument that fixed period extension would erode confidence in the NPT, endangering the non-proliferation regime. This implicitly rejected the non-aligned countries position that limited extension sought to strengthen rather than weaken the NPT ... South Africa's stance also stemmed from the position that the NWS had an upper hand in the negotiations. It rejected the linkage on the grounds that '...(this) raises the question, inter alia, of what would happen if for one or other reason, the conditions were not met' – implying that nothing would. Therefore, it claims to have sought a middle course between the two positions.[47]

The value that the US saw in using South Africa's nuclear policy as a legitimising agent of the current nuclear order was important as 'South Africa could produce a far wider margin of consensus for an indefinite extension than the United States could achieve alone'. As one observer asserted, 'the South Africans ... offered [Washington] a bridge to the non-aligned, one that the United States should walk over' for 'with their help, [the US] could get an overwhelming vote for extension'.[48] Indeed, the weight the US gave to South Africa's role in the nuclear issue was illustrated early on in Washington's support for Pretoria's membership of the Nuclear Suppliers Group – an organisation of states who supplied nuclear technology and which is aimed at preventing the supply of such technology to developing world nations.[49] As the only NAM member of this Group, South Africa's accession afforded the institution a certain legitimacy. Certainly, the notion that the Group was an elite body of developed nations (a notion that had the potential to delegitimise the group in the eyes of Southern observers) was blunted by South Africa's membership. Such membership can be seen as highly useful for those elements that desired legitimisation of the nuclear order.

At the same time, membership afforded the South African elite with a highly visible role in a contentious issue, thus raising the profile of the newly installed' leadership and indicating that the post-*apartheid* administration held the confidence of the developed nations – a welcome flagging of the government's credibility with 'international opinion' and an important boost for the new government in its attempt to attract investment. As one source put it,

> South Africa's return to international respectability under majority rule and a leader in the person of President Nelson Mandela ... has been reinforced by its constructive role in efforts at the Nuclear Non-Proliferation Treaty Review Conference to make the pact permanent through a consensus of the 178 signatories.[50]

This – and the rumour that 'membership of the Nuclear Suppliers Group was offered to South Africa as a reward for its support of a permanent NPT' – should not be lightly dismissed.[51]

As has been suggested, division at the Review endangered the Treaty. Both the Western and Eastern (ex-Soviet bloc) caucus groups favoured indefinite extension, yet could not muster more than around 55 votes between them, whilst the NAM were hampered by a failure to construct a coherent caucus or policy.[52] Such deadlock threatened to weaken if not delegitimise the NPT regime, particularly if a vote was simply taken on a majority basis and a number of NAM states decided to abstain from voting. This caused alarm in Pretoria, which felt itself in a difficult position. South Africa consequently 'broke ranks with NAM' and sought a 'compromise solution'.[53] The time-bound issue regarding extension was seen as causing deadlock at the Review, and South Africa viewed with concern the possibility of the Treaty breaking down.[54] As a South African delegate to the Review admitted, Pretoria 'believed that any decision taken by a simple majority would weaken the treaty'.[55]

This was of the utmost concern for the NWS, who feared that any renegotiation of a new NPT would be opened up to all sorts of inputs and opinions and, as the American ambassador to South Africa put it, 'such a process [could] take years and the outcome [would not be] certain'.[56] South Africa's position at the NPT Review then was essentially to facilitate a compromise that continued to legitimise the position of the NWS whilst appearing on face value to address the concerns of the developing world. As one account had it,

> When the conference opened, the United States and its allies, among them Russia, faced formidable opposition to an indefinite extension of the treaty, and did not have enough declared votes for a simple majority had there been a ballot ... Over the weeks however, the opposition, led by larger developing nations – among them Mexico, Venezuela, Egypt, Nigeria and Indonesia – began to split. The eventual *collapse of the opposition to an indefinite extension was hastened by the decision of South Africa to back such a plan* and propose a package of confidence-building documents that would meet some of the concerns of the non-nuclear weapons nations.[57]

An official source has supported this analysis, arguing that South Africa sought to do 'something practical' and engage with the NWS whilst avoiding pushing the time-bound agenda. In short, a 'policy of bringing the two sides together was the only realistic policy'.[58] Thus having initially expressed tentative support for a fixed period extension, Pretoria moved to support the NWS position 'without any preconditions or linkage to other nuclear disarmament measures',[59] a remarkable volte face that deeply angered many other participants at the Review.[60] The position that Pretoria put forward was to accede to the nuclear powers' stance for an indefinite extension of the NPT, whilst at the same time attempting to put pressure on them by advocating that the NPT process be reinforced through a non-binding *Principles for Nuclear Non-Proliferation and Disarmament* (see below). This position was a clear attempt by Pretoria to bridge the gap between the NWS and those who favoured a much stronger regime, including palpable moves towards disarmament.

By appearing to minimise polarisation between the haves and have-nots whilst actually strengthening the former, Pretoria played a classical middle power role by 'seek[ing] to expand the area of common ground [making] it possible to curtail risk in the management of conflict'.[61] One source put this succinctly when it pointed out that South Africa 'focused on defining areas on which the maximum number of signatories ... could find common ground'.[62] By playing this role, South Africa was 'instrumental ... in achieving the widest possible consensus'.[63] Towards the end of the Conference, a resolution demonstrated that there were 111 co-sponsors for a non-time-bound extension, more than enough votes to support this option without a specific roll-call and a major body-blow to those delegations which still held out against the NWS position.[64]

The final Review conclusion was agreed without a vote on the indefinite extension of the NPT and furthermore, the Review agreed upon – again without any vote – to two collateral documents on *Strengthening the Review Process for the Treaty* and *Principles and Objectives for Non-Proliferation and Disarmament.* These were in line with the positions favoured by the NWS. Indeed, 'the developed countries have to thank South Africa for its role in 'delivering' the sceptical non-nuclear weapon states, particularly the Non-Aligned Movement',[65] though other commentators later remarked that 'criticism [of] what is perceived to be the [South African] government's pro-Western stance on nuclear disarmament issues [leads one to ask] if the government is working together with its non-aligned partners'.[66] Official sources however believe that Pretoria's role at the NPT Review 'gave South Africa credibility with the United States'.[67]

The documents agreed upon at the NPT Review were in line with what Alfred Nzo had pushed, and South Africa's proposals were seen as the 'key to persuading the non-nuclear countries' to accept the new review system.[68] The proposals agreed upon included:

- a restated commitment to the non-proliferation of nuclear weaponry;
- a strengthening of adherence to the safeguards under the IAEA agreement;
- providing access to nuclear technology for peaceful purposes;
- a movement towards reducing nuclear arsenals;
- the endorsement of the establishment of an increased number of nuclear-free zones; and
- enforcing binding security assurances for non-nuclear powers.[69]

This raft of proposals left the South African leadership open to the charge that Pretoria had indulged in 'turning its back on the Third World and cosying up to the United States by supporting the Big Five powers in their bid to hold on to their nuclear bombs'.[70] Not least, this was because South Africa's position 'removed the only source of leverage on the nuclear weapons states, because the Treaty's extension [was] no longer ... linked to dismantling their arsenals', and 'in the absence of a binding time-frame, the nuclear powers [were] free to adopt their own notions of the right time to disarm'.[71] Indeed,

> [t]he key objection to South Africa's position is that it removed the only source of leverage on the NWS, because the treaty's extension can no longer be linked to dismantling of their arsenals. The

'Principles' which it proposed and were adopted to ensure strengthened review processes are not binding and do not set deadlines for
their goals. In the absence of a binding time-frame, the nuclear powers are free to adopt their own notions of the right time to disarm.
This was a logical consequence of South Africa's endorsement of the
restrictive reading, since a time-frame would have implied a form of
linkage.

South Africa claims to have bridged the gap between the two sides at
the review and extension conference – that it nudged the conference
towards a compromise. However, this is strictly not true. The review
conference deadlocked on language addressing the implementation on
Article VI. Despite agreement on indefinite extension, the 1995
extension conference ended without narrowing the divide between
the conflicting positions on nuclear disarmament. In the view of
some, this was partly due to the NWS stressing extension at the
expense of a review of the treaty's implementation. The NWS were
more concerned about the survival of the treaty than in pushing
forward the disarmament agenda.[72]

Such comments undermine the argument put forward by observers such
as Jean-Jacques Cornish that South Africa's proposals were an advance
for they qualified the indefinite extension with a declaration of principles binding the nuclear powers to quicker disarmament and that the
Treaty would be strengthened with an ongoing review process. Yet with
no date fixed upon this, such supposed principles were from the start
weakened by the indefinite extension.[73]

Indeed, it is not hard to assert that South Africa's role at the NPT
conference secured the relationship between South Africa and the
'certain realities' of the extant world order. 'Within days of Nzo's speech
in New York, the announcement came that South Africa [was] to receive
a billion dollar loan from the US-dominated World Bank'.[74] Another
source has claimed that South Africa wanted to impress the Big Powers,
with an eye on attracting investment.[75] Whilst one must be circumspect
in making any direct causal link between this and the NPT Review, it is
apparent that Pretoria's behaviour earned the new administration
gratitude in Washington and strengthened the 'mutual interests'
between Washington and Pretoria. Indeed, much of the South African
press were highly enthusiastic about Pretoria's role, exclaiming for example that 'it is achievements such as the one at the NPT conference which
will keep us on the map as a recognized player to be taken seriously, to be
consulted and, most importantly, to be traded with and invested in'.[76]

Such a scenario was achieved by South Africa pursuing an essentially middle power role that legitimised the global nuclear order whilst *appearing* to have the potential for de-legitimisation – 'providing countries with the means to vent frustration' as one source pointed out.[77] This exhibited 'a new conception of the tactics of achieving [the NPT] goal, through incremental short steps which are both unobjectionable in themselves and which have some value in reinforcing the nuclear non-proliferation regime'.[78] In other words, a continuation of the ongoing order through both avoidance of controversy and various tactics of inclusivity that, in the final analysis, does little to challenge the dominant powers' position. Such a policy of pragmatism was pursued by Pretoria at the NPT Review and 'pulled Washington's fat from the fire on the Nuclear Non-Proliferation Treaty',[79] presenting 'a major foreign policy victory for the Clinton administration'.[80]

South Africa's position post-1995

However, in the post-Review period, the legitimacy (and effectiveness) of the NPT has been under serious strain, not least because within two days of the Treaty's indefinite extension China conducted nuclear testing whilst France quickly announced that it too was going to resume testing. Furthermore, in mid-1997, Washington conducted a high-explosive underground test involving nuclear materials. Indeed, it quickly became apparent that for all South Africa's bridge-building efforts, the practicalities of the compromise pushed by Pretoria did nothing vis-à-vis the NWS disarmament obligations. Later, at the first PrepCom in April 1997, to review the Treaty mid term, the shaky 'consensus' around the NPT had clearly evaporated with demands for greater commitment to disarmament and security assurances.[81]

Ironically, despite being the state that contributed heavily to the scenario where the NWS are under very little pressure to disarm, Pretoria has since 1995 taken a leading role in ostensibly pushing forward the agenda of disarmament. According to one analyst, 'frustration with the United States' position (i.e. resumption of testing) has lead to South Africa taking on a more activist position'.[82] For example, Pretoria joined Brazil, Egypt, Ireland, Mexico, New Zealand, Slovenia and Sweden in signing a joint declaration entitled 'Towards a Nuclear Free World: The Need for a New Agenda', which called on the nuclear power states and those states who had just then tested weapons – India and Pakistan – to commit themselves to the elimination of their respective weapons.[83]

This new initiative of middle-ranking powers stemmed from the common perception that the disarmament process had gone 'cold'.[84] Furthermore, Pretoria has signed the CTBT and agreed to base monitoring facilities on its territory.[85] The CTBT was adopted on 10 September 1996 by the United Nations General Assembly. Prohibiting all nuclear test explosions, the CTBT was opened for signature on 24 September 1996 and was initially signed by 71 states, including the NWS. South Africa signed the Treaty on the 24 September 1996, though ratification only came into effect on 30 March 1999. South African activity regarding the CTBT was substantial, with Jackie Selebi serving as the first chair of the PrepCom of the CTBT, whilst the country was a member of the core group that managed the process of the resolution on the CTBT that was adopted in September 1996.[86]

Importantly, South Africa (alongside Canada) took an active role in PrepCom II ahead of the NPT Review in 2000. South Africa argued that considerable time had to be afforded to discussing the practicalities regarding progress towards disarmament as embarked upon by the NWS – a proposal they vigorously opposed. This had the potential to delegitimise the nuclear states' position as their 'rejection of South Africa's attempts to launch focussed discussion ... reveal their intransigence, which the [NNWS] increasingly find unacceptable'.[87]

As a result, Pretoria asserted that at the Review 'We are tasked to ensure that the bargain that was struck in 1995, and that provided the basis and the rationale for the agreement to extend our Treaty indefinitely, is met and fully implemented'.[88] Reflecting the disappointment South Africa felt in the way in which the NPT had played out after the Review of 1995, the Deputy Director-General went on to claim that

> The review period of 1995 to 2000 is not one of the most auspicious in our Treaty's history, especially with regard to the nuclear disarmament obligations contained in Article VI. It may be an exaggeration to say that the NPT is under threat, but it would be fair to say that developments since 1995 in areas directly related to, or having a direct impact on, the nuclear non-proliferation and nuclear disarmament provisions of the NPT contradict, and are counter productive to, the achievement of the NPT's objectives.[89]

Consequently, 'As a first step on the pathway to nuclear disarmament the Nuclear Weapons States (China, France, Russian Federation,

United Kingdom, United States) should make an unequivocal undertaking to accomplish the total elimination of their nuclear arsenals'.

The question is how can such activism vis-à-vis nuclear disarmament and the now quite hostile tone regarding the NWS be explained in the light of Pretoria's controversial role during the NPT conference in 1995? First, stung by criticism that South Africa had betrayed its allies in the developing world and brought its much-touted non-aligned credentials into disrepute, South Africa evidently opted for a policy that was less obviously in line with the NWS. This 'demonstrates South Africa's readiness to contribute towards efforts to enhance international peace and security', thus projecting Pretoria's overall posture on the international stage.[90] More importantly, such activism appears to demonstrate Pretoria's 'independent' stance with regard to Washington. Not only can this be usefully deployed domestically by the government against its critics who charge that its foreign policy is too close to the capitalist hegemon (and the NPT issue saw this charge being levelled with some vigour), but it can also be projected externally to demonstrate the proof of South Africa's apparent independence. After all, by pursuing the NWS over nuclear disarmament, South Africa appears to be delegitimising their position by striking out an autonomous policy position through asking the NWS to take the relevant articles of the NPT on disarmament seriously.

Yet, this must be contextualised: South Africa is pushing this ostensible agenda within a treaty framework *which it helped deliver* that means that there is very little pressure on the NWS to consent to a real disarmament process. As one analysis put it, 'had nuclear powers accepted legally binding time frames for nuclear disarmament, perhaps the US would desist from ... refining its nuclear arsenal'.[91] Indeed, after the 1995 NPT Review Conference the position of the nuclear powers and Washington in particular has been strengthened, as 'the NPT is devoid of any sense of urgency to achieve a nuclear-free world. The nuclear powers feel at liberty to determine their own pace of disarmament'.[92] The calls for disarmament by Pretoria, though they do fit within South Africa's overall foreign policy stance regarding disarmament, are compromised by the scenario where the current NPT has been indefinitely extended. In short, 'an inherent flaw' in the extended NPT 'is the assumption that [disarmament] measures could be negotiated without time-bound frameworks'.[93]

Furthermore, appearing to challenge and confront the dominant powers over nuclear weapons *after* the NPT has been indefinitely extended throws up the imagery of autonomy in which a country such as South Africa can challenge the developed world. Of course, there *is* agency, but what my analysis might suggest is that this has been largely confined to technical interventions, emasculated as it has been by the indefinite extension of the NPT and the reification of the nuclear powers' possession of their existing weaponry. Indeed, by appearing to challenge the NWS position over nuclear disarmament, South Africa contributes to *legitimising* the wider global nuclear order. This is particularly so when the fundamentals of the nuclear regime have been safeguarded (to Washington and its allies' satisfaction) by Pretoria's middle power activity at the Review. In other words, and in keeping with problem-solving multilateralism in general, such policies seem to accept the immutability of the current world order and seeks to ameliorate its worse aspects, rather than promote debate regarding the future organising principles of a more equitable international order. Incremental change is the order of the day – a fundamentally pragmatic policy stance.

Yet, by doing so Pretoria opens itself up to criticism that it was duped by the NWS, particularly after the resumption of testing by France and China and Washington's indications that it wanted to renew underground testing. This all makes Pretoria's 'brilliant package' – the president of the conference, Sri Lanka's Jayantha Dhanapala's words – appear rather hollow.[94] As sources have put it, 'South Africa foolishly trusted the nuclear powers not to start testing',[95] and 'South Africa fears it [was] betrayed as one nuclear power after another [have] announce[d] plans to go ahead with nuclear testing'.[96]

Why Pretoria's newfound energies over the disarmament issue might be termed ironic is, as I have pointed out above, because it was South Africa that helped craft and deliver this very scenario. Pretoria now usefully uses this situation to posture a supposedly less accomodatory role but, at the final analysis, this is devoid of any real substance – South Africa constantly fails to bring up nuclear disarmament when its leaders pay visits to the NWS.[97] Indeed, Pretoria's nuclear policy lacks any potency to seriously undermine the existing nuclear order – rhetoric against NWS intransigence over disarmament notwithstanding.

By abandoning a principled position in pursuit of 'bridge-building' and 'consensus', South Africa's nuclear policy is now largely restricted to urging the nuclear powers to hold themselves accountable to the provisions of the NPT. But, with no time-bound agreement in place it is likely that this will occur only when the NWS decide for themselves that disarmament is the way to go, particularly as most NNWS consider their relations with the NWS as more important than pushing for nuclear disarmament. Therefore the question should be posed: how seriously do the NNWS want a nuclear free world since their actions seem to suggest that this is only a relatively minor consideration, compared to ensuring good relations with the NWS states on other issues? South Africa is no different.

Notes

1. Bischoff, P.-H. and Southall, R., 'The Early Foreign Policy of the Democratic South Africa' in Stephen Wright (ed.), *African Foreign Policies* (Boulder: Westview Press, 1999) p. 166.
2. Cox, R., 'Middlepowermanship, Japan and Future World Order', *International Journal*, 44:4 (1989) p. 825.
3. Nel, P., 'Approaches to Multilateralism', Paper presented at biennial conference of the South African Political Science Association, Saldanha, 29 June–2 July 1999, p. 6.
4. Cox, R., 'Social Forces, States, and World Orders: Beyond International Relations Theory' in Robert Keohane (ed.), *Neo-Realism and Its Critics* (New York: Columbia University Press, 1986), footnote 2: p. 249.
5. See *The United Nations and Nuclear Non-Proliferation* (New York: United Nations Department of Public Information, 1995).
6. Rathjens, G., 'Rethinking Nuclear Proliferation', *The Washington Quarterly*, 18:1 (1994) p. 181.
7. 'Treaty on the Non-Proliferation of Nuclear Weapons (1968)' in *United Nations Treaty Series*, 729:10485 (New York: United Nations, 1970).
8. Simpson, J. and Howlett, D., 'The NPT Renewal Conference: Stumbling Toward 1995', *International Security*, 19:1 (1994) pp. 41–71.
9. See Walker, W., 'Nuclear Weapons and the Former Soviet Republics', *International Affairs*, 68:2 (1992) pp. 255–77.
10. Paul Kennedy *The Rise and Fall of the Great Powers* (New York: Vintage Books, 1989) p. 505.
11. *Asian Age* (New Delhi, 14 August 2004).
12. Following talks with the United States, North Korea suspended its decision to pull out of the NPT in June 1993. In January 1994 the CIA estimated that North Korea may have produced one or two nuclear weapons. In January 2003 North Korea left the NPT.
13. See Walker, 'Nuclear Weapons and the Former Soviet Republics'.
14. The NPT stipulates that five years after its entry into force a review conference would be held. The first conference was in 1975 and it was decided thereafter that Review Conferences should be held every five years to review the implementation of the Treaty and to make proposals for strengthening the NPT and encourage all states to sign up to the NPT.
15. Moore, J.D.L., *South Africa and Nuclear Proliferation: South Africa's Nuclear Capabilities and Intentions in the Context of International Non-Proliferation Policies* (Basingstoke: Macmillan, 1987).
16. Howlett, D. and Simpson, J., 'Nuclearisation and De-nuclearisation in South Africa', *Survival*, 53:3 (1993) pp. 154–5.
17. Howlett, D. and Simpson, J., 'Nuclearisation and De-nuclearisation', p. 158.
18. *The Star* (Johannesburg, 14 November 1986).

19. See Cohen, A., *Israel and the Bomb* (New York: Columbia University Press, 1998).
20. *Sunday Independent* (Johannesburg, 4 May 1997).
21. Interview with senior official, Non-Proliferation and Nuclear Matters Directorate, Department of Foreign Affairs, Pretoria, 8 July 1999.
22. Burgess, S. and Purkitt. H., *The Rollback of South Africa's Chemical and Biological Warfare Program* (USAF Counterproliferation Center, Air War College, Maxwell Air Force Base, Alabama, 2001) p. 42.
23. Ibid.
24. Denis Goldberg 'A Nuclear Policy for a New Democratic South Africa', Paper presented at the ANC-Organised 'Nuclear Policy of the Democratic South Africa' conference, 11–13 February 1994.
25. Masiza, Z. and Landsberg, C., 'Fissions for Compliments: South Africa and the 1995 Extension of Nuclear Non-Proliferation', *Policy: Issues and Actors*, 9:3 (1996) p. 23.
26. State Department, 'A Declaration by the President on Security Assurances for Non-Nuclear Weapon States Parties to the Treaty on the Non-Proliferation of Nuclear Weapons' (Washington D.C.: State Department, 1995) available at http://www.acda.gov/factshee/wmd/nuclear/npt/nonucwp.htm
27. Collina, T. Z., 'South Africa Bridges the Gap', *Bulletin of Atomic Scientists* (July/August, 1995) p. 30.
28. Threshold states are countries developing or producing nuclear weapons for near-term deployment.
29. See Taylor, I., *Stuck in Middle GEAR: South Africa's Post-Apartheid Foreign Relations* (Westport, CT: Praeger, 2001).
30. Interview with senior official, Non-Proliferation and Nuclear Matters Directorate, Department of Foreign Affairs, Pretoria, 8 July 1999.
31. Masiza, Z. and Landsberg, C., 'Fission for Compliments: South Africa and the 1995 Extension of the Nuclear Non-Proliferation Treaty', *Policy: Issues and Actors*, 9:3 (1996) p. 23.
32. *Washington Post*, 17 April 1995.
33. Cirincione, J., 'Evaluation of the Nuclear Non-Proliferation Treaty Review and Extension Conference', Presentation to the Arms Control Association Breakfast, 17 May, 1995, http://www.stimson.org/campaign/aca.htm
34. *Cape Argus* (Cape Town, 19 April 1995).
35. Interview with senior official, Non-Proliferation and Nuclear Matters Directorate, Department of Foreign Affairs, Pretoria, 8 July 1999.
36. See *Mail and Guardian* (Johannesburg, 21–27 April 1995).
37. *Washington Post* (12 May 1999).
38. Department of Foreign Affairs, *South African Foreign Policy Discussion Document* (Pretoria: Department of Foreign Affairs, 1996) p. 12.
39. Beri, R., 'South Africa's Nuclear Policy', *Strategic Analysis: A Monthly Journal of the IDSA* (online journal), 22:7 (October 1998), available at http://www.idsa-india.org/an-oct8-2.html
40. See Howlett, D. and Simpson, J., 'Nuclearisation and De-nuclearisation in South Africa'.
41. *Cape Argus* (Cape Town, 19 April 1995).
42. *Business Day* (Johannesburg, 16 May 1995).

43. Interview with senior official, Non-Proliferation and Nuclear Matters Directorate, Department of Foreign Affairs, Pretoria, 8 July 1999.
44. Collina, T. Z., 'South Africa Bridges the Gap', p. 30.
45. *New York Times* (23 April 1995).
46. Alfred Nzo quoted in *Cape Times* (Cape Town, 21 May 1998).
47. Beri, 'South Africa's Nuclear Policy'.
48. *New York Times* (23 April 1995).
49. See Masiza, Z., *Hunting With the Hounds, Or Running With the Hares? South Africa and Nuclear Export Control Regimes* (Johannesburg: Foreign Policy Series, Policy: Issues and Actors, 11:5, 1998).
50. 'South Africa Offers Hope in NPT Talks', *Diplomatic World Bulletin*, 24–30 April 1995.
51. *Cape Argus* (Cape Town, 19 April 1995).
52. Simpson, J., 'The Birth of a New Era? The 1995 NPT Conference and the Politics of Nuclear Disarmament', *Security Dialogue*, 26:3 (1995) p. 249.
53. Interview with Zondi Masiza, policy analyst, Centre for Policy Studies, Johannesburg, 9 July 1999.
54. Interview with senior official, Non-Proliferation and Nuclear Matters Directorate, Department of Foreign Affairs, Pretoria, 8 July 1999.
55. Abdul Minty quoted in *Mail and Guardian* (Johannesburg, 23 June 1995).
56. *Mail and Guardian* (Johannesburg, 28 April–4 May 1995).
57. *New York Times*, 12 May 1995.
58. Interview with senior official, Non-Proliferation and Nuclear Matters Directorate, Department of Foreign Affairs, Pretoria, 8 July 1999.
59. Alfred Nzo quoted in *Cape Times* (Cape Town, 21 May 1998).
60. Simpson 'The Birth of a New Era?', p. 247.
61. Cox 'Middlepowermanship', p. 826.
62. *Business Day* (Johannesburg, 16 May 1995).
63. Breytenbach, W., 'South-North Bargaining: What Role for South Africa', *Africa Insight*, 25:4 (1995) p. 231.
64. Joseph Cirincione 'Evaluation of the Nuclear Non-Proliferation Treaty Review and Extension Conference', Presentation to the Arms Control Association Breakfast, 17 May 1995, available at http://www.stimson.org/campaign/aca.htm
65. Motumi, T., 'South Africa and the Nuclear Non-Proliferation Treaty – Diplomatic Coup or Pyrrhic Victory?', *African Security Review*, 4:2 (1995) p. 46.
66. *The Sowetan* (Johannesburg, 26 August 1997).
67. Interview with senior official, Non-Proliferation and Nuclear Matters Directorate, Department of Foreign Affairs, Pretoria, 8 July 1999.
68. *Washington Post* (12 May 1995).
69. Nzo, A., 'Statement by the Foreign Minister of the Republic of South Africa, Mr Alfred Nzo, at the 1995 Review and Extension Conference of the Parties to the Treaty on the Non-Proliferation of Nuclear weapons (NPT)', New York, United States, 19 April 1995, Issued by the Department of Foreign Affairs.
70. *Mail and Guardian* (Johannesburg, 21–27 April 1995).
71. Beri, 'South Africa's Nuclear Policy'.
72. Ibid.
73. See Cornish's argument in *Pretoria News* (Pretoria, 11 May 1995).
74. *Mail and Guardian* (Johannesburg, 29 April–4 May 1995).

75. Interview with Zondi Masiza, policy analyst, Centre for Policy Studies, Johannesburg, 9 July 1999.
76. *The Star* (Johannesburg, 15 May 1995).
77. *Business Day* (Johannesburg, 16 May 1995).
78. Simpson 'The Birth of a New Era?', p. 252.
79. *Business Day* (Johannesburg, 16 May 1995).
80. *Washington Post* (12 May 1995).
81. Pande, S., 'Post-NPT Extension: Nuclear Non-Proliferation Challenges', *Strategic Analysis: A Monthly Journal of the IDSA* (online journal), 21:9 (December 1997), available at http://www.idsa-india.org/an-dec-2.html
82. Interview with Zondi Masiza, policy analyst, Centre for Policy Studies, Johannesburg, 9 July 1999.
83. 'Nzo Reaffirms Call for Nuclear Disarmament', Pretoria, 28 September 1998, Issued by Department of Foreign Affairs.
84. The Irish Foreign Minister referred to the eight-nation declaration as a process of 'warming up something that's gone cold', quoted in *South African Press Agency* (New York, 23 September 1998).
85. *South Africa Press Agency* (Pretoria, 21 May 1999).
86. 'Media Statement on South Africa's Ratification of the Comprehensive Test-Ban Treaty (CTBT)', Pretoria, 30 March 1999, Issued by Department of Foreign Affairs.
87. Roche, D., 'An Analysis of the Second Preparatory Committee Meeting for the 2000 Review of the Non-Proliferation Treaty', available at http://waterserv1.uwaterloo.ca/~plough/98prepcom.htm, Accessed 12 July 2002.
88. Statement by Abdul Minty, Deputy Director-General Multilateral Affairs, South Africa, New York, 24 April 2000.
89. Statement to the NPT 2000 Review Conference by H.E. Mr. Abdul S. Minty, Deputy Director-General Multilateral Affairs, South Africa, New York, 24 April 2000.
90. 'Media Statement on South Africa's Signature of Agreement of the Comprehensive Test-Ban Treaty ', Pretoria, 21 May 1999, Issued by Department of Foreign Affairs on behalf of the SA Permanent Mission to the CTBT PrepCom, Vienna.
91. *The Sowetan* (Johannesburg, 26 August 1997).
92. *The Sowetan* (Johannesburg, 20 August 1996).
93. *The Sowetan* (Johannesburg, 26 August 1997).
94. Dhanapala is said to have 'immediately seized upon the South African position and heavily promoted it', motivated, according to one analyst, by a desire to advance his diplomatic career – interview with Zondi Masiza, policy analyst, Centre for Policy Studies, Johannesburg, 9 July 1999.
95. Ibid.
96. *The Star* (Johannesburg, 23 June 1995).
97. *The Sowetan* (Johannesburg, 20 August 1996).

8
Pragmatic Multilateralism?
South Africa and Peace
Operations

Paul D. Williams

> The cornerstone of our foreign policy will be to end conflicts peacefully, to achieve a new world order that is more equitable and people-centred and to create conditions for sustainable development. This demands that we strengthen and not weaken multilateralism.
>
> Deputy-Minister Aziz Pahad, Response to
> State of the Nation Address, 18 February 2003.[1]

Unfortunately, the sort of vague rhetoric expressed by Pahad raises more questions than it answers. How exactly can South Africa end Africa's wars? In which forums should South Africa strengthen its commitment to multilateralism? Upon what principles and values will Pretoria's multilateralism rest? And if the official answer is neoliberal principles, how will this produce 'more equitable' and 'sustainable development' when the weight of evidence suggests that such policies have the opposite effects?[2] On one point at least, Pahad is clear: the choice facing the ANC government is whether to strengthen or weaken its commitment to multilateralism not, as is frequently assumed, to choose between adopting either multilateral *or* unilateral policies. Multilateralism is an unavoidable part of living in what Hedley Bull described as an 'anarchical society'. The South African government thus has no choice but to work with others to achieve its objectives.[3] Consequently, the most important practical questions include what forms of multilateralism should Mbeki's government pursue, in what forums should it pursue them, and what objectives is Pretoria's mulitlateralism intended to achieve?

As discussed in the Introduction to this volume, rationalist definitions of multilateralism in academic International Relations have focused upon state-to-state diplomacy.[4] In contrast, neo-Gramscian thinkers have highlighted some of the limitations of state-centric discussions of multilateralism and the ways in which, in practice, multilateral forums tend to reinforce the hegemonic norms of the existing world order.[5] Analysing peace operations and issues of war and peace in contemporary Africa also highlight at least two limitations of the rationalist agenda. First, focusing on issues of peacekeeping and conflict resolution highlights how important it is not to exclude non-state actors from discussions of multilateralism. Ending Africa's wars requires would-be mediators to engage with a wide variety of non-state actors, including local civic associations, INGOs, private corporations and rebel insurgents. As a result, this chapter endorses the conclusion reached by Nel, Taylor and van der Westhuizen that any new multilateral architecture will be unsustainable if it disregards the significance of non-state actors.[6] At least with regard to peace operations, therefore, Pretoria should seek out suitable transnational actors and local civic associations as potential allies in the struggle to end the continent's wars and support those non-state groups who seek recognition and political representation in the continent's war zones through non-violent means.

A second limitation is the way in which rationalist approaches to multilateralism – and the United Nation's (UN) approach to conflict resolution and peacebuilding – have been wedded to liberal assumptions about the relationship between politics and economics, the underlying harmony of interests between states and other actors, and – in relation to warfare – the assumption that war is an irrational activity and hence the belligerents will have an obvious interest in terminating the violence.

These assumptions are problematic for at least two reasons. First, they downplay the logical conclusion that taking multilateralism seriously in international politics should require efforts to engineer transformative rather than reformist policies, including moves towards reducing the many stark inequalities of the current world order.[7] Second, the hurried international attempts to turn war-shattered states into market democracies has at times had the unintended effect of exacerbating social and political tensions and thus increased the likelihood that violence will re-ignite.[8] Given Mbeki's support for the market-driven agenda that underpins both the NEPAD and his vision of an African Renaissance, this argument, which I find persuasive, has important implications for South Africa's approach to peace operations.

I explore the challenges thrown up by South Africa's approach to peace operations in four parts. The first section briefly summarises two contemporary debates about international peacekeeping relevant to Pretoria's situation. The second and third sections describe Pretoria's peacekeeping philosophy and its practical participation in peace operations focusing on its missions in Lesotho, the Democratic Republic of Congo (DRC) and Burundi. The final section reflects upon the main challenges that have emerged from Pretoria's current agenda. To preempt the argument somewhat, peace operations present Mbeki's government with several difficult challenges. Arguably the most immediate problem is that the SANDF has reached (or is nearing) breaking point with its peacekeeping commitments in Burundi and the DRC, and its attempts to help the South African police force maintain law and order at home. Yet partly because South Africa is the continent's major military and economic power and partly because Mbeki has vociferously championed the African Renaissance and NEPAD initiatives and made no secret of his desire to obtain a permanent seat at the UN Security Council, Pretoria needs to be seen to play a leading role in ending Africa's wars. This, in turn, exacerbates the strain on Pretoria's resources and lends credence to those suspicious of the motives behind South Africa's Africa policy (see also Chapter 5). Of course, peace operations alone cannot solve the continent's problems but they provide one important mechanism with which to encourage the stability necessary for more peaceful and just orders to flourish. In the short term at least, as Lieutenant-General Siphiwe Nyanda put it, 'There can be no "African Renaissance" without the military'.[9]

Contemporary debates in international peacekeeping

Two important debates are currently shaping the nature of peace operations across the globe. One concerns the political purpose of peace operations while the other is about which entities can legitimately authorise them. Both of these debates have a direct bearing on peace operations in Africa, which is where South African peacekeepers have primarily been engaged.

First, there is an ongoing debate between those who see the role of peace operations in global politics in Westphalian terms and those who see it in more ambitious, post-Westphalian terms.[10] Both conceptions support ideas about the broadly positive relationship between liberalism and peace. Supporters of Westphalian notions of peacekeeping, such as the governments of China, Russia, India and many – although by no means all – developing states, argue that it should focus on facilitating the peaceful settlement of disputes and orderly relations *between* states.[11]

From this perspective, the ideological persuasion and political organisation of states and the societies within them should not concern peacekeepers, so long as states subscribe to the Westphalian norms of sovereign autonomy and non-intervention and do not upset international order. The post-Westphalian conception of peacekeeping, whose most vociferous supporters include Western states such as the United Kingdom (UK), Canada and France as well as NGOs such as Human Rights Watch and the International Crisis Group, suggests that liberal relations between states ultimately require liberal-democratic societies within states, because the way that a particular state conducts its international affairs is inextricably connected to the nature of its domestic society. Threats to international peace and security are thus not limited to acts of aggression between states but may also result from violent conflict and illiberal governance within them. Consequently, understood in post-Westphalian terms, peace operations should not be limited to maintaining order *between* states but instead take on the much more ambitious task of ensuring peace and security *within* states. In the medium- to long-term this is to be achieved by creating liberal democratic polities, economies and societies within states that have recently experienced, or are undergoing, violent conflict. In practice, peace operations guided by these post-Westphalian principles have been committed to implanting the seeds of liberal-democratic statehood in war zones.

As discussed below with respect to the cases of Lesotho, the DRC and Burundi, Pretoria's current philosophy on peace operations shares a great deal with the post-Westphalian view, although this does not rule out its participation in or support for more traditional missions, such as the UN Mission in Ethiopia and Eritrea (UNMEE). The struggle between the Westphalian and post-Westphalian approaches to peace operations is also reminiscent of – and to some extent mirrors – the ongoing struggle within Africa to define the hegemonic values guiding pan-African projects such as the African Renaissance, the NEPAD and the African Union (AU). In this struggle two blocs of states have emerged. The first has been referred to as a revisionist/reformist bloc (including South Africa, Nigeria, Algeria, Egypt, Ghana, Botswana, Mozambique and Tanzania). On paper at least, this bloc has signed up to liberal and market-led visions of politics in Africa exemplified by the NEPAD. In contrast, a counter-revisionist bloc led by Libya, but including Zimbabwe, Côte d'Ivoire, Guinea, Burkina Faso and Swaziland, has emerged and been defined by its resistance to 'substantive democratic change' on the continent.[12]

The second ongoing debate is concerned with which international bodies can legitimately authorise peace operations. Since the end of the Cold War, the main contenders have been the UN Security Council, regional arrangements and ad hoc coalitions of states.[13] There is even an NGO, the Henry Dunant Centre for Humanitarian Dialogue, running an unarmed civilian peace operation in Aceh, Indonesia. In South Africa's case, its primary legal and political obligations with regard to peace-keeping are within the UN, the AU and the Southern African Development Community (SADC), as well as to its own citizens. Not surprisingly therefore, South Africa's troops, police and civilian experts have participated in peace operations authorised by the UN Security Council and the AU, and (as discussed below) in operations where it is not entirely clear whether they were authorised by Pretoria alone or under SADC auspices. As the three cases analysed here illustrate, Pretoria's recent experiences involve diverse notions of which entities can legitimately authorise peace operations.

The successive ANC governments have all consistently suggested that where peace operations are concerned their primary obligations and responsibilities fall within Africa in general and Southern Africa in particular. It is thus important to briefly examine how these debates have influenced current trends in peacekeeping in Africa. Here four points are worth making. First, since the end of the Cold War, Africa has witnessed an increase in peace operations authorised and undertaken by regional organisations.[14] These have included five by ECOWAS (two in Liberia and one each in Sierra Leone, Guinea-Bissau and Côte d'Ivoire), two (in Lesotho and the DRC) ostensibly under the mantle of SADC, one by the Economic and Monetary Community of Central African States in the Central African Republic, and two by the AU in Burundi and Darfur, Sudan. South Africa played a leading role in operations in Lesotho and Burundi.

Second, since the death of 18 US soldiers in Mogadishu, Somalia in October 1993, the so-called P-3 states (France, the UK and the US) have contributed very few of their own soldiers to UN peace operations on the African continent – in August 2004 the P-3 states had deployed just 215 troops, 186 of which were in the French contingent of UN operation in Côte d'Ivoire (UNOCI). These states have deployed troops to Africa for a variety of reasons since 1993 (including for non-combatant evacuation missions, humanitarian operations and combat operations) but they have done so primarily outside UN command and control structures. Instead, the P-3 states have been powerful advocates of the idea that Africans should take primary responsibility for containing, policing and solving wars in their own continent. As a result, each of the P-3 states designed their own programmes to support the development of African peacekeeping capacities under the mantra of 'African solutions to African problems'. The US proposed a series of initiatives including the African Response Force, the African Crisis Response Initiative and African Contingency Operations Training Assistance; the UK developed the African Peacekeeping Training Support Programme and sent a BMATT to South Africa, which by 2004 was slimmed down and focused to a 40-strong Peace Support Team; and France offered Africans RECAMP (*Renforcement des capacities Africaines de maintien de la paix*).

Third, despite constant pleas for resources concomitant to UN peace operations in the Balkans, for instance, most peace operations in Africa continue to lack adequate human or financial resources and have been downsized in their planning stages by the great powers at the UN Security Council. In August 2004, for instance, UN peace operations in Africa were understaffed by 13,175 personnel (calculated by subtracting the numbers of personnel deployed from the authorised strength of the operation). Finally, although more traditional types of peacekeeping can be found in Western Sahara and Ethiopia/Eritrea, most contemporary peace operations in Africa have taken place in environments where there are numerous belligerent parties acting as spoiler groups; consent is at best variable and tenuous, and more often than not warfare is ongoing.[15] As a consequence, Africa more than most continents needs multidimensional peace operations involving military, political, humanitarian and judicial components. These need to be capable of both managing precarious political transitions based on fragile peace agreements and of defeating spoiler groups that have vested interests in prolonging the violence.

Pretoria's peace operations philosophy

Since 1994, many states both inside and outside Africa have expected Pretoria to play a leading role in keeping the peace on its continent. But until the very end of the 1990s it was unprepared in political, financial and human terms to undertake anything but the most limited of missions such as providing four observers to the Bosnian operations, nine engineers to MONUA in Angola and various logistic contributions to UN operations such as UNAVEM II and III and ONUMOZ. By the end of the decade, however, Pretoria had pledged to join the UN's Standby Arrangements System was developing a National Office for the Co-ordination of Peace Missions,[16] and had provided approximately

6000 soldiers and 15 foreign affairs officials with training in peacekeeping, conflict resolution and civil military relations.[17]

In the absence of much direct peacekeeping experience until relatively recently, South Africa's philosophy on the subject has been heavily influenced by the country's own recent history of conflict resolution. However, external events have also played their part.[18] The first significant event was US Secretary of State Warren Christopher's visit to drum up support for the US proposal of creating an African Crisis Response Force. However, the South African armed forces were preoccupied with their own internal reconfiguration, and peacekeeping remained well down their agenda. The second event was the government's rather lethargic reaction to the crisis in the refugee camps in eastern Zaire in 1996. Although the Canadian proposal calling for a Multinational Force to be deployed to the area failed to materialise, this was not before South Africa had been approached to contribute to the force. As it turned out, the Department of Foreign Affairs (DFA) supported the idea whereas the Ministry of Defence was much less keen, arguing that South Africa's troops were not trained for such an operation and that the public may not tolerate the casualties that might result.

It was against this backdrop that the Ministries of Foreign Affairs and Defence, and the intelligence community initiated a process to develop South Africa's position on what they preferred to call 'peace missions'.[19] After some initial criticism from outside government, the process was later broadened to include a small number of NGOs and groups within civil society.[20] The results emerged in October 1998 as the *White Paper on South African Participation in International Peace Missions*, which was accepted by parliament the following year.

Several aspects of the *White Paper* are worth mentioning as they provide the philosophical rationale for Pretoria's engagement in peace operations.

1. The document emphasised that it was in South Africa's national interest to participate in such operations, 'when properly authorised by international authorities' (section 4.2).
2. Within the SANDF, peace operations are understood as a secondary function compared with the primary task of defending the South African state. As a consequence the armed forces did not create dedicated structures for peace operations but performed them in an ad hoc manner within primary force structures, for instance, through the army's Rapid Deployment Ground Force. The earlier Defence Review stated that where core national interests are not threatened,

only two battalion groups should be prepared for peace operations with only one on active duty in such missions at any given time. Where Chapter VII operations are required, these forces may be augmented by mechanised and parachute forces (section 5.4).[21]

3. Principles were established for South Africa's participation in peace operations including a clear international mandate, sufficient means, a domestic mandate and budget, volunteerism, clear entry and exit criteria, regional cooperation, and foreign assistance (section 6.1). What exactly constituted a 'clear international mandate' was left rather vague as to whether it needed to be authorised by the UN, the AU and SADC or just one of the three. At home, parliament was supposed to play a significant role in ensuring that any participation in peace operations had a domestic mandate. In practice, however, real authority to authorise and deploy peace operations has lain with the president's office with parliament doing little more than legitimising deployments after the fact.[22]

4. Importantly, the *White Paper* emphasised the need to counter 'unrealistic expectations of South Africa's potential role in third-party interventions' (section 1.1).

5. The document warned against the dominance of a single nationality in any given peace operation as this could weaken the mission's legitimacy (section 2.4).

6. Finally, the *White Paper* acknowledged the importance of peacebuilding and the need to address the root causes of violent conflict rather than just its symptoms.

Despite this elaborate attempt to offer a clear conceptual rationale and a set of principles for South African peacekeeping, the practice has not been nearly as neat as the theory.

Pretoria's participation in peace operations

Although the ANC's first major peace operation abroad took place in 1998, South Africa is one of the few states to have conducted a peace operation within its own borders. The idea for a national peacekeeping force (NPKF) emerged from a variety of civic associations who feared that violence might erupt during the transition process, especially in the East Rand, and because the South African Police were widely seen as being unfair instruments of white power.[23] Despite the potential complications of establishing a home-grown force, the idea of foreigners policing South African streets was viewed as neither necessary nor desirable. As it turned out, the process of assembling the NPKF required its architects to engage in multilateralism of sorts inasmuch as it involved the government ensuring cooperation between two traditional adversaries, the South African Defence Force and Mkhonto we Sizwe South Africans were also given a first-hand introduction to some of the perennial problems of command and control that face commanders of UN peace operations as the NPKF included troops from five armies and nine police forces and received external training from experts from France and the Commonwealth. Despite the government's best efforts the public quickly became disillusioned with the NPKF because of a number of so-called teething problems (racism, insubordination, desertion, violence, criminality and strikes); its deployment to the East Rand in April 1994 was little short of shambolic; it suffered a hostile welcome from Inkatha supporters, including stone throwing and gun battles which resulted in local fatalities; and in practice, there was much confusion as to whether the force's mandate was peacekeeping or peace enforcement. The NPKF was disbanded on 2 June.

This episode provides some important clues about the limitations of peace operations: they are extremely difficult to conduct effectively, even with good local knowledge; they require skills that take time to learn and are notoriously difficult to apply in practice; the consent and support of large sections of the local population is necessary to avoid a peace operation simply becoming an additional belligerent; they are costly; and they are unavoidably political. Despite these first-hand experiences of the challenges involved, Pretoria has felt obliged to engage in a variety of peace operations on the African continent.

Since 1998, South Africa has played a leading role in five major peace operations in three different countries, namely, Lesotho, the DRC and Burundi. The fact that Pretoria has focused its peacekeeping efforts in its own backyard, the wider southern African region and the Great Lakes reflects the way in which the Mandela and Mbeki governments both prioritised the search for peace in 'its' region and Africa as a whole.

Lesotho

On 22 September 1998, approximately 600 SANDF troops crossed into Lesotho on the instructions of the acting state president Chief Mangosuthu Buthelezi. They were deployed to quell the violence that had erupted between supporters of the Lesotho Congress for Democracy (LCD) and opposition parties. The LCD's opponents claimed the May elections were fraudulent and a commission headed by South African Judge Pius Langa was established to investigate any electoral irregularities. However, when the Langa Report was eventually released on 17 September its conclusions were rather ambiguous and only fuelled rather than quelled the violence in Lesotho.[24] Consequently, the LCD's opponents continued their aggressive protests and urged King Letsie III to dissolve the newly elected Parliament and install a government of national unity. On 23 September a further 300 troops arrived from Botswana to support the SANDF contingent. The foreign soldiers arrived in response to an appeal made by Lesotho's prime minister, Pakalitha Mosisili. Fearing a military coup was imminent, Mosisili had appealed to the four states which had sponsored the Langa Commission (South Africa, Botswana, Mozambique and Zimbabwe) for assistance. With the addition of Mozambique, the other three states made up the troika that had been established by the OAU and SADC to deal with the repercussions of the 1994 coup when King Letsie III and part of the army overthrew the government of Dr Ntsu Mokhehle. After the 1994 coup the troika oversaw the production of a Memorandum of Understanding that left them as the de facto guarantors of democracy in Lesotho. Some analysts have claimed it was on the basis of this Memorandum that Mosisili had appealed for assistance.[25]

In spite of what was code named Operation Boleas, the violence, looting and destruction of property continued. In response, South Africa despatched a further 450 troops to Lesotho on 27 September. The final casualty figures suggested the fighting resulted in the deaths of 9 South African soldiers, 58 Lesotho Defence Force soldiers and 47 civilians. It also resulted in over 4000 refugees and expatriates fleeing to South Africa.[26] By the end of September order was restored but not before much of Maseru's business district (and parts of neighbouring Mafateng and Mohale's Hoek) had been reduced to rubble. Pretoria subsequently deployed nearly 4000 troops to Lesotho where they stayed until the end of 1994.

Operation Boleas was notable for several reasons. First and foremost, resort to the military instrument represents a clear failure of preventive diplomacy and a collective regional failure to address the sources of disaffection and exclusion within Lesotho.[27] Second, Boleas attracted much criticism for its bungled initial stages (especially the poor intelligence and the insufficient numbers of troops deployed in the first instance) and the degree of suffering caused to the citizens of Lesotho.[28] The legal and political justifications for the operation also proved controversial. At the time, Boleas was justified on the grounds of a draft SADC policy position that urged against permitting unconstitutional changes of government. In South Africa, however, several senior parliamentarians were excluded from the decision-making process. Internationally, the operation also found itself without a clear authorising organisation. Boleas was clearly not authorised by either the UN Security Council or the OAU. And despite South African claims to the contrary, nor was it authorised by SADC, since this could only have been done at the level of a SADC summit and no such summit took place. At the time, the newly developing Organ on Politics, Defence and Security (set up to deal with precisely such issues) was ineffectual owing to disagreements over its nature and purpose between South African- and Zimbabwean-led blocs within SADC.[29] Hence, while Pretoria claimed it had intervened to support a democratically elected government in the spirit of the 1994 Memorandum of Understanding, the government's critics saw Boleas as an operation devised, led and authorised by Pretoria to protect not only its interests and investments in the tiny mountain kingdom but also its dominant status within wider regional politics.[30]

The Democratic Republic of Congo

The war that has raged on-and-off in the DRC since August 1998 is commonly thought responsible for the deaths of over three million people and involved armed forces from eight external states.[31] But it was not until November 1999, under Security Council Resolution (SCR) 1279 that the UN authorised MONUC to oversee and assist in the implementation of the Lusaka Accords, which the war's major belligerents had signed in mid-1999. In February 2000 under SCR 1291, MONUC was authorised to expand to over 5500 military personnel. These were to be deployed with a Chapter VII mandate in accordance with the phased implementation of the Lusaka Accords. In practice, however, the planned timetable was disrupted as fighting continued in spite of the Lusaka peace process. Following the continued fighting and massacre of civilians around the town of Bunia in the eastern Ituri district of the DRC, MONUC was authorised to expand to 10,800 military personnel (although by March 2004 only some 10,200 had actually arrived in the DRC). In August 2004, Kofi Annan recommended that MONUC should be expanded from 10,800 to 23,900 personnel and its civilian police component be increased to 507 personnel.[32] On 1 October, however, Security Council Resolution 1565 authorised only a further 5900 personnel, including 341 civilian police.

Given the importance both the Mandela and Mbeki governments have attached to building a peaceful southern African region, it was hardly surprising that Pretoria's representatives would become heavily involved in mediation in the DRC. As Aziz Pahad warned in November

1996, there is no 'Great Wall' to protect South Africans from the negative repercussions of the war.[33] There are of course many reasons why South Africa would welcome peace in the DRC but at least part of Pretoria's motivation revolved around the commercial potential of the country's vast natural resources. Such commercial interests also help explain why South Africa was keen for the DRC to join SADC, which it did in 1997. Despite the continuing violence, commercial opportunities have attracted a variety of South African multinationals to the DRC. Fourteen such companies, including Anglo-American, De Beers, ISCOR, Saracen, Banro and Mercantille CC, gained notoriety for their activities in the DRC when they were named by the *UN Report of the Panel of Experts on the Illegal Exploitation of Natural Resources and Other Forms of Wealth in the DRC* (2002) as having violated the ethical guidelines on corporate accountability and human rights formulated by the Organisation of Economic Cooperation and Development. A more positive example is the South African cellular phone company Vodacom which invested nearly $40 m in Congolese Wireless Network and has attracted 22,000 customers with a license until 2020.[34] In addition, Afrikaner businesses have also been eager to pursue investment opportunities in the DRC as part of their own 'Afrikaner-renaissance'.[35] But whatever role Mbeki envisages for private actors in helping to achieve South Africa's foreign policy objectives, it is also clear that while the war in the DRC persists there will be little hope of attracting the sort of foreign investment needed to realise his vision of an African Renaissance or the NEPAD.

Pretoria's mediation started in 1996 when the government tried to broker agreements between President Mobutu and Laurent Kabila.[36] These efforts intensified after Mobutu was overthrown and Pretoria pushed for the DRC's inclusion within SADC. They intensified still further when Mbeki assumed the presidency – indeed, Mbeki's first day in office was taken up with the subject of conflict resolution in the DRC and the new minister of foreign affairs, Nkosazana Dlamini-Zuma, ranked the war as her top priority.

However, despite the flurry of diplomatic activity South Africa remained unwilling to participate in MONUC, preferring mediation to peacekeeping. It was not until April 2001 that South Africa sent 150 technical personnel to participate in MONUC. At this stage, Pretoria's diplomatic strategy revolved around persuading Zimbabwe and Rwanda to pull their soldiers out of the DRC. Following Laurent Kabila's assassination in early 2001, Mbeki tried to persuade his son Joseph that establishing an inter-Congolese Dialogue within South Africa would be a positive way forward. The Dialogue eventually began in Sun City in late February 2002 but in the luxurious surroundings the participants took 80 days to hammer out a shaky agreement. Arguably the major breakthrough, however, came when South Africa played an important role in persuading Rwanda and Uganda to withdraw their soldiers from the DRC. In August 2002 Rwanda agreed to withdrawal in exchange for the authorities in Kinshasa taking effective action against the Interahamwe and ex-Rwandan government forces hiding in the DRC. The next important breakthrough came in Cape Town on 8 April 2003 when Yoweri Museveni was persuaded to withdraw his troops from Ituri by 24 April. The withdrawal was to be monitored by South Africa's Third Party Verification Mechanism, working alongside the UN. However, with a staff of just 20 this was hopelessly overstretched. In June 2003, over 1300 additional South African troops were deployed to Ituri as part of a reinvigorated MONUC at a cost to the South African tax-payer of R619m ($78m). This followed the withdrawal of Ugandan troops from this area and coincided with the arrival of a French-led Interim Emergency Multinational Force (IEMF) to the eastern town of Bunia.[37] The fact that the IEMF withdrew in September led many people to concur with Museveni's description of these peacekeepers as 'dangerous tourists'.[38] The IEMF was gradually replaced by MONUC peacekeepers, mainly from Uruguay. By April 2004, Pretoria had just under 1450 personnel participating in MONUC and until renewed fighting broke out around the town of Bukavu in June 2004 there were tentative signs that an end to the war might be in sight.

Burundi

In October 1993, Burundi's elected president, Melchior Ndadaye, was killed along with the next two officials in line to succeed to the presidency. The coup sparked sporadic waves of violence between the minority Tutsi and majority Hutu population that have claimed between 250,000–300,000 lives, mainly civilians.[39] Although the UN Security Council deployed a small number of civilian observers it refused to offer military assistance to the stricken country.[40] Consequently, African initiatives were the main source of external mediation, primarily the Regional Peace Initiative on Burundi, the personal mediation efforts of Julius Nyerere and (from November 1999) Nelson Mandela, the South African Protection Support Detachment (SAPSD, 2001–2003) and the African Union's Mission in Burundi (AMIB, 2003–2004). On 1 June 2004, the UN Operation in Burundi (ONUB) took over from AMIB signalling the UN's return after more than a decade of refusing to deploy its peacekeepers to the stricken country.

South Africa's involvement in Burundi's civil war began in earnest in November 1999 when Nelson Mandela succeeded the late Julius Nyerere as the primary external mediator. Despite accusations of pro-Hutu bias and strong-arming President Pierre Buyoya into accepting his preferred terms, on 28 August 2000, Mandela successfully helped negotiate the Arusha agreement. Six months later, Mandela announced a more concrete three-year peace process that involved power-sharing between Tutsi (G10) and Hutu (G7) political parties. However, several rebel groups, most notably Pierre Nkurunziza's Forces for the Defence of Democracy (CNDD-FDD) and Agathon Rwasa's National Liberation Front (FNL), were not invited. Consequently, the peace process saw only a minimal reduction in the fighting.[41]

In an attempt to get the peace process back on track, Mandela unilaterally called for South African troops to form part of a VIP protection operation to help guard 26 Hutu politicians (mainly from Frodebu) who had returned from exile and were anxious about the predominantly Tutsi army.[42] In October 2001, 30 South African police arrived as reconnaissance for a larger South African force. Initially, they faced some local hostility and had to be protected by Burundian gendarmes. But shortly afterwards, some 750 SANDF troops arrived in Burundi tasked with protecting the VIPs and training a local, multi-ethnic VIP protection force.

The SAPSD was Mandela's personal initiative. The force was not authorised by the UN Security Council, nor did it have an explicit peacekeeping mandate to intervene in the civil war – the troops were to evacuate should the hostilities resume in earnest and they become targets. However, several factors imbued the operation with a high degree of legitimacy. First, with the occasional exceptions of France and Belgium, since the 1993 coup the UN Security Council had consistently signalled it would not send peacekeepers to Burundi. Mandela's (and Nyerere's) efforts were thus widely seen as helping the Council deflect criticism that it was ignoring Burundi's conflict. Second, the Security Council strongly endorsed the SAPSD only a few days after its deployment.[43] Finally, the SAPSD was deployed at the request of Burundi's government.

The question of whether the mission accomplished its mandate is more problematic, however. Despite the South African presence, the security and humanitarian situations in Burundi continued to worsen throughout 2002.[44] However, on 2 December another ceasefire agreement was signed in Arusha between Burundi's Transitional Government and the CNDD-FDD. This included provision for an African mission to monitor the ceasefire, supervise the cantonment of fighters and ensure the two sides observed commitments to halt arms shipments, free political prisoners and withdraw foreign troops. Speaking in the Security Council shortly after this agreement, South Africa's Deputy President, Jacob Zuma, suggested that the envisaged African force was a practical example of Chapter VIII of the UN Charter in action and would 'act as a bridging instrument, opening the situation for the UN to come in when we have perfected the conditions'.[45] Zuma's argument was later endorsed by the Security Council, which subsequently called for donors to help set up the African mission as soon as possible in liaison with the UN.[46]

Following discussions with the UN about the mandate, financing and logistics of the SAPSD force, in February 2003, AU heads of state approved their first armed peace operation. In April over 900 SANDF troops were deployed to Burundi as part of the AU Mission in Burundi (AMIB) for an initial period of one year.[47] As well as the tasks set out in the Arusha Agreement, AMIB was also mandated to support the delivery of humanitarian assistance and the disarmament, demobilisation and reintegration (DDR) process. At the end of April, the AU appointed Mamadou Bah as head of AMIB and on 1 May the SAPSD was integrated into AMIB becoming its advance party. However, for several months the South African troops were forced to operate without the Ethiopian and Mozambican contingents, which arrived in late September and mid-October respectively. Both states cited concerns about the fragility of Burundi's ceasefire and a lack of funds as reasons for their late arrival.[48] By December 2003 AMIB's strength stood at 2645 troops.[49]

AMIB quickly faced military, political and financial problems. In military terms, it could not avoid being caught up in the civil war. Almost immediately after its arrival, Burundi's capital, Bujumbura, suffered heavy shelling in April and July from CNDD-FDD and Rwasa's FNL troops respectively. And on 30 June, AMIB troops killed four CNDD-FDD rebels while defending their cantonment zone in Muyange (the zone was not attacked again). Conversely, earlier that month South African troops stood by and watched CNDD-FDD militia kill one person and loot houses and shops in the town of Burumata, much to the anger of locals.[50] However, after AMIB's arrival, and especially after the signing of the two Pretoria Protocols,[51] the CNDD-FDD joined the peace process and politically motivated violence did decrease – only to be replaced by violence of a more criminal nature.[52] AMIB also faced enormous difficulties in trying to disarm approximately 70,000 rebel fighters. Not only were several factions reluctant to participate, many individuals and splinter groups remained intent on keeping their weapons, and even by September 2003 AMIB lacked the resources to meet the basic needs of approximately 200 ex-combatants gathered at the Muyange

Demobilization Centre.[53] In addition, AMIB lacked a finalised disarmament, demobilisation and reintegration plan as late as November 2003 (including no clear definition of a combatant) and the World Bank was also reluctant to provide funding for DDR because the December 2002 ceasefire arrangements allowed the CNDD-FDD troops to keep their weapons in the cantonment zones.[54]

Politically, AMIB became entangled in international differences over how best to resolve the civil war. Specifically, Uganda and Tanzania objected to the strategy supported by the UN, the AU, Rwanda, Burundi and South Africa.[55] This prompted Zuma to question the Ugandan and Tanzanian role in supplying various factions (especially the CNDD-FDD) and object to Ugandan or Tanzanian troops being deployed as part of AMIB.[56] AMIB also faced serious financial difficulties. As Mamadou Bah pointed out in late 2003, of the $120m required to fund AMIB's operations for a year, only $20m had been made available.[57] In addition, the 2003 Consolidated Appeal for Burundi has received only $21m of the promised $72m of non-food assistance.[58]

On balance, however, AMIB did contribute to a far more stable security situation in Burundi than which existed upon its arrival. Indeed, by the end of 2003 Zuma considered the situation stable enough to ask the UN to take over from the AMIB as set out in the Arusha agreement and the AU's Addis Ababa communiqué which had created the force.[59] After a period of vacillation owing to the precarious nature of Burundi's peace process, in May 2004 the UN SCR 1545 authorised ONUB to take over from AMIB. The handover took place on 2 June. ONUB was placed under the command of South African Major General Derrick Mgweti and was given an authorised strength of 5650 with contingents expected from Angola, Nepal and Pakistan (although by August only 3322 personnel had actually been deployed).

Despite some disagreements within the AU, AMIB was widely seen as a legitimate operation, although strictly speaking it conducted enforcement activities without UN Security Council authorisation. Operationally, AMIB's key problems were its inability to make serious progress on DDR and deter all spoiler groups, who are now engaging primarily in criminal as opposed to political violence. More fundamentally perhaps, despite pledges of support from other African states, South Africa was the only state to commit troops from the deployment of the SAPSD in 2001 until late 2003. Nevertheless, under South Africa's leadership, AMIB acted as an important support mechanism for building confidence in the Arusha agreement and was able to respond flexibly to developments on the ground through the brokering of the two Pretoria Protocols. In the longer term, ONUB will have the difficult task of building stable peace in Burundi probably without the necessary funds.

Pretoria's ongoing challenges

Five currently unresolved issues stand out from this survey of South Africa's approach to peace operations as having the potential to influence Pretoria's new multilateralism more generally. First, there is the issue of which institutions can legitimately authorise peace operations. Here, Pretoria's actions have sent mixed signals. Officially, as the DFA's *Strategic Plan 2003–2005* makes clear, South Africa wants to establish 'a rules based international system'.[60] In practice, however, Pretoria has not stuck to the rules governing peace operations. While in the DRC, Pretoria did operate with a mandate from the UN Security Council, in Lesotho and Burundi the picture is more complicated. Despite official claims to the contrary, Operation Boleas was designed, led and authorised from Pretoria. In addition, even if one accepts that Boleas was authorised by SADC, Chapter VIII of the UN Charter is clear that while regional organisations may undertake peaceful operations without prior Security Council authorisation, all enforcement action requires a Security Council mandate, and this was not granted in Lesotho's case. In Pretoria's defence, it was acting upon a request from Lesotho's Prime Minister. In Burundi, the situation is more complicated for although the SAPSD was Mandela's unilateral initiative it did have the consent of Burundi's government and gained many supporters within the UN. Similarly, while the AMIB broke the letter of the law by conducting enforcement action without first obtaining a UN Security Council mandate, the Council quickly endorsed the operation as a legitimate regional response to the civil war. This evidence suggests that Pretoria does not consider the UN to be the sole or even primary multilateral forum in which to authorise peace operations in Africa.

South Africa's use of African multilateral forums raises related questions about whether the AU or SADC are in fact the most appropriate organisations in which to create and organise peace operations. Aside from issues of capability, SADC's failure to establish a consensus concerning the deployment of peace operations would suggest it is entirely unsuited to either authorising or conducting peacekeeping in the region. For its part, the AU has envisaged that with the help of EU and G8 funding it will create five regional brigades of peacekeepers in two phases (2005 and 2010). This vision is optimistic to say the least but it was given a modicum of credibility in May 2004 when the AU established its Peace and Security Council. The two main problems with relying on AU peacekeeping are political will and resources. As the AMIB demonstrates, it is highly unlikely that the AU can gather together the funds necessary to conduct even a small-scale peace operation for a period of more than one year. Nor can it afford a well-trained, well-equipped and professional peacekeeping force complete with the transportation necessary to get it in and out of war zones. Indeed, in May 2003 the AU excluded ten members from its meetings because they were more than two years in arrears.[61] At present, the AU is high on grandiose statements of intent and low on substance, funding and genuine capabilities. Moreover, even if it could prove successful on its own terms, there would be problems. Not only would it duplicate mechanisms that already exist at the UN but given the OAU's track record, it could become an instrument of 'Autocrats United' to support incumbent regimes presiding over unjust and therefore unstable political orders.[62] The Union's decision in February 2003 to extend its criteria for collective intervention under Article 4(h) of its charter to include the undefined notion of a 'serious threat to legitimate order' is a case in point.

The next three issues revolve around South Africa's domestic politics, namely, consultation, cost and capability. In relation to Burundi, for instance, the Democratic Alliance suggested that although it favoured Pretoria's participation in peace operations in principle, it was concerned by the uncertain legal basis of the operation, the lack of parliamentary consultation on the deployment and the apparent lack of an exit strategy.[63] However, while the lack of consultation outside the ANC is a problem, the other concerns can be exaggerated. Indeed, where domestic anxieties about South Africa's participation in the DRC and Burundi missions have surfaced they have been primarily to do with the financial cost of the operations.[64] In a country where houses, water, electricity and medical care are often in short supply large peacekeeping bills need to be carefully explained and justified. And here, the government has done itself no favours by often failing to consult parliament let alone justifying its decisions to the wider public. The cost of three years of operations in Burundi, for instance, was estimated at $180m (only $20m of which will be met by donors), with another $190m for operations in the DRC.[65] However, the cost of peacekeeping is not only measured in financial terms it can also be measured in body bags. To date, only nine South African peacekeepers have been killed in combat, although two more have died under peculiar circumstances while on duty in Burundi.[66] It would however be unrealistic for South Africans to expect relatively casualty free peacekeeping to continue indefinitely, especially given the unstable environments in which South African troops are currently deployed. The problem is that gauging public support for dangerous enforcement operations is difficult. However, as domestic tolerance of SANDF casualties weakens it is likely that calls will increase for South Africa's private security sector to play a bigger role in peace operations, as it did in relation to the war in the DRC.[67]

The issues of costs and capabilities have been starkly brought together in the debate about Pretoria's infamous $4.5bn arms deal, which is almost entirely comprised of material designed to fight conventional wars rather than help the SANDF undertake effective peace operations.[68] So while the SANDF's budget has risen in recent years, the money has not been spent on material suitable for peacekeeping.[69] In addition, a leaked Department of Defence document in July 2002 revealed the parlous state of the SANDF: only 3000 of 76,000 troops could be deployed operationally; only 4 out of 168 tanks were operational; the air force usually ran out of fuel in September; much training has been stopped; and 7 out of 10 deaths in the army were HIV/AIDS related.[70] The last point about HIV/AIDS and the SANDF is particularly important for South Africa's peacekeeping capabilities. By 2001, the SANDF was acknowledging infection rates among its soldiers of 17 per cent, although independent analysts suggest the figure is nearer 40 per cent with some units reporting rates as high as 90 per cent. By mid-2004, the SANDF was acknowledging an infection rate of 23 per cent.[71] Unless the spread of HIV/AIDS is stopped among the SANDF, South Africa's ability to conduct peace operations will be severely restricted.[72] The effects of all these factors on the SANDF's operational efficiency was borne out by the fact that the South African contingent in Burundi required external logistical help and funding for medical support for its troops. These statistics also explain why, despite Pretoria's vocal role in the 2003 Liberian peace process and pledges that it would deploy 200 troops to UNMIL, the government was only able to send a symbolic presence to the stricken country (in April 2004 UNMIL contained just 3 South African troops).[73]

As far as peace operations are concerned, the current ANC government remains in a difficult position. Having consistently claimed a leadership role within Africa since the end of apartheid, Pretoria has been under considerable pressure – generated in part by its claims to champion an African Renaissance and the NEPAD – to be at the forefront of attempts to bring peace to both the southern African region and the continent as a whole. The problem is that, as the cases of Burundi and the DRC attest, most African states clearly lack the political will and capability to conduct the sort of peace operations required on the continent and South Africa has been left playing a leadership role often without African followers. Moreover, since the debacle in Somalia in 1993, the world's most powerful states have been loath to send their troops to Africa with peacekeeping mandates. This has left UN peace operations under-resourced and often incapable of achieving their mandates. In this situation it seems likely that Pretoria will continue its rather pragmatic approach to multilateralism where peace operations are concerned.

Notes

1. Cited in Department of Foreign Affairs (DFA), *Strategic Plan 2003–2005*, available at www.dfa.gov.za, p. 24.
2. For some of the evidence that neoliberal policies have the opposite effects see United Nations Development Programme, *Human Development Report 2003, 2005* (Oxford: UNDP/Oxford University Press, 2003, 2005).
3. See Hill, C., *The Changing Politics of Foreign Policy* (London: Palgrave, 2003) p. 284.
4. See, for example, Keohane, R., 'Multilateralism: An Agenda for Research', *International Journal*, 45:4 (1990) p. 731; and Ruggie, J. G., 'Multilateralism: The Anatomy of an Institution' in Ruggie (ed.), *Multilateralism Matters: The Theory and Praxis of an Institutional Form* (New York: Columbia University Press, 1993) p. 11.
5. See, for example, Cox, R. W., 'Multilateralism and World Order', *Review of International Studies*, 18:2 (1992) pp. 161–80; and Gill, S., 'Global structural change and multilateralism' in Stephen Gill (ed.), *Globalization, Democratization and Multilateralism* (Basingstoke: Macmillan, 1997) pp. 1–18.
6. Nel, P., Taylor, I. and van der Westhuizen, J., 'Multilateralism in South Africa's Foreign Policy: The Search for a Critical Rationale', *Global Governance*, 6:1 (2000) pp. 43–60.
7. Ibid.
8. See Paris, R., *At Wars End* (Cambridge: Cambridge University Press, 2004).
9. 'Damned If We Do, Damned If We Don't', *Mail & Guardian* (19 August 2003).
10. Here, I am drawing directly upon Bellamy, A. J., Williams, P. and Griffin, S. *Understanding Peacekeeping* (Cambridge: Polity, 2004).
11. It should be noted that individual states often shift their position between these two approaches when it is politically expedient for them to do so.
12. See Schoeman, M. and Alden, C. 'The Hegemon that Wasn't: South Africa's Foreign Policy towards Zimbabwe', *Strategic Review of Southern Africa*, 25:1 (2003) pp. 20–1.
13. See Bellamy, A. J. and Williams, P. D., 'Who's Keeping the Peace? Regionalization and Contemporary Peace Operations', *International Security*, 29:4 (2005) pp. 157–95.
14. For a useful overview see Boulden, J. (ed.), *Dealing with Conflict in Africa* (New York: Palgrave, 2003).
15. See Bellamy, *et al.*, *Understanding Peacekeeping*.
16. NCOMP remains understaffed and sidelined with only three full-time staff members in April 2003 instead of the suggested ten. See Kent, V. and Malan, M.,

Decisions, Decisions: South Africa's foray into regional peace operations (Pretoria: ISS Occasional Paper 72, 2003) p. 12.

17. Nhlapo, W., 'South Africa and Peacekeeping: Looking to the future' in J. Cilliers and G. Mills (eds), *From Peacekeeping to Complex Emergencies: Peace Support Missions in Africa* (Natal: SAIIA/ISS, 1999) pp. 128–9.

18. The following account draws on Williams, R., 'From Peacekeeping to Peacebuilding? South African Policy and Practice in Peace Missions', *International Peacekeeping*, 7:3 (2000) pp. 85–6.

19. Use of the word 'mission' was meant to carry less militaristic overtones than the narrower concept of a peace operation, with its emphasis on the military dimensions of peacebuilding. Ibid., pp. 88–9.

20. Ibid., p. 88.

21. For a defence of the practical importance of the SANDF's so-called secondary functions and a relevant critique of the Defence Review's position on this issue see Williams, R., 'Defence in a Democracy' in Rocky Williams *et al.* (eds.), *Ourselves to Know: Civil-Military Relations and Defence Transformation in Southern Africa* (Pretoria: ISS, 2002) pp. 205–23.

22. See Kent and Malan, *Decisions, Decisions*.

23. My account is taken from Anglin, D. G., 'The Life and Death of South Africa's National Peacekeeping Force', *Journal of Modern African Studies*, 33:1 (1995) pp. 21–52.

24. Vale, P., *Security and Politics in South Africa: The Regional Dimension* (Boulder: Lynne Rienner, 2003) pp. 126–7.

25. Barber, J., *Mandela's World* (Oxford: James Currey, 2004) p. 111.

26. Vale, *Security and Politics in South Africa*, p. 128.

27. Ibid., p. 131.

28. See Matlosa, K., 'The Dilemma of Security in Southern Africa: The Case of Lesotho' in Nana Poku (ed.), *Security and Development in Southern Africa* (London: Praeger, 2002) pp. 83–100 and Barber, *Mandela's World*, p. 115.

29. See Williams, 'From Peacekeeping to Peacebuilding?', pp. 97–101.

30. Vale, *Security and Politics in South Africa*, pp. 126–34.

31. Angola, Chad, Namibia, Sudan, Zimbabwe, Rwanda, Uganda and Burundi.

32. UN doc. S/2004/650, 14 Aug. 2004, para. 120.

33. Annual Address to the SAIIA, 7 November 1996.

34. *Africa Confidential*, 43:20 (2002) pp. 6–7.

35. *Africa Confidential*, 42:6 (2001) p. 3.

36. For more detail on South Africa's policy towards the war in the DRC see Taylor, I. and Williams, P., 'South African foreign policy and the Great Lakes crisis', *African Affairs*, 100 (2001) pp. 265–86; and Landsberg, C., 'The Impossible Neutrality? South Africa's Policy in the Congo War', in John F. Clark (ed.), *The African Stakes of the Congo War* (London: Palgrave, 2002) pp. 169–83.

37. South Africa contributed 22 SANDF personnel and two helicopters to the IEMF.

38. Cited in *Africa Confidential*, 44:10 (2003) p. 8.

39. S/2003/1146 (4 December 2003) p. 10.

40. For details see Ould-Abdallah, A., *Burundi on the Brink 1993–1995: A UN Special Envoy Reflects on Preventive Diplomacy* (Washington, DC: US Institute of Peace, 2000).

41. According to Jan van Eck, far from 'representing a genuine national consensus among Burundians', the Arusha process became 'one of the major sources of dispute and contention'. 'We Can't Guarantee Their Safety', *Mail & Guardian* (3 March 2003).
42. The protection force was originally intended to be a multinational operation with troops from South Africa, Ghana, Nigeria and Senegal. However, the other contingents did not arrive, claiming that the security situation remained too precarious.
43. See, for example, SCR 1375 (29 October 2001) and S/PV.4406 (8 November 2001), Statements by the president of the UNSC and the Ugandan representative as chairman of the Regional Peace Initiative on Burundi, pp. 4–5; and S/PV.4417 (15 November 2001), Statement on behalf of the Security Council by Mr Knight (Jamaica) p. 2.
44. See S/2002/1259 (18 November 2002).
45. S/PV.4655 (4 December 2002) p. 4.
46. See S/PV.4675 (18 December 2002) p. 3 and S/PRST/2002/40.
47. See Communiqué of the Ninety-first Ordinary Session of the Central Organ of the Mechanism for Conflict Prevention, Management and Resolution at Ambassadorial Level, 2 April 2003, Addis Ababa, Ethiopia. AMIB was authorised to comprise some 3500 troops from Ethiopia, Mozambique and South Africa. The Arusha agreement envisaged its deployment by end of December 2002 but logistical and political difficulties delayed its arrival.
48. Both contingents received crucial bilateral funding from Britain and the US, and Italy, Germany and Denmark also made contributions to AMIB.
49. 866 from Ethiopia, 228 from Mozambique, 1508 from South Africa and 43 military observers from Benin, Burkina Faso, Gabon, Mali and Tunisia. S/2003/1146, p. 7.
50. Louw, L., 'On the streets of Bunia and Burundi', *eAfrica* (July 2003), pp. 12–13.
51. The Pretoria Protocols were signed on 8 October and 2 November 2003 respectively. They set out commitments regarding political, defence and security power-sharing. For details see S/2003/1146, pp. 3–4.
52. S/2003/1146, p. 8.
53. See Human Rights Watch, *Everyday Victims: Civilians in Burundi's War* (New York: 15:20(A), December 2003) pp. 9–15.
54. Gasana, J. M. and Boshoff, H., *Mapping the Road to Peace in Burundi: The Pretoria sessions* (Pretoria: ISS Situation Report, November 2003) p. 5.
55. Gasana, J. M. and Boshoff, H., *Burundi: Critical Challenges to the Peace Process* (Pretoria: ISS, Situation Report, September 2003) p. 2.
56. *Africa Confidential*, 44:16 (2003) p. 6.
57. *Africa Research Bulletin*, 40:11 (2003) p. 15532B.
58. S/2003/1146, p. 11.
59. S/2003/1146, p. 6.
60. DFA, *Strategic Plan 2003–2005*, pp. 8 and 15.
61. 'AU peace force under threat', *Mail & Guardian* (26 May 2003).
62. Jett, D., 'Standby Force a Mission Impossible?', *eAfrica* (July 2003) p. 9.
63. wa ka Ngobeni, E. and Mthembu-Salter, G., 'Under Pressure to Act', *Mail and Guardian* (2 November 2001).
64. See, for example, 'What South Africa's International Role Costs the Taxpayer', *Mail & Guardian* (1 November 2002).

65. *Africa Confidential*, 44:14 (2003) p. 2.
66. One was found strangled in a Bujumbura suburb, and the other was shot by a sergeant after he had shot and wounded one of his officers in the SAPSD's base in Bujumbura.
67. For example, Brooks, D., 'South Africa's Private Peacekeeping Option', *The Star* (Johannesburg, 3 November 1999).
68. Indeed, the Democratic Alliance called for the government to cancel the third tranche of the arms deal precisely because the materiel involved was incompatible with the SANDF's role in peace operations. 'DA wants debate on troop deployment', *Mail & Guardian* (12 August 2003).
69. *Africa Confidential*, 41:8 (2000) pp. 1–3.
70. Keith Somerville cited in House of Commons (UK) Foreign Affairs Committee (FAC), *South Africa: Fifth Report of Session 2003–04* (London: TSO, HC 117, 2004) p. EV107.
71. Hosken, G., 'SA Unlikely to Send More Troops to the DRC', *Pretoria News* (25 June 2004).
72. International Crisis Group (ICG), *HIV/AIDS as a Security Issue* (Brussels: ICG Report, 19 June 2001), pp. 20 and 22.
73. Somerville cited in FAC, *South Africa*, p. EV107.

Conclusions
Reflections on a Decade of Multilateral Diplomacy

Donna Lee, Ian Taylor and Paul D. Williams

There can be no doubt that multilateralism has become a central plank of the 'new' South Africa's diplomacy. It is also apparent that the African National Congress (ANC) government has little option but to cultivate a robust multilateral diplomatic strategy. As a developing middle power state, South Africa lacks the opportunities and capabilities to achieve its foreign policy goals unilaterally. Like many states South Africa has a limited ability to influence – let alone set the agenda of – most international institutions. This includes Pretoria's struggle to facilitate multilateral cooperation within its own region/sub-region because many of its neighbours either resent or are very wary of its influence within Africa in general and Southern Africa in particular. Unilateral options are rare for Pretoria – such opportunities remain the privilege of more powerful actors such as the United States, the European Union and China. And in any case, multilateral institutions matter since they now regulate much of the security, economic, and judicial dimensions of the international system, with a remit of governance that is continually expanding into all areas of economic, social and political life at the international, regional, sub-regional and domestic levels.

It is also worth recalling that South Africa's new multilateralism occurred during a newly forming post-Cold War era characterised by complexity and uncertainty. With ever increasing numbers of multilateral conferences and summits, a rapidly growing number of state and non-state actors involved in multilateral processes, a mounting list of agenda items, and the increasingly technical nature of issues under negotiation, contemporary multilateralism is a strategic and technical challenge for most states to master, not least for the 'new' South Africa. In this context, several key international organisations have struggled to be effective governing institutions. One need only to think of the World

Trade Organisation (WTO), which has lurched from the collapse of one set of negotiations to another, or the United Nations (UN), which has long been in stalemate over reform proposals and suffered allegations of irrelevance in the war against Iraq. In one sense, South Africa's return to active involvement in multilateral institutions and negotiations after its apartheid-induced isolation has helped mitigate against this sense of crisis. Indeed, as a self-proclaimed 'voice of Africa' and by casting its diplomatic strategy as a responsible problem-solver and bridge-builder between North and South, Pretoria has sought to reinvigorate multilateralism, despite its manifold problems. Nevertheless, given the constraints upon its own ability to influence international agendas, as well as this difficult period for several key multilateral institutions, it is not surprising that the first decade of South Africa's new multilateralism contained fewer examples of concrete impact than the government's statements suggest.

In this concluding chapter we briefly reflect upon the first decade of the 'new' South Africa's diplomacy with reference to three themes evident within the book's previous chapters. The first concerns South Africa's role within several emerging coalitions of mainly Southern states. Despite the structural constraints and their limited material power these coalitions have started to push for reform of the international system in a variety of ways. The second theme involves Pretoria's shift from an object to a subject of multilateralism. We refer to this as the 'dual embrace' of multilateralism, that is, the 'new' South Africa's embrace of multilateralism and multilateral institutions' embrace of South Africa. The third theme is that of Pretoria's pragmatism and the contradictions this has thrown up. The contradictions at the heart of South Africa's new diplomacy have stemmed primarily from its projection of a rather schizophrenic identity that proclaims to be both the G7's facilitator and a contemporary champion of a distinctly African renaissance. Arguably, it is how these contradictions are resolved that will shape the next decade of South African multilateralism.

South Africa and emerging coalitions

One interesting development in Pretoria's diplomacy is the idea that a coordinated approach within the developing world is vital. This has encouraged a renewed activism within institutions such as the G20+ and the IBSA Forum (India-Brazil-South Africa). Attempts to build coalitions of developing countries to influence global governance is now a relatively mature aspect of Pretoria's foreign policy. Eight years ago, for instance, Thabo Mbeki addressed the Non-Aligned Movement (NAM) ministerial meeting and asserted that

> it is vital that the NAM and the Group of 77 plus China should have a common, co-ordinated and strategic approach in their interactions with organisations of the North such as the G8 and European Union. We must ensure that the benefits of the twin processes of globalization and liberalization accrue to all of our countries and peoples and that its potential threats and risks are accordingly mitigated. It is therefore incumbent upon the Movement to continue being in the forefront of efforts to ensure the full integration of the developing countries' economies into the global economy. It is to our mutual benefit that we continue advocating for a new, transparent and accountable financial architecture.[1]

In recent times South Africa has exerted considerable energy to construct a united bloc from which such an agenda can be launched. Foreign Minister Nkosazana Dlamini-Zuma, for instance, suggested that a select group of developing countries should 'form a nucleus of countries in the South that can interact on behalf of developing countries'. This 'is a serious priority for SA', she went on to say.[2]

In March 2000, South Africa took a step towards operationalising this objective in Cairo when it met with Brazil, India, Nigeria and Egypt to launch a trading bloc of developing nations to challenge the G7 in the post-Seattle round of WTO negotiations. In Africa, such impulses were crystallised by the October 2001 launch of the New Partnership for Africa's Development (NEPAD) which sought a bargain between Africa and the G7 to promote a reformist developmental agenda. This agenda has been criticised for accepting market-driven mechanisms as its starting point.[3] This is a fundamental point in evaluating Pretoria's stance towards global governance and its perspective on what globalisation implies. Indeed, NEPAD's designers saw liberal globalisation as providing glowing opportunities. 'The world', they argued,

> has entered a new millennium in the midst of an economic revolution. This revolution could provide the context and means for Africa's rejuvenation. While globalisation has increased the cost of Africa's ability to compete, we hold that the advantages of an effectively managed integration present the best prospects for future economic prosperity and poverty reduction.[4]

Similarly, the NEPAD gels with the policy aims of Mbeki's much-touted African Renaissance, which has underpinned post-apartheid

South Africa's foreign policy, particularly since Mandela stepped down. Yet this Renaissance and the concomitant posture towards globalisation has been criticised as being under undue influence from the dominant neoliberal orthodoxy.[5] To answer such criticism, Mbeki has pursued a policy which embraced neoliberalism while simultaneously claiming that multilateral diplomacy could alleviate the worst aspects of globalisation. Thus South Africa has promoted a tactical and reform-minded agenda that revolved around the promotion of a rules-based trading regime. Pretoria's membership of the G20 and G20+ reflect this policy.

Such a stance served the important function of helping to persuade the ANC's constituency on the Left that it is actively striving for the benefit of the less advantaged both at home and abroad, while signalling to the G7 and the IFIs that the government can be trusted to play by the rules of the game. Adopting a reformist element to its foreign policy regarding the global political economy is one way in which this could be achieved. Indeed, this type of reformism has been described as 'a way of deflecting the perceived negative effects of globalization on the South African state, and of displaying a commitment to change for the sake of domestic coalition partners to the Left'.[6] Again, this is reflected in Pretoria's involvement in initiatives such as the G20, the G20+ and the IBSA.

The appeal to a rules-based regime under the WTO is a good example of where Pretoria sought to fit rhetoric with practice, as is South Africa's membership of the Cairns Group, its stance at forums such as the NAM and UNCTAD, and the G20 and G20+. All are attempts to get the G7 to take its responsibilities seriously and act in 'partnership' with the developing world to alleviate problems and be more sensitive towards the needs of the less developed. None of these institutions reject outright neoliberal globalisation. Rather they have pushed for increased access to the global market, partly for material gain and partly because there appears to be a genuine belief that it will encourage development.[7]

This policy received a major boost at the G77 meeting in Havana in April 2000 when the body adopted a resolution that agreed with Mbeki's vision of a united developing world within trading bodies such as the WTO. Indeed, the G77 summit was cast as the starting point of a collective process which would come to affect the future of the global system. It was reported as sending 'a clear message to the developed countries that their reluctance to reform the international financial system is a major threat to international peace and security'.[8] The G77 agreed to drive this process of consolidation by establishing a directorate that included Mbeki, Olusegun Obasanjo of Nigeria and Mahathir Mohamed of Malaysia.[9]

By constructing a reformist-inclined coalition with key strategic partners, Mbeki apparently hopes to build an alliance that will be taken more seriously by the G7 than the G15 and G77 groups. With a form of credibility derived from Mbeki's self-image as a philosopher king as well as his G7-friendly credentials as the architect of South Africa's Growth, Employment and Redistribution (GEAR) programme, he seems ideally placed to pursue a reformist agenda at the various multilateral bodies that deal with global trade issues.

An emerging example is the IBSA Forum. This builds on already existing and fairly strong bilateral ties between the IBSA members such as negotiations for a fixed preference agreement between Mercosur and the SACU, as a means to establish a future free-trade agreement, as well as a preferential trading deal between India and Mercosur, which will enable the two sides to select the products that will have reduced tariffs in bilateral trade. The IBSA may however also be the first step toward a full free-trade agreement among the G20 developing countries.

The IBSA Forum was set up in Brazil in June 2003 and formally launched by Presidents Thabo Mbeki and Lula da Silva and Prime Minister Atal Bihari Vajpayee at the UN General Assembly in September 2003. The Forum's vision is set out in the Brasilia Declaration (June 2003) which aspired to making the global political economy work for all of the planet's people. This plan has both political and economic ingredients. Politically, reform of the UN, in particular the Security Council, is emphasised, with the Declaration stressing the need to expand the number of permanent and non-permanent members and to involve developing countries in both categories. India and Brazil are already supporting each other's membership bids and the IBSA Forum has committed itself to combining energies in order to obtain reform, as well as enhancing the effectiveness of the UN system.

Economically, the IBSA Forum might be seen as a concentrated effort by key states in the developing world to push a more 'friendly' form of globalisation:

The Foreign Ministers of Brazil, India and South Africa expressed their concern that large parts of the world have not benefited from globalization [and they] agreed that globalization must become a positive force for change for all peoples, and must benefit the largest number of countries. In this context, they affirmed their commitment to pursuing policies, programmes and initiatives in different international forums, to make the diverse processes of globalization inclusive, integrative, humane, and equitable.[10]

Following on from this, the IBSA pushes a now familiar position, decrying protectionist policies in the G7 and stressing the need to advance the Doha Development Programme as well as working on the current round of trade negotiations as a means to reverse protectionist policies and trade-distorting practices. Furthermore, IBSA is based on the restated importance of a predictable, rules-based, and transparent multilateral trading system as a means through which developing countries could maximise their development via trade and their competitive advantage. As part of this, IBSA cooperation towards making the international financial architecture responsive to development and towards increasing its effectiveness in preventing and addressing national and regional financial crises was placed as a key objective.

Pretoria and multilateralism: From object to subject

This book has provided a critical insight into Pretoria's embrace of multilateralism in the post-apartheid era by detailing its willingness and enthusiasm to become a full and active member of the key multilateral institutions and processes at international, regional and sub-regional levels. These include the UN, where it is currently actively seeking permanent membership of the Security Council to add to its already significant presence in the UN General Assembly and other UN organs and agencies; active involvement in several peacekeeping operations, the Commonwealth and the WTO; as well as successful multilateral negotiations such as the Kimberly and Ottawa Processes. Added to this, Pretoria has assumed leadership roles in the NAM, the African Union and SADC, and in so doing became the self-styled leader of an African Renaissance, although this has not been unproblematic.[11] South Africa's multilateral diplomacy has a truly global reach and, unlike many middle powers such as Canada and Australia which have pursued a niche diplomatic strategy that has a regional or issue specific concentration, Pretoria has engaged with a relatively full complement of global multilateral institutions and processes. In this context the new multilateralism in South African diplomacy seeks to reposition Pretoria as a subject of international relations rather than their object.

Equally, the key multilateral forums and processes, at least at the international level (markedly less so at the sub-regional level), have fully embraced the new South Africa. Major multilateral economic forums such as the WTO, as well as the G8, G20 and Davos economic summits, have turned to Pretoria as a trustworthy voice of Africa, not least because this element of African representation adds a degree of inclusivity and legitimacy to such proceedings.[12] Thus South Africa's multilateral diplomacy plays a crucial symbolic role in justifying and reinforcing existing international power structures in which Western states are dominant. In this context, international multilateral institutions and processes continue to objectify South Africa.

Clearly there is a mutually advantageous association in this dual embrace. South Africa has been able to enhance its influence in the international system and position itself as a pivotal if not major player in some important international organisations. Simultaneously, Pretoria's participation has enhanced the legitimacy of these organisations – particularly the WTO – which can now claim to be more representative and thus democratic with a South African delegate seated around the negotiating table. In these international negotiations South Africa is often expected to 'deliver Africa'. Mandela pointed to this symbiotic relationship when he claimed that political and economic development in Africa could only be achieved by multilateral cooperation with the rich developed countries.[13]

But what and who is this dual embrace for as far as South Africa is concerned? To what extent has this dual embrace transmitted South Africa's principles onto the international stage? Indeed, given South Africa's neoliberal trade policy within the WTO – compared to its more assertive pan-Africanist stance within the Commonwealth and NAM – it is not unreasonable to ask what the ANC government's policy priorities and values actually are. On trade policy, at least, they would appear to be contradictory and opaque.[14]

In some international forums South Africa behaves in ways which reinforce the existing world order and its dominant knowledge claims by appealing to the powerful states in the North as a reliable bridge-builder, capable of facilitating a productive North–South dialogue. Yet in others, Pretoria champions an assertive pan-Africanist stance as a challenge to the hegemonic order and its liberal values in order to appear as a reliable partner to its African neighbours.[15] In this sense, South African diplomacy has exhibited a variety of *multilateralisms* depending on the setting, the issue and the audience in question.

The evidence in this book suggests that these contradictions, added to the structural constraints, present fundamental obstacles to Pretoria pursuing a coherent multilateral strategy. South Africa has largely failed to promote a consistent foreign policy across the plethora of international institutions, though it has succeeded in advancing its economic interests within Africa and Southern Africa.[16] The NEPAD project in particular has helped facilitate South Africa's economic penetration of other

African economies but has largely failed to advance the economic, social and political well-being of most Africans.[17] Instead, South Africa's multilateralisms have served primarily to promote the further assimilation of the neoliberal agenda into the South so that what was once a set of policy prescriptions for advanced post-industrial economies has become a global policy prescription for all economies, large or small, post-industrial or pre-industrial, developed or underdeveloped, North or South.

The failures of pragmatic multilateralism

A number of chapters in this book adopt a critical perspective on South African multilateralism and understand Pretoria's diplomacy as a pragmatic response to long established constraints. Multilateralism is viewed as a difficult strategy to pursue, especially for a developing middle power country like South Africa which faces obvious and formidable constraints at the international, regional and sub-regional level which, it can be argued, prevent the successful pursuit of a more transformative multilateral agenda and tend to encourage instead a reformist pragmatic strategy. Such constraints include a lack of adequate resources in peacekeeping missions, a lack of relative power capabilities and an inability to win the trust and confidence of its fellow African countries. Most of the commentaries in this book argue that South African diplomacy is primarily driven by a pragmatic thrust that largely works for South Africa's elites within the confines of what they see as possible. In this perspective, the practice of South African multilateralisms in the WTO, SADC, the NAM, the EU–SADC negotiations, the UN, as well as its peacekeeping missions is compelled by a seemingly rational calculation about what is achievable for a middle power developing state lacking relative hard and soft power capabilities at the international, regional and sub-regional levels.

At this level of explanation the various multilateral negotiations under scrutiny in this volume are characterised chiefly as a set of procedural political processes, operating on the basis of compromise between states of disparate power. States know that defining what constitutes the national interest as well as the content of framework agreements are often products of lowest common denominator bargaining. In this context it is perhaps unsurprising to find that in the practice of multilateral diplomacy key principles are often diluted and redefined in ever-broader terms as the negotiations proceed. This certainly appears to be a characteristic of the practice of South African diplomacy in the Doha Development negotiations of the WTO where key principles on development in general and agricultural trade reform in particular were abandoned by South Africa's delegates in the hope of reaching a compromise position vis-à-vis the major powers on the Singapore Issues. Yet this bridge-building strategy failed miserably. South Africa lacked the diplomatic know-how and capability to carry its developing country partners in the negotiations, and it was equally constrained by the lack of a viable alternative to neoliberal development strategies within the WTO writ large.

Such tensions and contradictions in diplomatic strategy are also evident in the regional and sub-regional dimensions of South Africa's multilateralism. While South Africa can rightly claim that its period as chair of the NAM was successful – Pretoria did after all guide the 'moderate majority' in the NAM and help develop a deeper sense of South–South common interests – there are notable failures in similar attempts by South Africa to forge South–South dialogues within SADC, the G20+ and the UN.

It is interesting to note that South Africa's attempts at consensus-building are particularly problematic in Southern Africa where tensions and resentment run high over South Africa's assumed leadership of the region. The disagreement within SADC over how to respond to the war in the Democratic Republic of Congo (DRC) was an important case in point. Pretoria's close neighbours have often been wary of South Africa's pan-Africanist posturing. Consequently, the ANC government lacks soft power capacities to lead effectively in its own region. South Africa thus often retreated from a robust promotion of democratic principles into a racialised model of Africanism in order to build a rather insular coalition of Southern African states. This was exemplified in Pretoria's response to Zimbabwe's ongoing crisis. Rather than challenge Mugabe's policies as a dangerous shift away from the democratic principles of good governance, Mbeki lent support to the regime in order to build a consensus in Africa. South Africa's prioritising of this rather perverse form of pan-Africanism has simply lent credibility to Zimbabwe's own racist model of undemocratic government.[18]

While South Africa may worry that it lacks the diplomatic capabilities to lead within its own sub-region it does not lack material power relative to its neighbours. It is by far the largest and most developed economy within Southern Africa, and its 'keen multilateralism', to use Qobo's phrase, aims to facilitate a deeper economic penetration into the economies of its neighbours. Yet the economic disparities give rise to dilemmas for South Africa in the sub-region. As the economic hegemon South Africa must tread carefully for fear of being branded a neo-imperial power in its own backyard, especially since its neighbours harbour long-standing fears over its predominant economic position. Sensitive to these criticisms and sentiments, Pretoria links it sub-regional diplomacy to the perceptions of South Africa held by its neighbours. Thus within its immediate neighbourhood Pretoria is a keen multilateralist – at least publicly – out of fear of being perceived as a unilateral bully. Indeed, multilateralism within SADC enables South Africa to project an image of benevolent diplomacy in contrast to an image of a neo-colonial power. This pragmatism has enjoyed some successes – notably the trade negotiations within SADC – but these are overshadowed by a total failure to resolve the crisis in Zimbabwe and its resort to an effectively unilateral response to Lesotho's crisis in 1998. Consequently, rather than develop a distinct sub-regional foreign policy, Pretoria has presided over policy drift within SADC.

Limitations on South Africa's multilateral diplomacy are most apparent where Pretoria is engaged in long-term broadly-based multilateral negotiations (such as the development negotiations in the WTO, UN, G8 and G20). By constructing middle power diplomatic strategies of bridge-building between North and South, facilitating consensus and managing conflict in Africa, South African foreign policy becomes less principled, less assertive and thus ultimately less effective. These limitations, however, are not quite as apparent where Pretoria is engaged in short-term issue based negotiations such as the recent Kimberly and Ottawa Processes. In these multilateral negotiations South Africa's middle power diplomacy proved far more effective since this model of multilateralism brings like-minded participants together around a single, clearly defined issue. The Kimberley Process around conflict diamonds is a case in point.

The Kimberley Process began with NGOs, primarily based in Canada, pushing the issue of conflict diamonds as a major concern for human security. Actors from the non-governmental sector, the corporate world and state governments then came together to try and resolve what was fast becoming a major scandal in international commerce. In contrast to other activist-driven issues pertaining to Africa, such as debt relief, the levels and provision of development assistance, or aid conditionalities, the issue of conflict diamonds rapidly achieved a rare broad consensus, with Pretoria playing host to the first meeting (held in Kimberley). South Africa, along with Botswana and Namibia, has economies heavily linked to the global diamond industry and Pretoria was keen to play a leading role in heading off any potential boycott of the diamond industry. The Kimberley Process, chaired by South Africa, thus began with about

35 participants involved in producing, processing, importing and exporting rough diamonds. It then quickly became a major vehicle in seeking to clean up the world's diamond industry. The UN General Assembly passed Resolution 55/56 on 1 December 2000 to mandate an expanded Kimberley Process, giving the forum the task of drawing up detailed proposals for an international certification scheme for rough diamonds. Subsequent meetings of the Kimberley Process saw the adoption of minimum standards for certifying rough diamonds and the implementation of an international certification scheme. The Process finally mandated the UN Security Council to pass a resolution, which would be endorsed by the General Assembly, to put in place a set of legally binding trade mechanisms to ensure that in the future rough diamonds will be exported in sealed containers accompanied by a certificate of origin. Throughout, South Africa provided technical and logistical support and the Process was seen as a triumph for Pretoria's new multilateralism.

Conclusions

Some of the more critical perspectives on multilateralism in this volume understand the role of international institutions very differently from those adopting liberal perspectives. Neo-Gramscians see international organisations such as the UN and WTO not as rule-based forums for cooperation, but rather as sites of political conflict and confrontation. By highlighting the normative underpinnings of multilateral behaviour, neo-Gramscians argue that multilateral institutions act to transmit hegemonic norms as well as forums for counter-hegemonic norms.[19] Multilateral institutions are sites of political struggle and, in the context of South African diplomacy, a space in which Pretoria might challenge the power of the North. South Africa's adoption of neoliberalism, first evident in the GEAR and then in the NEPAD, however, is one reason why we have not seen the emergence of counter-hegemonic norms within the NPT negotiations as well as the UN, WTO, NAM and SADC. In sum, South Africa's multilateralisms have projected its own foreign policy interests *within* the neoliberal agenda rather than as a challenge to it.

South African diplomacy, therefore, operates in multilateral forums in which hegemonic forces and knowledge claims constrain state behaviour and narrow states' options for action. This contrasts sharply with the liberal view that multilateralism is a rule-based negotiation framework facilitating and encouraging cooperation and coordination between interest-maximising states behaving pragmatically. A more critical approach readily identifies how and why neoliberal values and the hegemonic power of the North is institutionalised in international organisations and processes. In this way, the multilateral strategies of developing countries such as South Africa face embedded structural and ideational constraints to effective participation and influence so that they tend to remain marginalised within the multilateral process. Yet, developing countries like South Africa can enjoy greater levels of participation in such forums. What has been lacking is the influence and the ability – even willingness – to build counter-hegemonic norms. Consequently, South Africa's rather uncritical participation in international organisations such as the WTO and other multilateral processes such as the NPT negotiations has served to legitimise existing hegemonies.

The neo-Gramscian perspectives of South African diplomacy in this book make explicit claims that international and domestic capital interests have benefited from Pretoria's chosen policies. Arguably, the interests of the ruling classes have been advanced at the expense of the ruled. South Africa's chosen diplomatic strategy as bridge-builder has smoothed the progress of neoliberal global, regional and domestic markets. This, in turn, has bolstered the power and wealth of the North vis-à-vis the South as well as elite interests within all states – including those in Africa.

In sum, the dual embrace of multilateralism is supposed to encourage an African Renaissance that would stimulate economic development and encourage democratically accountable governments, human rights and the rule of law on the continent. Yet the new multilateralisms in South African diplomacy are often serving to legitimise and entrench existing global, continental, regional and national power structures. Despite the celebratory rhetoric, Pretoria's diplomacy remains schizophrenic and deeply contradictory.

Notes

1. Mbeki, T. (1998) 'Speech of the Deputy President of the Republic of South Africa, Thabo Mbeki, at the Opening of the Ministerial Meeting of the XII Summit Meeting of Heads of State and Government of the Non-Aligned Movement'.
2. *Financial Mail* (Johannesburg, 18 February 2000).
3. Taylor, I. and Nel, P., ' "Getting the Rhetoric Right", Getting the Strategy Wrong: "New Africa", Globalisation and the Confines of Elite Reformism', *Third World Quarterly*, 23:1 (2002) pp. 163–80.
4. Nepad Secretariat, *New Partnership for Africa's Development (Nepad)* (2001) p. 8, www.dfa.gov.za/events/Nepad.pdf

5. Taylor, I. and Vale, P. 'South Africa's Transition Revisited: Globalisation as Vision and Virtue', *Global Society*, 14:3 (2000) pp. 399–414.
6. Nel, P. (1999) 'Conceptions of Globalisation among the South African Elite', *Global Dialogue*, 4:1 (April) p. 35.
7. Lee, K. (1995) 'A Neo-Gramscian Approach to International Organization: An Expanded Analysis of Current Reforms to UN Development Activities' in A. Linklater and J. Macmillan (eds), *Boundaries in Question: New Directions in International Relations* Basingstoke: Macmillan, 1995, p. 156.
8. *Business Day* (Johannesburg, 14 April 2000).
9. *Financial Mail* (Johannesburg, 21 April 2000).
10. Embassy of Brazil, London (2003) *Meeting of Foreign Secretaries of Brazil, South Africa and India Brasilia Declaration*, 6 June.
11. See Taylor, I. and Williams, P., 'South African Foreign Policy and the Great Lakes Crisis: African Renaissance Meets Vagabondage Politique?', *African Affairs*, 100:399 (2001) pp. 265–86.
12. See Ian Taylor 'South Africa: Beyond the Impassse in Global Governance' in John English, Ramesh Thakur and Andrew Cooper (eds), *Reforming from the Top: A Leaders' 20 Summit* (Tokyo: United Nations University Press, 2005) pp. 230–59.
13. See James Barber 'The New South Africa's Foreign Policy: Principles and Practice' *International Affairs* 81:5 (2005) pp. 1079–96.
14. See Taylor, I., 'The Contradictions and Continuities of South African Trade Policy' in Dominic Kelly and Wyn Grant (eds) *The Politics of International Trade: Actors, Issues, and Regional Dynamics* (Basingstoke: Palgrave, 2005) pp. 295–308.
15. For a discussion of the importance of contradictions in both South Africa's domestic and foreign policies see Herbst, J., 'Mbeki's South Africa', *Foreign Affairs*, 84:6 (2005) pp. 93–105.
16. See Alden, C. and Soko, M., 'South Africa's Economic Relations with Africa', *Journal of Modern African Studies*, 43:3 (2005) pp. 367–92.
17. See Taylor, I., *NEPAD: Towards Africa's Development or Another False Start?* (Boulder, CO: Lynne Rienner, 2005).
18. See, for example, Ian Taylor, ' "The Devilish Thing": The Commonwealth and Zimbabwe's Denouement', *The Round Table*, 94:380 (2005) pp. 367–80.
19. See, for instance, Taylor, I., 'Legitimisation and De-legitimisation Within a Multilateral Organisation: South Africa and the Commonwealth', *Politikon*, 27:1 (2000) pp. 51–72.

Index